The New Authoritarianism in the Middle East and North Africa

Indiana Series in Middle East Studies

Mark Tessler, *general editor*

The New Authoritarianism
in the Middle East and North Africa

STEPHEN J. KING

Indiana University Press
Bloomington and Indianapolis

This book is a publication of

Indiana University Press
601 North Morton Street
Bloomington, IN 47404-3797 USA

www.iupress.indiana.edu

Telephone orders   800-842-6796
Fax orders   812-855-7931
Orders by e-mail   iuporder@indiana.edu

♾ The paper used in this publication meets the minimum requirements of the American
National Standard for Information Sciences—Permanence of Paper for Printed Library
Materials, ANSI Z39.48-1992.

Manufactured in the United States of America

Library of Congress Cataloging-in-Publication Data

King, Stephen J. (Stephen Juan), date
    The new authoritarianism in the Middle East and North Africa / Stephen J. King.
        p.   cm. — (Indiana series in Middle East studies)
    Includes bibliographical references and index.
    ISBN 978-0-253-35397-9 (cloth : alk. paper) — ISBN 978-0-253-22146-9
(paper : alk. paper)
    1. Middle East—Politics and government—1979– 2. Africa, North—Politics
and government. 3. Authoritarianism—Middle East. 4. Authoritarianism—
Africa, North. 5. Democratization—Middle East. 6. Democratization—Africa,
North. 7. Political culture—Middle East. 8. Political culture—Africa, North.
9. Middle East—Social conditions. 10. Africa, North—Social conditions. I. Title.
    JQ1758.A58K56   2009
    320.530956—dc22
                                                                            2009019547

1 2 3 4 5 14 13 12 11 10 09

CONTENTS

ACKNOWLEDGMENTS

In completing this book I have incurred many debts. My foremost thanks are to a Georgetown University colleague and friend, Thomas Banchoff, who read the entire manuscript and offered very useful suggestions at a critical stage in the process. A number of other colleagues made helpful comments and suggestions and provided support along the way. These include Lisa Anderson, John Bailey, Harley Balzer, Catherine Evtuhov, Atul Kohli, Sam Mujal-Leon, Judith Tucker, John Waterbury, and Clyde Wilcox. I must also acknowledge the help of graduate students at Georgetown, especially Zeinab Abul-Magd, April Longley, Marten Peterson, and Katrien Vanpee who were exceptionally able research assistants.

Anonymous reviewers from Indiana University Press were very helpful with suggestions that increased the analytic clarity and empirical focus of the book. The book's copyeditor, Joyce Rappaport, is exceptionally able. Dee Mortenson, my editor at Indiana University Press, provided needed encouragement and support.

A substantial portion of the research and writing was completed during a year spent at the Woodrow Wilson International Center for Scholars in Washington, D.C. Georgetown University also provided a semester without teaching and administrative responsibilities and funded a summer of field research.

Finally I would like to note the help of loved ones. Joan Yengo and our daughter Marley Carmina Yengo-King provided the warmth, distractions, and motivation necessary to manage the ups and downs of book writing. My mother, Frankie King, provided the foundation necessary to accomplish anything. To Arne Tangherlini, I wish we had had more time.

The New Authoritarianism in the Middle East and North Africa

Political Openings and the Transformation of Authoritarian Rule in the Middle East and North Africa

The authoritarian regimes in the Middle East and North Africa (MENA) survived the "third wave" of democracy that took place in the late twentieth century.[1] However, they did not survive it without undergoing fundamental changes. This book contributes to closing the gaps in our understanding of what sustains authoritarian rule during global democratic waves and what might have caused such rule to unravel in an important subset of the MENA countries that emerged in the post-independence era: the single-party, Arab socialist regimes of Egypt, Syria, Algeria, and Tunisia.[2] In addition, through highlighting how authoritarianism in the MENA is both persistent and dynamic, this book provides a new understanding of how politics currently operate under authoritarian rule in these countries.

There was a turn toward democracy in the MENA during the third wave. Egypt, which began holding regular multiparty legislative elections in 1976, appeared to be genuinely moving toward the rule of law, liberalization, and democratization in 1990, at which time the country's High Constitutional Court dissolved a parliament that the court ruled had been elected under an unconstitutional electoral law.[3] In 2000, the same court ruled that the legislative elections of 1990 and 1995 had been unconstitutional because the electoral process failed to provide for full judicial supervision. Algeria's state party was defeated first in local elections in 1990 and subsequently in legislative elections in 1990–1991 by an Islamist party, before the military moved in to annul the results, thereby setting off waves of bloodshed that lasted some fifteen years. Tunisia introduced multiparty legislative elections in 1989 along with a national pact to guide the transition to democracy after President Ben Ali had taken power in a constitutional coup in 1987. Nominally competitive presidential elections were inaugurated in the mid-1990s. In order to reflect Ben Ali's new platform of democratic reform, the president even changed the name of the political party that led the country to independence, from the Socialist Destour to the Democratic Constitutional Rally (RCD). In 1990 Syria held elections to its People's Assembly. Even though only tame parties running as part of a coalition with the ruling Ba'th party were allowed to participate, independent candidates increased their share of seats. At a congress of the Ba'th party in 2005, delegates endorsed the idea of independent political parties and the relaxation of emergency laws that had been in place since 1963.[4]

Concurrent with these political openings, leaders of the Arab socialist republics accelerated a process of comprehensive economic reforms toward outward-looking, market-oriented capitalist economies that granted dominant roles to the private sector. Privatization of state-owned enterprises and land, which increased dramatically in the 1990s in the MENA, is taken by all significant local and international actors to be the main index of a regime's sincerity on the issue of creating a liberal economic order.[5]

How did authoritarian leaders in Egypt, Syria, Algeria, and Tunisia initiate these political openings and economic transformations yet maintain authority and control? This book argues that the authoritarian leaders of the Arab socialist republics made timid turns toward democracy in the 1980s and 1990s, but then utilized single-party organizational resources and patronage-based economic liberalization to subvert full democratization and reinforce control over a new authoritarian system that included liberal economic policies, new ruling coalitions, some controlled political pluralism, and electoral legitimation strategies.

In Egypt, Syria, Algeria, and Tunisia, state-led economic liberalization and experiments in multiparty politics led not to a full opening but actually were crafted to support the new authoritarianism. Economic reform policies created and favored a rent-seeking urban and rural elite supportive of authoritarian rule and took resources away from the workers and peasants who increasingly had the most to gain from democratization. Thus, the privatization of state assets provided rulers with the patronage resources to form a new ruling coalition from groups that would be pivotal in any capitalist economy: private-sector capitalists, landed elites, the military officer corps, and top state officials, many of whom moved into the private sector and took substantial state assets with them. At the same time, ruling parties maintained elite consensus and contained the disaffection of the lower strata in the new multiparty arena by offering them a dwindling share of state resources. In the end, political openings in the four countries culminated in transformed authoritarian rule.

Even as I contend that economic liberalization characterized by the distribution of patronage to economic elites and robust single-party institutional structures provided autocrats with resources to sustain authoritarianism in the MENA republics, this does not mean that other factors were not involved.[6] However, the tasks for analysts seeking to explain resilient authoritarianism in the MENA are both to identify the most salient factors for particular countries and to provide an explanatory framework that can weigh those factors that influence regime outcomes. This framework will be provided in chapter 2. At this point, we note that in explaining why authoritarian rule is so entrenched in the MENA, scholars tend to emphasize how incumbent elites utilize formal institutional arrangements to disrupt the construction of coalitions that threaten their hold on power or focus on the initial causes of authoritarianism in the region.[7] This book enriches the literature on persistent authoritarianism in the MENA by examining how regime elites created political support during a period of dynamic economic and political change. The study offers additional insight on the causal mechanisms that sustain authoritarian rule.

The book aims to do more than contribute to understandings of persistent authoritarianism in the Arab world. It argues that Middle East authoritarianism is both persistent and dynamic. The book demonstrates how changes have occurred within authoritarianism in an important subset of Arab countries, by focusing on four regime dimensions: policies, ruling coalition, political institutions, and legitimacy. In highlighting the conceptualization of a new authoritarianism that has emerged in a subset of Middle Eastern states, I hope to push the inquiry beyond the issue of determinants to include the critical question of the effects of reconfigured authoritarian rule on the political and economic welfare of the people in the region.

Dimensions of Change:
From the Old Authoritarianism to the New
Authoritarianism in the Middle East and North Africa

While countries in the Middle East and North Africa have not made the transition from authoritarianism to democracy, the process of change that has occurred in the region is too fascinating and important to be ignored. To understand continuity and change, we need a rigorous typology that can describe MENA authoritarianism over the last few decades. This analytical framework will be useful for understanding other regions as well. Indeed, transitions from one form of authoritarianism to another, or to hybrid regimes, are among the most pronounced outcomes of numerous political openings around the world. Many of these transitions had previously been grouped under the third wave of democracy.[8]

In this book, as noted, regimes are conceptualized as composites of four dimensions: policies, ruling coalition, political institutions, and legitimacy. These are four elements that must be understood in order to grasp the change within continuity of Middle Eastern authoritarian regimes. This approach combines a concern for both political structure and the socioeconomic relations that affect who governs and who benefits in an emerging political economy. Over the past three decades, all four of these dimensions have been altered in the former Arab socialist single-party republics.

Policies

In the immediate post-independence period, the progressive Arab states staked their legitimacy on populist policies that enabled workers and peasants to make important economic and political gains. Landowners and owners of private capital faced the threat, and in some instances the realization, of nationalization and redistributive land reform. These new policies established social relations that crippled the old oligarchies in these states.

The regimes implemented state-led, import-substituting industrialization (ISI) development strategies in which the states took the lead in industrial and agricultural development. Newly created state-owned enterprises, behind protectionist walls, produced a variety of consumer products for domestic markets. Steady employment in these enterprises often provided the funds for ordinary workers to pay for the Egyptian, Syrian, Algerian, and Tunisian products that supported the countries' break away from a heavy dependence upon agriculture and the export of primary commodities that characterized the colonial era.

State–society relations in this period also included the development of a social contract that increased the states' role in the provision of welfare and social services. New state programs were implemented that provided wage guarantees, food subsidies, education, health care, housing, and other benefits to the general population.[9] Tacitly, many citizens accepted authoritarian rule in exchange for these benefits and anticipated success in the struggle for development.

For a number of reasons in the 1970s and 1980s, the Arab socialist republics began shifting development policies from the ISI interventionist and redistributive model to a liberal economic model frequently called the Washington Consensus. The Washington Consensus advocates fiscal discipline, including cutting welfare outlays; the privatization of state-owned enterprises and land; and the liberalization of policies on finance, trade, and interest rates.[10] The rising influence of this consensus in global economic policies has been tied to the collapse of the Soviet Union and the Eastern bloc; trends in the International Financial Institutions, especially the World Bank and IMF; the internationalization of markets and production; large debts; stagnant economic growth rates; and the inability of ISI industries to accumulate sufficient capital for investment.

Ruling Coalition

The shift toward a market economy and to export-oriented growth led by the private sector has been accompanied by a shift in ruling coalitions. Regimes typically cultivate sets of allied interests and coalition partners that buttress their ability to govern. In the old authoritarianism of the Arab republics, this coalition initially consisted of organized labor, peasants, the public sector, the military, and white-collar interests.[11] Once entrenched, these populist coalitions acted to maintain their share of state benefits in their countries' political economies.

Beginning earlier, but accelerating in the 1990s, the populist ruling coalitions in the Arab republics have been replaced by coalitions that still include the military, but rely more on commercial agriculture, private industrialists, export sectors, and upper-echelon state agents who have moved into the private sector usually with the benefit of privatized state assets.[12] Furthermore, the convergence of state officials and economic elites in a new ruling coalition has been fueled by economic liberalization characterized by patronage and rent seeking, as noted in the Egyptian case by Nader Fergany, lead author of the UNDP Arab Human Development Report 2002–2005:

> Egypt's privatization and structural adjustment programs . . . have led to a [brand] of crony capitalism. The operative factor is a very sinister cohabitation of power and capital. The structural adjustment program is helping to reconstruct a kind of society where a small number of people own the lion's share of assets. . . . Privatization in effect has meant replacing the government monopoly with private monopoly. . . . The middle class has been shrinking while there has been an enlargement of the super-rich. State-owned enterprises have been sold to a minority of rich people. The record of private sector enterprises creating jobs is very poor. We are not reaping the benefits of an energetic bourgeoisie, what we have is a parasitical, comprador class. . . . The consequences will be no less than catastrophic. This society is a candidate for a difficult period of intense, violent social conflict, and the kind of government we have will not do.[13]

Political Institutions

Institutionally, the hallmark change in the MENA Republics has been the adoption of multiparty elections after years of justifying the legitimacy of single-party rule. Egypt under Sadat in the 1970s began the multiparty electoral trend in the Arab republics. Hosni Mubarak then built on the political reforms undertaken by Sadat, which had been undone by political unrest and Sadat's assassination in 1981. Mubarak held parliamentary elections in 1984, 1987, 1990, 1995, 2000, and 2005. Multiparty direct presidential elections were held for the first time in 2005. In Syria, under current President Bashar Al-Asad, the son of the late president, Hafez Al-Asad, the country has attempted to modernize authoritarianism along Egyptian lines by implementing controlled political pluralism.[14] Tunisia held multiparty legislative elections in 1989, 1994, 1999, and 2004, and its first multiparty presidential elections in 1999. Algeria conducted competitive multiparty national assembly elections in 1991, and less competitive ones after the 1992 military coup; these occurred in 1997, 2002, and 2007. Multicandidate presidential elections were held in 1995, 1999, and 2004.

While some analysts believe that "every step toward political liberalization matters, both for the prospect of a transition to democracy and for the quality of political life as it is daily experienced by abused and aggrieved citizens,"[15] on balance the new multiparty context and occasional loosening of state control over society in the Arab republics have not improved the political lives of many of these countries' citizens, in particular those of workers and peasants.

These political openings in some instances did provide the first significant experience in political participation by the general population since independence; many social groups, social movements, associations, and political parties sprang up to participate in the new institutional context. However, multiparty politics largely have not benefited ordinary citizens for two reasons. First, workers and peasants, who were largely disadvantaged by the new economic policies, realized that it was extremely unlikely that any opposition party could win these state-controlled elections and that opting for political opposition ran a high risk of political marginalization and even retaliation from the state. The lower strata were captive voting blocks for the ruling parties, living too close to the edge to support opposition political parties that lacked access to state patronage. Opposition meant losing their chance to obtain the diminished levels of social spending available after the implementation of economic reforms. With no viable alternatives, they largely maintained their support for state parties in elections or abstained even as state policies shifted against labor and the small peasantry. In a fundamental sense the dramatic institutional change was not the introduction of multiparty politics; rather, it was the transformation of ruling populist parties such as the Arab Socialist Union and the Socialist Destour (constitution), into parties of rural and urban economic elites, even as these ruling parties maintained their hegemony in the political arena.

There is a second, related reason why the introduction of multiparty politics has not improved the political lives of most ordinary Egyptians, Syrians, Algerians, and Tunisians. One salient result from the implementation of these democratic institutions has been the creation of lopsided political reforms that favor the strong over the weak.[16]

The limited political liberalizations in these countries and multiparty elections have provided an avenue for landed elites and business classes to press for their material interests and personal freedoms in the new parliaments, while largely excluding the mass public from these same opportunities.[17] Landed elites and business classes have utilized their growing representation in parliaments, whether in opposition or more commonly as members of the state parties, to contribute to designing economic reform policies in a manner that best suits their interests.[18] The expansion of judicial powers has been utilized primarily to ensure new property rights, while secondarily protecting the right of the masses to assemble and protect themselves from state abuses.[19]

In sum, workers and peasants often fared better politically under single-party rule than they have in the new multiparty arenas, which are a sham, with the partial exception of the Algerian case. While the historic single-party systems certainly utilized state corporatist organizations and coercion when deemed necessary to control labor and peasants, these groups participated in the governing coalitions substantively, and regime policies reflected this. In the new authoritarianism, ruling elites and their ruling parties have been correct for the most part to gamble that they can switch their core constituency of support toward urban and rural economic elites, while retaining the continued support of popular sectors. In the new electoral competition, the lower strata lack viable alternatives and need whatever state patronage might survive increasing marketization. The state, of course, also utilizes coercion when protests erupt from the rollback of populist policies.

With little hope of improving their lot through the new multiparty elections, workers and peasants have exerted pressure within the state corporatist organizations affiliated with the state parties that were designed to mobilize their support and control them during the establishment of the old authoritarianism. In contrast to the liberal pluralist tradition, in a corporatist concept of society, groups become cogs in the state machinery. The exclusive representation of organized interests along functional lines—workers, farmers (small and large scale), capitalists, students, professionals, and others, takes the place of political representation based on universal suffrage and free individuals all equal before the law.[20]

The shift in policies and ruling coalitions in the MENA republics have strained these corporatist arrangements, splitting leaders from their base. While the leadership of national trade unions for labor and peasants generally has supported the regimes' new focus on developing a market economy and private enterprise, the base has turned to wildcat strikes, protests, and spontaneous demonstrations, which have led to repression and more overtly authoritarian states.[21] Workers and the small peasantry have heatedly protested privatization schemes in the Arab republics. Mass layoffs due to privatization policies have provided fuel for potential social explosions. Wildcat strikes and demonstrations have numbered in the hundreds in Egypt and Algeria. Hunger strikes in Tunisia have caught the media's attention. Sit-ins and waves of protests accompanied land reform measures in Egypt, while soldiers flooded privatized land in Tunisia to prevent organized opposition.[22] These protests have only slowed privatization policies, and except for a small program here or there, have been unable to redirect the distribution of state assets to the displaced workers and peasants. Protests have been more successful at applying pressure, resulting in early retirement schemes and unemployment insurance to compensate for their losses. Still, most view these programs as too limited in scope, and often unfulfilled in practice. Protests by workers and peasants have also been largely unsuccessful at changing labor laws to provide greater leeway to strike. Over time, privatization has become the most contested piece of economic reform initiatives.[23]

Beyond the dynamics of a ruling party and affiliated state corporatist organizations moving into the multiparty era there is another striking, and widely recognized, feature of the evolution of multiparty politics in the Arab republics: the rise of political Islam. The presence of Islamist cultural and political movements complicates the controlled multipartyism pursued by authoritarian incumbents in the MENA in a number of ways. First, these are mass movements that are well organized, well embedded in the social fabric, and capable of mobilizing considerable followings.[24] Indeed, if allowed to compete freely, Islamist political parties could possibly win national elections in Egypt, Syria, Algeria, and Tunisia. Faced with this real challenge the governments of Tunisia, Syria, and Egypt have outlawed altogether political parties based on religion, and have utilized the state's coercive power more fiercely against Islamists than against any other political opposition. The Egyptian government does allow them to compete as independents. The Algerian government banned the Islamist party with mass support after the bloody battles between it and the FIS, while permitting much weaker Islamist parties to compete in subsequent electoral contests.

In historical terms, Islam has consisted of varied interpretations, and there are multiple strands of political Islam.[25] This both poses challenges and offers opportunities for regime incumbents seeking to implement multiparty elections while maintaining power and control. There is a minority, transnational, violent, terrorist brand of political Islam that frightens people at home and abroad and can be reasonably described as neo-Islamic totalitarianism.[26] Its presence gives authoritarian incumbents wide scope in their use of repressive measures. Often that repression is utilized against both religious and secular oppositions, and against Islamists who renounce violence.

In contrast to the violent face of political Islam, certain political movements claim to want to attain their goals by peaceful means, competing for power democratically with non-Islamist political parties. These movements interpret Islam as compatible with democracy and civil liberties. This trend is often called Liberal Islam.[27] Somewhere in the middle, between neo-Islamic totalitarianism and Liberal Islam, are Islamists who claim to support democracy and denounce violence, but their actions arouse some doubts about the claims. The Muslim Brotherhood in Egypt and offshoots in other countries lie in this middle ambiguous zone. Egypt's Muslim Brotherhood has garnered enough public support to make it difficult for the regime to both repress them and claim to promote genuine electoral competition.

Finally, political Islam poses a fundamental challenge to the region's new authoritarianism and its state-controlled elections by offering an alternative that appeals to broad audiences. Their ideology prescribes a simple solution to the persistent crises of contemporary Arab societies —a return to the fundamentals, or true spirit of Islam, and to political programs based on Islamic principles.[28] They attack the rampant corruption in government and society with calls for piety.[29]

Increasing presidentialism represents another institutional change in the Arab republics. During the early populist phase, these regimes were highly presidential, with charismatic figures—backed by the military—such as Gamel Abdel Nasser, Habib Bourguiba, and Houari Boumédienne towering over their political systems. However, in the region's new authoritarianism, presidential power has increased even more. Economic reform in the region and globally has been accompanied by a shift in the policymaking process to privilege-insulated technocratic change teams under presidential auspices. This insulation of technocrats and the presidents' closest advisors has even been recommended by the international financial institutions pressing for the implementation of stabilization and structural-adjustment policies in the Arab world.[30] Stronger presidentialism weakens the state parties in relationship to executive branch elites, even more so when multiparty politics are adopted. In such circumstances, historic ruling parties to some degree have to compete with other parties for privileged access to presidential power. Presidents probably calculate that the new multiparty systems weaken both the single party and the bureaucracy relative to themselves. The new institutional arrangements reduce structural resistance to policies, which transfer economic management from the state–single-party alliance to the new state–bourgeoisie–private sector alliance.[31]

Legitimacy

A profound shift in policies, coalitions, and political institutions in the Arab republics has forced changes in strategies of legitimation. Building on Max Weber, Hesham Al-Awadi usefully conceptualizes how legitimacy, defined as political stability without the need for coercion, is pursued in the Arab World.[32] Al-Awadi disaggregates legitimacy. Legitimacy includes charismatic legitimacy of the type that Nasser, Bourguiba, and Boumédienne possessed in abundance; traditional legitimacy that encompasses the struggle over the mantle of Islam by both regime incumbents and Islamists; rational legal legitimacy that emphasizes the value and procedures of formal institutions; ideological legitimacy; and eudaemonic legitimacy that is largely based on promises to improve peoples' living standards and welfare. Finally, Al-Awadi adds the notion of nationalist legitimacy, which refers to the political discourses of leaders who evoke nationalist sentiments by protesting against foreign powers, especially the United States and Israel.

In the old populist authoritarianism of the Arab republics, the nationalist movements against colonialism, foreign powers, and traditional indigenous oligarchies led to widespread support for the nationalist and revolutionary leaders in Egypt, Syria, Algeria, and Tunisia and the regimes they sought to construct. These leaders professed vague commitments to Arab socialism and utilized populist rhetoric and policies to gain support, but in terms of legitimacy they relied more on promises to improve people's living standards than on ideological fervor. The authoritarian bargain or social contract was pivotal as a legitimacy resource, committing the state to provide goods and services in exchange for political docility and quiescence.

As leaders in the Arab world commit to neo-liberal economic models and roll back populist policies, they quickly endanger their base of legitimacy. The rampant rent seeking by the wealthy and the powerful during the switch to capitalism compounds this risk, and undercuts the potential of a new ideological resource: support for the capitalist ethic and shared economic gain. It is hard to argue that competitive markets, private enterprise, and free trade will lead to marked improvement in both national and individual welfare when average citizens see corruption and experience great uncertainty about their place in the new market arrangements.

To counter their legitimacy deficits regimes have created a veneer of market populism through coerced charity. Urban and rural economic elites who have been favored in state policy under neo-liberalism are coerced by the regimes to contribute to charity for the economically disadvantaged. In Tunisia, for example, President Ben Ali operates the 2626 program (the post-office box number to mail contributions). His office distributes these funds to the needy. A similar dynamic operates in Egypt where Mubarak pressures rich private-sector entrepreneurs into contributing to nominally voluntary charitable programs operated by the state.[33] In rural areas in Tunisia during economic liberalization, wealthy farmers are coerced by the most powerful central state representatives in the area into contributing to welfare mechanisms organized along the Islamic calendar.[34] While coerced charity helps leaders maintain a degree of eudaemonic legitimacy, the drop-off in welfare benefits conferred by the old social contract is readily observable.

The starkest change in legitimation strategies between the old and new authoritarianism in the Arab republics is the switch to legitimacy based on the state-led introduction of democratic institutions. With all of their shortcomings in practice, the legalization of multiple parties and competitive elections between them signaled new steps at building legitimacy in the Arab republics. In addition to electoral legitimacy, authoritarian incumbents attempt to sustain the nationalist and revolutionary legitimacy that helped them consolidate power during the period of the old authoritarianism. Finally, an indicator of legitimacy gaps is the use of the military and police to coerce and demobilize populations. Spikes in state coercion have been associated with the implementation of neo-liberal reforms.[35]

In sum, authoritarianism in the Middle East is both persistent and dynamic. In focusing on the conceptualization of a new authoritarianism that has emerged in an important subset of Middle Eastern states, this work examines the effects of reconfigured authoritarian rule on the welfare of millions of Egyptians, Syrians, Algerians, and Tunisians.

Organization of the Book

The book is organized in the following fashion. Chapter 2 presents the theoretical framework, which weighs the influence of a number of variables in sustaining MENA authoritarianism. It also justifies the book's focus on institutional legacies of single-party rule and patronage-based economic liberalization in the Arab republics. Chapter 3, "The Old Authoritarianism," provides historical background structured around the typology introduced in this chapter and the two main causal variables asserted in the study.

Chapter 4 makes the full case for the emergence of a new MENA authoritarianism characterized by changes from the old authoritarianism in development policies, new rent-seeking ruling coalitions, political institutions, and new legitimation strategies. It also contributes to the comparative literature on the links between economic and political liberalization by making the case that the authoritarian leadership in four typical Middle Eastern and North African countries has succeeded in utilizing economic liberalization to support a new form of authoritarian rule.

Chapter 4 also explores the forms and dynamics of authoritarianism in cross-regional perspective, asserting that the emerging literature on hybrid regimes, cases of stalled democratization, and transitions to rather than from authoritarian rule is weakened by a near-singular focus on the competitiveness of elections.[36] It argues that we should also theorize the social foundations of these new forms of authoritarian rule and identify other traits that matter to the people who live under them. Within the realm of political institutions it is notable that the new MENA authoritarianism resembles emerging forms of authoritarian rule in other regions of the world. For example, Gretchen Bauer and Scott Taylor argue that states in southern Africa have often stopped at the dominant party stage of evolution while increasing the concentration of power within the hands of an executive presidency. They also point out that state-led economic liberalization reorganized opportunities for rent seeking in Sub-Saharan Africa rather than eliminating them.[37]

Chapter 5 adds contrasting cases outside of the region in order to highlight the asserted causal arguments about authoritarian incumbents utilizing single-party institutions and patronage-based economic liberalization to sustain authoritarian rule. The book concludes in chapter 6 by exploring possible ways to foster democracy by undermining single-party rule and undercutting the foundations of patronage politics through the design and enforcement of market competition legislation in Egypt, Syria, Algeria, and Tunisia.

A Note on Methodology and Case Selection

This book seeks to integrate an important subset of MENA states, the Arab single-party republics, into the comparative and theoretical literature on authoritarian persistence and transformation. It examines a limited number of regimes in order to look at common themes and to try to isolate critical variables through the methodology of comparative case studies. Utilizing the abundant and well-developed descriptive case studies of economic reform in the Arab world and fieldwork, I highlight how the combination of ruling-party institutional structures and patronage-based economic liberalization helped to sustain authoritarian rule during a period of political openings in the Middle East and North Africa.

The four cases in this study also warrant analysis due to important contemporary concerns. New economic and political arrangements in Egypt are important because Egypt is the most powerful, populous, and influential Arab state. Algeria is the most powerful and populous North African state. Syria has long been the Arab world's leading frontline state in the Arab–Israeli conflict. Tunisia, although small, has served as the region's leader in terms of economic reform. All four of the cases harbor Islamist social movements that range from Neo-Islamic totalitarianism to interpretations of an Islamic heritage that share "Western" concerns for liberal rights and democracy.

TWO

Sustaining Authoritarianism during the Third Wave of Democracy

Due to a growing recognition of transitions toward rather than away from authoritarianism in recent years, the comparative study of political regimes has increasingly shifted from a focus on democratic transitions and consolidation to the analysis of authoritarian regimes.[1] Within the global context, a depiction of the emergence of a new form of authoritarian rule in parts of the Arab world in the late twentieth and early twenty-first centuries can potentially inform and illuminate regime-transition processes elsewhere in the world.

Despite the increasing scholarly attention paid to the analysis of nondemocratic regimes, analysts are impeded by a near absence of theories about authoritarian politics, especially in comparison to the intensive theory-building developed to explain democratization in recent decades.[2] To contribute to filling this void, this chapter builds on an integrative analytical strategy for understanding regime transitions, the funnel approach; its aim is to introduce a partly new conceptual model to the social science literature on authoritarianism.[3]

In terms of regime transitions globally we are currently experiencing "the low tide after the third wave."[4] Samuel Huntington coined the term *the third wave* for a period of global democratic expansion that began in Southern Europe in the 1970s.[5] His underlying theme was that transitions from undemocratic to democratic regimes in this period, just as in the first wave (1828–1926) and the second wave (1922–1944), far outnumbered transitions in the other direction. This assumption has been challenged in recent years. One study claimed that the third wave of regime change culminated in 77 percent new authoritarian regimes and 23 percent new democracies.[6] In retrospect, the bountiful literature that analyzed "democratic transitions," "democratic con-solidation," and "stalled democracies" clearly included many cases of transitions from one form of authoritarian rule to another, albeit admit-ting that the newer forms of authoritarianism would usually include a façade of multiparty politics.

Notably, the lead authors of the study that spurred the democratic transitions literature, Guillermo O'Donnell, Philippe C. Schmitter, and Laurence Whitehead, argued that transitions from authoritarian rule (the title of their foundational four-volume series, instead of transi-tions to democracy)[7] could lead to democracy, authoritarian regres-sions, revolutions, or hybrid regimes.[8] It is also noteworthy that due to normative commitments to democracy, and hopefulness about transi-tions away from authoritarian rule in the 1980s and 1990s, the litera-ture that followed the transitions framework established by O'Donnell, Schmitter, and Whitehead often underemphasized the possibility of new authoritarian outcomes and argued that any country moving away from authoritarian rule—operationally, countries implementing multi-party elections—could be considered a country in transition toward democracy.[9]

Examining regime transitions from the vantage point of the twenty-first century when democracy is still the only broadly legitimated regime type, and yet authoritarianism is alive and well, it seems sensible to focus on the mechanisms that allowed autocrats to maintain author-ity and control during the third wave of democracy. Furthermore, it is important to gain a greater appreciation of what political life is like for the millions of people who live under the reconfigured authoritarian regimes.

Analytical Challenges

A wide range of interconnected factors explain both authoritarian and democratic outcomes of political openings in authoritarian regimes. Scholars generally recognize five types of variables. First, there are macro-structural level variables that influence regime outcomes such as economic development, national culture, and international forces. Second, the domestic structural level encompasses objective social groups defined by factors such as socioeconomic position and changes in the balance of power among them. Third, the institutional level comprises formal domestic organizations and their rules and procedures. Political parties, military and security organizations, state bureaucracies, and regime components such as constitutional or legislative rules and procedures are institutional variables that are important for the choices and preferences of actors, and for the outcome of regime transitions. Fourth, the social-group level of analysis encompasses subjectively defined groups that can sway regime trends. These include social movements, ideological factions within the military, regime hard-liners and soft-liners, and moderate and maximalist oppositions. Fifth, the leadership level of analysis, elite choices, are important for regime outcomes. Democracy may be something, within the crevices of structural restraints, that elites give to the masses.

In an initial effort to explain why some developing countries became democratic and others did not, scholars emphasized macro-structural variables such as socioeconomic development and corresponding cultural change that fostered democratic politics.[10] The literature on the socioeconomic and cultural prerequisites of democracy provided only a partial explanation for regime transformations and was particularly weak in explaining how and when propitious macro-structural and cultural conditions were translated by particular actors in particular times and places who took the steps to establish democratic institutions. In other words, "inert, invisible structures do not make democracies or dictatorships. People do. Structural factors such as economic development, cultural influences, and historical institutional arrangements influence the formation of actors' preferences and power, but ultimately these forces have causal significance only if translated into human action."[11]

In response to these weaknesses and as an escape from what seemed to be an overdetermined structuralism with pessimistic implications for democracy, an actor-based perspective largely supplanted structural approaches to regime change.[12] In O'Donnell and Schmitter's influential study of transitions from authoritarian rule, elite dispositions, choices, calculations, and pacts are the primary catalysts for transitions away from authoritarian politics and toward the construction of democratic alternatives.[13] The authors argue that during periods when authoritarian incumbents concerned about legitimacy become factionalized and unstable enough to initiate political openings, structural factors become looser guides to political calculations and actor behavior than they are in more stable periods of established authoritarian regimes.[14] During these critical junctures, individual heroics aimed at fostering democracy can be rewarded with success.

The literature that built on O'Donnell and Schmitter's study of regime transitions increasingly sought to refute structural approaches and highlight the choices of individual elites as the central drivers of regime change.[15] The excessive voluntarism in many of these studies, however, led many analysts to argue that the next stage in the study of regime change should synthesize approaches. The emerging consensus, which I share, is that structural approaches that characterized the first generation of work on regime transformation, and the voluntarist approaches, which characterized much of the second, must be synthesized to provide a fuller understanding of the outcomes of political transition processes.

In my view, two goals should guide the third generation of comparative studies of political regimes. First, we should construct theories that integrate structural and actor-based approaches.[16] Second, the explanatory framework should be able to facilitate the understanding of both democratic and authoritarian outcomes of political transitions in order to avoid the weakness of some transition studies that do not have a category for authoritarianism once a political opening begins.[17] In an effort to contribute to achieving both of these goals, here I modify the funnel approach introduced by James Mahoney and Richard Snyder.[18]

The growing consensus that the study of regime-transition processes requires an integrative agenda raises issues for scholars that have not been fully addressed. "Advocates of integrative approaches have said little about what empirical analyses of regime change that employ these approaches should look like. Nor have they offered guidelines for constructing theories that integrate structural and voluntarist approaches."[19]

To begin addressing these challenges, Mahoney and Snyder developed an integrative strategy that they termed the funnel approach. According to the authors, integrative approaches to regime change use both choices of actors and objective conditions as primary causal variables. The strategy should employ both the methodological and theoretical building blocks of both voluntarist and structural approaches. The funnel approach deploys an integrative strategy that constructs explanations of regime outcomes using systematic jumps across five levels of analysis, working downward from the macro-structural level to the level of individual choices or leadership. The jumps consist of the sequential introduction of variables from new levels of analysis after the explanatory power of variables at already examined levels has been exhausted. Variables at a particular level of analysis are understood to explain part of a regime outcome; hence, one must consider variables from all levels to approximate a full explanation. Movement across levels of analysis is systematic because it is guided by the analyst's judgment that variables at a particular level cannot contribute further to the explanation: they are necessary but not sufficient causes. This judgment justifies moving to a different level in order to find additional causal factors. In general these jumps follow the hierarchical ordering of levels of analysis, moving vertically down from the macro-structural toward the leadership level where the range of possible outcomes is narrowest. Macro-structural and domestic structural factors are understood to filter down the funnel of causality, constraining social groups and political leaders to make choices at the narrowest part of the funnel. The five levels of analysis are the same as stated at the beginning of this chapter; here they appear in Table 2.1.

The explanatory power of the funnel integrative strategy derives from a model of causation in which variables from different levels of analysis are treated as independent vectors with distinct forces and directions. For example, some variables may foster democratic trends and others authoritarian trends. Regime outcomes are explained by summing forces and directions of variables. Thus, world system conditions, domestic structural conditions, institutional factors, leadership choices, and so forth become equivalents for the purpose of explanation because they are all converted into directional forces contributing to regime outcomes. As Mahoney and Snyder note, "Converting different types of variables into vectors transforms the difficult problem of bridging levels of analysis into a simple question of adding the explanatory weight of vectors."[20] The analyst who knows the cases determines the explanatory weight of each level of analysis.

Despite its strengths, the funnel approach has two weaknesses. One is the approach's insensitivity to interactive causation across levels of analysis. Because the analyst cannot move back up the funnel after a level's explanatory power has been exhausted, causation becomes a one-way street. The second weakness is an agent bias that does not

Table 2.1. The Funnel Approach to Regime Transitions

LEVELS OF ANALYSIS	DESCRIPTIONS
Macro-Structural	International dimension Political culture
Domestic Structural	Objectively defined social groups based on factors such as socioeconomic position and changes in the balance of power among them Socioeconomic conditions
Institutional	Formal domestic organizations and their rules and procedures Political parties, military and security organizations, state bureaucracies, and regime components such as constitutional or legislative rules and procedures
Social Group	Subjectively defined social groups: social movements, ideological factions within the military, regime hard-liners and soft-liners, and moderate and maximalist oppositions
Leadership	Individuals who lead subjectively defined social groups or institutional-level organizations such as political parties, governments, and militaries

allow the possibility of structures determining identity and choices. With the funnel approach, the analyst assumes that a margin of maneuverability for actors always exists among the crevices of structural constraints. To address these weaknesses, the next section modifies the funnel approach and frames it in a way that facilitates increased understanding of authoritarian outcomes of political openings in the Arab single-party republics.

Structures as Resources for Social Actors during Political Change

Integrative explanations for regime change such as the funnel approach seek a middle ground between voluntarist and structural extremes that have dominated work on regime change. As Mahoney and Snyder explain, "A fully integrative approach requires an integrative methodological conceptual base that goes beyond under-socialized and over-socialized conceptions of agency as well as constraint and generative models of structure."[21]

A persuasive way to handle the reality of structures both constraining and offering new possibilities for actors is the strategy followed in some works in social theory that conceptualize structures as resources that provide actors with tools to pursue their political projects while also constraining action by delimiting the range of possible projects.[22] The funnel approach to regime change can be improved by adopting the conceptualization of structures as resources. Additional improvement to the funnel explanatory framework can be made through the addition of a reflexive conception of human agency. This conception emphasizes how actors self-consciously deploy structural resources and modify their behavior and redefine their interests and goals in response to changing situations.[23]

How does this modified funnel approach anchor the analysis of regime change presented in this book? In the 1980s and 1990s, the former Arab single-party socialist republics faced serious economic and political challenges, which exerted pressures on two of their central features: the dominance of a single party and a social base of support among workers and peasants.[24] New economic conditions, including persistent economic crises, the apparent exhaustion of statist development strategies, and transformations in the global economy, changed the preferences of key actors. The structural conditions produced dilemmas and strategic questions for ruling party leaders and other state officials, the bourgeoisie, large landowners, workers, and peasants.

Ultimately, regime elites reacted to these altered structural conditions by gradually accepting and implementing the tenets of the neo-liberal Washington consensus. While partially constrained by the apparent choice between persistent economic stagnation and a marketizing project that would alienate their traditional social base,[25] these elites also recognized that they could utilize the new economic policies as a patronage resource to build a new core base of support among a rent-seeking bourgeoisie and rural elite, and enrich themselves in the process.

The new economic policies clashed with the interests of workers and peasants. Wages were held down to cut costs and boost exports, while extensive privatization reduced industrial sectors, increased unemployment, annulled labor contracts, and reduced access to land for the small peasantry. Ultimately the governments recognized that their marketizing economic project was inconsistent with a labor- and peasant-support base of the state. The rent seeking involved in the privatization process made this an even more glaring reality. The solution that state elites chose for these issues was to increasingly change the legitimacy claim of the regime from populist policies to electoral legitimacy. Of course, what the regime incumbents envisioned was not that ruling parties would actually ever lose power, but that they would win more competitive elections and share their power somewhat more.

The shift in the core constituencies of the regimes was premised on the ruling party's ability to retain the support of the popular sectors as a captive voting block: with no visible alternative, the popular sectors would remain loyal to the ruling parties. Single-party regimes that had previously built a strong and broad-based party organization proved to be resilient during later crises and better able to cope with alienated constituencies than military and personalist regimes.[26] In addition, ruling parties limited elite factionalism during hard times and served as sites for institutional innovation, including movement from single-party systems to limited multiparty systems.[27]

Workers and peasants were severely challenged by the macro and domestic structural conditions of the 1980s and 1990s and the responses of regime leaders to them. Labor and the peasantry generally opposed the new economic direction but were hesitant to break with ruling parties politically. Since no opposition party seemed capable of winning, workers and peasants opting for political opposition ran a high risk of political marginalization, could suffer material losses from state patronage (however much reduced such patronage became in the market reform era), and even could experience physical retaliation from the state and its party. Still, the base of national labor and peasant federations increasingly mounted protests against economic reforms while union leaders largely remained loyal to the incumbent regimes and continued to help deliver the votes of their constituents. In the end, authoritarianism was transformed but sustained.

The transition dynamics just described differ from the pattern found in the general literature. The transitions literature argues that the introduction of democratic institutions by authoritarian incumbents to bolster legitimacy often acts as a slippery slope in which political dynamics—interplay between regime hard-liners and soft-liners, and moderates and radical groups in society about full democratization—spin out of regime control and culminate in substantive democratization whether incumbents intend this outcome or not. The context for regime elites is obviously a challenging one, or they probably would not consider allowing multiparty elections. Reacting to the challenges by initiating political liberalization emboldens the mobilization of various social forces living within a context of socioeconomic distress. Numerous authoritarian regimes break down during these difficult junctures. However, the Egyptian, Syrian, Tunisian, and Algerian single-party authoritarian regimes of the late 1980s and 1990s did not.

Why were democratic impulses contained in the Middle East and North Africa? The thesis of this book was presented in the opening chapter. I highlight the capacity of state parties to contain the discontent of workers and peasants and the use of new sources of state patronage from economic liberalization to create a new social base of support for transformed authoritarian rule. Other leading approaches to persistent authoritarianism in the MENA highlight the importance of various institutional arrangements for choices made by actors that served to perpetuate authoritarian rule.[28] Winner-take-all electoral systems hindered the formation of political party pluralism.[29] Divide-and-rule tactics utilized against opposition parties were effective.[30] The well-financed coercive apparatus of the states efficiently served regime needs when necessary.[31] Autocratic elites utilized their geo-strategic positions to dampen international pressure for democracy. International powers that pursued democratic foreign policy agendas in other regions supported autocrats in the Arab world if they were moderate in the Arab–Israeli conflict, provided access to oil reserves, and later in the twenty-first century could present themselves as a bulwark against Islamist terrorism.[32] Autocratic leaders developed a cult of personality and manipulated symbols and rhetoric to immobilize political action. Insincere rituals of public obedience and compliance with autocratic regimes' self-presentation acted as self-disciplinary devices that generated a politics of public dissimulation and populations depoliticized by decades of slumbering civic life.[33] Historical patterns of patronage and patriarchy infused new institutions and perpetuated authoritarianism.[34] In some cases, oil rents that accrued to autocratic states provided the resources for the purchase of public compliance.[35] A bourgeoisie and organized labor sponsored by authoritarian states made these historical agents of democracy disinclined to play that role.[36] An exceptionally high level of conventional and non-conventional warfare created a burden of arms and deference to the military. This has been combined with praetorians who, in a context of war, tensions, and civil strife, claim to rule in order to carry forward a sacred mission. These ends-oriented Middle Eastern states discouraged the emergence of time-limited electoral legitimacy.[37]

The factors mentioned above certainly contributed to the authoritarian outcomes of political openings in the Middle East and North Africa in the 1980s and 1990s. Still, there are sound and convincing reasons to highlight new patronage resources from economic liberalization and single-party institutional structures; these can be especially effective resources for regime incumbents to transform authoritarian rule while maintaining power and control.[38] The reasons will be expounded upon in the next section.[39]

Tools of Autocrats: Single-Party Institutional Structures and New Patronage Resources

Single-Party Regimes

Different forms of authoritarianism break down in characteristically different ways. Some forms are more resilient than others.[40] Among the three major forms of authoritarian rule—single party, military, and personalist—single-party regimes are the most robust, and military regimes the most fragile.[41] Military regimes survive an average of nine years, personalist regimes an average of fifteen years, and single-party regimes an average of twenty-three years.[42] Authoritarian regimes are most vulnerable to collapse when poor economic performance undermines their ability to purchase social compliance and when elite fragmentation weakens their capacity to manage economic and political problems.[43] Single-party regimes are more capable of containing elite fragmentation and withstanding challenges caused by economic crisis and political difficulties of various sorts than military or personalist authoritarian regimes.

It is difficult for military regimes to contain elite conflicts and factionalism, partly because different factions all have access to instru-
ments of force. When conflicts between rival factions become intense,
one group might try to topple the other.[44] Military regimes carry
within them the seeds of their own rapid destruction in another way
as well. In many instances, soldiers place a higher value on the survival
and efficacy of the military itself than on anything else. They desire a
maintenance of hierarchy, discipline, and cohesiveness within the military. In contrast to single-party and personalist regimes, military rulers
may not want to retain power. They may instead prefer going back to
the barracks so long as military resources and autonomy from civilian
interference in military internal decision making can be maintained.[45]
Military regimes also have weak roots in society, which means they
find it hard to control or to withstand popular protest. For these reasons, when challenged by economic and political problems that induce
elite fragmentation, military regimes often disintegrate and seek to
return to the barracks under favorable terms.

Personalist regimes are also more fragile than single-party regimes.
During and after a seizure of power, personalist cliques are often formed
from the networks of friends, relatives, and allies that surround every
political leader. Over time in personalist regimes, factions form around
potential rivals to the leader within those networks, but during normal
times the participants have strong reasons to continue supporting the
regime and leader. Recruited and sustained with material inducements,
lacking an independent political base, and thoroughly compromised in
the regime's corruption, insiders are dependent on the survival of the
incumbent and rally around him or her during times when economic
and political problems lead to strong challenges from society.

Personalist regimes are usually rooted in a narrow slice of society.
This situation fosters more challenges to their rule when economic
and political problems arise than is the case in single-party or military
authoritarian regimes. If the personalist authoritarian regime breaks
down, the retaliatory consequences may be severe and life-threatening,
so factions on the inside tend to circle the wagons during such junctures. These regimes typically do not last long and may have a bloody
end if they suffer abrupt and large losses of resources that prevent the
continued serving of patronage networks.[46]

Single-party authoritarian regimes are better able to withstand challenges from economic crisis and various political problems than military and personalist authoritarian regimes. This robustness is partly due to the greater ability of single-party regimes to contain elite fragmentation. Rival factions in single-party regimes have strong incentives to cooperate with each other. Factions form in single-party regimes around policy differences and competition for leadership positions, but everyone is better off if all factions remain united and in office.[47] In addition, one-party regimes typically build up an elaborate system for rooting themselves, and thus have greater control of both the state apparatus and the larger society than other types of authoritarian rule. Consequently, single-party regimes are more resistant to opposition. Compared to military and personalist regimes, they have access to a stronger organization of supporters within the population, and at the same time find it easier to control dissidents.[48]

For authoritarian regimes, ruling parties bring elite cohesion, social and electoral control, and political durability. Ruling parties provide a site for political negotiation within the ruling elite that represents more than reliable patronage distribution. By offering a long-term system for elites to resolve differences and advance in influence, state parties generate authoritarian durability. They provide the site for individuals to pursue political influence and material interests while also ameliorating conflicts between competing elite factions by providing a place for debates and future chances to revisit issues for losing factions.[49] Ruling parties are both durable and dynamic. They are adept at creating new social bases of supports or abandoning old ones to stay in power. They are flexible enough to make shifts in their bases of support to stay in power and are rapidly and effectively able to respond to the grievances of new constituencies.[50]

Finally, single-party regimes are robust in part because their institutional structures make it relatively easier for them to allow greater participation and popular influence on policy than in military or personalist authoritarian regimes.[51] During the statist era especially, union groups affiliated with ruling parties in corporatist arrangements allowed input on policy for the masses. Affiliated unions in the market era allow a conduit for dialogue between states that are reworking their constituency relations.

New Sources of Economic Patronage

Patronage politics exist in all political systems, including our own. Less than in Sub-Saharan African countries, and more than in advanced industrial countries, Arab rulers rely on patronage politics to administer, rule, and survive.[52] The political logic of this form of rule encourages autocratic rulers in the region to constantly seek new patronage resources to purchase compliance. In the early socialist era of the Arab single-party republics, the assets of former colonial rulers and the nationalization of the productive assets of indigenous urban and rural economic elites and new state-owned enterprises provided resources to build support among urban workers and the small peasantry.

Autocratic rulers in the region have also found other resources to distribute and maintain social compliance. Foreign aid and strategic rent based on geography and political alliances have served this purpose. The MENA region has the greatest amount of petrodollars in the world with which to purchase compliance.[53] Some analysts have argued that "the political logic of authoritarian regimes in the region—specifically, the reliance on selective patronage to survive—creates strong political incentives to resist economic reform that would diminish the regimes' discretionary power."[54] I want to make a different case. With weak to nonexistent regulation of the privatization of state assets, regimes have discretionary power over these very resources and have utilized them to create new forms of rent-seeking behavior that has altered the form and dynamic of authoritarian rule.

For the purposes of analysis, new sources of state patronage generated by economic liberalization can be considered part of the domestic structural conditions that changed the balance of class power in Egypt, Syria, Algeria, and Tunisia. In that light, it is a domestic structural variable. I also want to make the case that patronage politics in the region is a historically specific cultural factor that fosters authoritarian trends. Patronage politics exist alongside rational-legal, administrative, and bureaucratic behavior in the MENA, and may be a cultural relic that will diminish over time.[55] The crony capitalism and patronage politics that are a central feature of politics in the Arab republics today may decline or disappear in time as well, though they may be too well entrenched to change easily.

As conceptualized here, patronage politics are equivalent to constituency clientelism. Constituency clientelism has four elements that distinguish it from patron–client relations. First, the patron is the state, not individual elites. Second, entire social classes are clients. Third, class-specific public goods such as subsidies, support prices, and protected markets are exchanged for acceptance of strict controls on political participation.[56] Fourth, privatized state land and industries are collective assets that have been exchanged for the support of urban and rural economic elites.

Both patronage politics and constituency clientelism appear in the neoclassical political economy literature as rent-seeking behavior. In this literature, rent seekers are most prevalent in statist economies, where they pursue the benefits of subsidies, tariffs, and regulations created by the state's intervention in the economy.[57] Rent seeking is viewed as a socially wasteful activity because it reallocates resources from productive to unproductive activities. From this perspective, market reforms dismantle rents and dissipate rent-seeking behavior. I argue that market reforms, especially privatization policies, can generate new rents.[58]

In sum, single-party institutional structures and patronage-based economic liberalization in Egypt, Syria, Algeria, and Tunisia provided resources for authoritarian incumbents to manage difficult economic and political problems by preventing elite fragmentation, by helping them to withstand challenges from constituencies against whom state policy had turned, and by enabling efforts to create new core bases of support in transformed authoritarian regimes. Political elites in all the Arab republics seem to recognize that this is a viable strategy for them if they are to transform authoritarian rule while maintaining power and control. These strategies to sustain authoritarian rule may not be as accessible for personalist, military, and monarchical authoritarian regimes, though many have noted the rise of crony capitalism in those authoritarian regime types as well.[59]

The concluding chapter of this book will return to examining patronage-based economic liberalization and single-party resources in the Arab republics and will identify possible paths to surmount them as resources that sustain authoritarian rule. The next chapter, however, presents the old authoritarianism in detail with an emphasis on the emergence of single-party rule in Egypt, Syria, Algeria, and Tunisia, and the role of state patronage in consolidating it.

THREE

The Old Authoritarianism

In an effort to displace colonial powers and their domestic allies, and achieve their own aims—especially rapid industrialization, social justice, and greater equality—leaders of nationalist movements or revolutionary coups throughout the developing world often forged populist authoritarian regimes characterized by the following: statist, interventionist, and redistributive economic policies; primary coalitional support among the lower classes; vague-to-explicit socialist ideologies; and nationalist, charismatic, and eudaemonic legitimacy based on promises to utilize state power to improve people's living standards. Political power was institutionalized through state parties, their affiliated corporatist organizations, and powerful executives. This chapter describes the populist authoritarian regimes that were the outcome of nationalist movements and revolutionary takeovers in Egypt, Syria, Algeria, and Tunisia.

This description of the consolidation of the single-party Arab socialist republics will provide about as much straightforward history as is to be found in this book. The chapter's goals, however, are more ambitious. To present a structured comparison between the old authoritarianism and the new (the latter is the topic of chapter 4), I have organized the case studies in both chapters around four regime dimensions: political institutions, ruling coalitions, policies, and legitimacy. Moving beyond a snapshot comparison, the aim in both empirical chapters is also to capture the dynamics of regime change. This chapter will highlight the development of single-party institutions and policymaking characterized by patronage and rent seeking, both crucial elements in the consolidation of Arab socialism. Chapter 4 argues that incumbent authoritarian elites utilized the previously developed single-party institutions and new sources of patronage provided by the economic liberalization process as resources to transform authoritarian rule while maintaining power and control. The new authoritarianism, by contrast, is characterized by a façade of multiparty politics, increasingly powerful presidents, economic liberalization, a reconfigured regime coalition anchored by a rent-seeking urban and rural economic elite, and some form or degree of electoral legitimation.

At the outset of this chapter on the old authoritarianism, it is important to note that what the regimes' leaders themselves came to call Arab socialism could be more accurately termed state capitalism. At the height of this period, the market remained the principal means of distribution. The economically dominant public sectors developed by these regimes did not lead to the complete elimination of private enterprise, and state ownership was not accompanied by workers' control of the means of production.[1]

An important underlying element in this depiction of the Arab republics concerns what Aristide R. Zolberg called the one-party ideology and what I refer to as a corporatist ethos instead of a liberal pluralist ethos.[2] Corporatists believe that they will be able to adjust the clash of societal interests and render them all subservient to the public good. State corporatists seek to co-opt, control, and coordinate all factions in society, which are organized by functional roles in the economy, into a united whole working as one unit.[3] Leaders of nationalist movements in the developing world tended to cast themselves as leaders of a single, all-encompassing nationalist struggle to abolish the colonial order, with elites acting in the name of the masses and as spokesmen of the general will. Any opposition became virtually tantamount to treason as nationalist leaders sought and in large part succeeded in bringing all social sectors under their control while negating the power of their countries' traditional elites. Ruling parties and affiliated corporatist organizations were the primary institutions utilized in these efforts to create unanimity.

Before Single-Party Rule and Arab Socialism

Single-party rule and Arab socialism in Egypt were implemented by a group of young officers within the army led by Lieutenant Colonel Gamal Abdel Nasser, who engineered a successful military coup in

1952. The Free officers toppled King Farouk, a scion of the Khedive dynasty that had carved out autonomy from the Ottoman Empire more than a century earlier.

Prior to the 1952 revolution, a number of nationalist political parties in Egypt had emerged to combat British rule. The British dominated Egypt in the form of a colonial protectorate from 1882 to 1922. Partial independence was achieved in that latter year, with full independence attained in 1936. A representative assembly first established in 1866 provided a forum for the nationalist struggle in Egypt. Mustapha Kamil, an ethnic Egyptian, formed the National Party (al-Hizb al Watani) in 1907 to strongly protest British occupation. The National Party received broad public support. At about the same time, a rival but more moderate political party of large landowners and intellectuals, the Party of the Nation (Umma), emerged as well. Finally, a nominal nationalist party, the Constitutional Reform Party, was formed to directly support the Khedive's interests.[4]

Britain clamped down on parliamentary activity in Egypt during World War I; however, the end of the war provoked great nationalist fervor throughout the country. In 1918, a group associated with the Umma Party formed a delegation, Wafd, to participate in the post-war international peace conference. This group, led by Sa'ad Zaghul, demanded full Egyptian independence. When the British claimed that the Wafd members were not representatives of the Egyptian people, the population rallied around the Wafd. To repress this nationalist spurt, the British exiled Sa'ad Zaghul and some of his Wafd colleagues to Malta. That act angered the population, cemented the Wafd as the leading force in the Egyptian nationalist movement, and fortified Zaghul as a nationalist hero.[5]

By 1919, Britain was reeling from a country-wide revolt. In 1922 it formally ended the British Protectorate by granting Egypt formal independence. However, the British maintained the prerogative of defending Egypt against foreign aggression or interference, maintained authority over the Suez Canal zone, held dominance over policies in Sudan (officially an Anglo-Egyptian condominium), and protected foreign interests and minorities. They thus remained a force behind the scenes and continued to protect their strategic interests. Egypt's political system between 1922 and 1952 has been described as ambiguously independent.[6] The term oligarchic democracy has also been applied to describe Egyptian politics of that era. Multiparty parliamentary elections were held regularly, but the British, in pursuit of their own interests, played off the monarchy against the Wafd, which had become a political party to contest the elections that emerged from the adoption of a new constitution in 1923.[7]

As a political party, the Wafd had both popular appeal and oligarchic dimensions. Its leader, Zaghul, was the popularly acclaimed father of the nation. The Wafd was affiliated with the nationalist struggle; it developed organizational capacities throughout the country, and created ties to an emerging trade union movement, students, and other organizations.[8] On the other hand, once in power, the Wafd often targeted state policy to please blocs of big landlords, bankers, and manufacturers seeking privileged access to state power in pursuit of rents.[9] Overall, during Egypt's liberal parliamentary era, including the early post–World War II years, economic and social policies reflected the rule of an oligarchy. As Joel Beinin writes in *Workers and Peasants in the Modern Middle East,* "Projects recruited peasants and workers to send their children to school where they would learn to be productive citizens of secular nation states, to work to build the national economy, and to participate in national political life on terms determined by their social betters. Higher wages, access to agricultural land, and other social issues were postponed in the name of the national cause."[10] By 1950, some 60 percent of the rural population was landless: fewer than .05 percent of all landowners held 35 percent of the land. At the same time, urban manufacturing failed to provide work for the growing population migrating from the countryside to the cities.[11]

The Wafd was not the only organization to attract popular support from the Egyptian population during the country's liberal era. The society of the Muslim Brothers, a social and political movement founded by Hassan Al-Banna in 1928, spread quickly in Egypt and eventually to the region as a whole. Under Al-Banna, the Muslim Brotherhood sought to preserve Islamic morality and to foster Islamic revival in broad terms. The organization was animated in the early years by the British occupation and secular trends emanating from Turkey.[12] The son of a religious scholar, Al-Banna became a teacher of Arabic and was assigned to the Suez Canal Zone city of Isma'iliya, where he had direct contact with the British military occupation and with dispirited Egyptians working within British labor camps. Soon after arriving in

Isma'iliya, Al-Banna utilized school, mosque, coffeehouses, and night classes for his students' parents to teach and preach the cause of Islam to the community as a whole.[13]

Hassan Al-Banna defined the organization that he founded at age twenty-two as a "combination of Islamic renewal society, athletic club, economic corporation, and political organization aiming to reform the Egyptian political system along lines it judged as authentically Islamic."[14] In addition to providing an appealing message of cultural authenticity, religious revival, and nationalism in an occupied country, Al-Banna and his close associates used their organizational skills and leadership abilities to make the Muslim Brothers one of the most important organizations active in the Egyptian political scene by the start of World War II.[15]

Politics in post–World War II Egypt continued the prewar pattern of deformed versions of pluralism and democracy. These were combined with structural conditions that reproduced widespread poverty, low average incomes, high unemployment, and grossly inequitable divisions of property. In 1952 the Free Officers military group, a cabal of some three hundred young Egyptian officers led by Gamal Abdel Nasser, overthrew the British-backed monarchy in Egypt and ended British occupation.[16] Within a year, parliament was abolished and political parties were outlawed.

The nationalist revolution in Egypt led to Egyptian-born leadership in the country for the first time in centuries. It also created an institutional and organizational vacuum along with the need for the Free Officers to define their own political and economic projects for the country. The Wafd, with its ties to rich landowners and capitalist merchants, was rejected as a nationalist party, and the Free Officers held divergent attitudes about the Muslim Brotherhood. The development of ideology and social and economic policies under the rule of the Free Officers occurred alongside multiple attempts to create a ruling party and affiliated state corporatist organizations to govern relations between state and society.[17]

In Syria, Arab socialism and single-party rule emerged from a society characterized by deep sectarian and ethnic cleavages and great inequality. A single elite, largely Arab and Sunni Muslim, was formed in Syria in the late nineteenth and early twentieth centuries, due largely to changes in property rights under the Ottoman Empire and French colonial rule, enabling a class of urban notables and absentee landlords to gain private ownership of large tracts of land. This elite established an agrarian oligarchy that dominated politics and government offices.[18] In prior times, Syrians had for generations practiced a type of collective farming known as *musha.'* Communal land was redistributed periodically to give each family a turn on the better plots. However, the new land laws resulted in local notables and tribal *shaykhs* seizing legal titles that greatly expanded their holdings, and reducing the majority of peasants to the status of sharecroppers.[19] This new elite, in many instances, took control of land on a scale large enough to be measured in villages, not acres or hectares. In Hama, into the 1950s, four families —the Barazis, the 'Azms, the Kaylanis, and the Tayfurs—owned 91 of the 113 villages of the Hama region.[20]

These wealthy landlords had ties to Syria's religious-mercantile establishment. They were sometimes members of the country's leading Sunni Muslim religious families, the *ulema,* who resided in the ancient quarters of various cities and acted as guardians of Islamic high culture in addition to controlling land held in pious trusts (*awqaf*). Absentee landlords and the religious establishment merged with wealthy merchants in the cities. A small number of this elite utilized their resources to invest in industrial projects.[21]

While new land laws under the Ottomans created great wealth for a merged Arab elite in Syria, Ottoman centralization policies, including that of placing more Turks in the provinces, threatened their new social, political, and economic power. For this reason, at the beginning of the twentieth century the Syrian elite turned to Arabism as a vehicle to maintain their privileges. Arab nationalism offered the elite in Syria some popular support and its best chance to maintain political and social influence against both the Ottoman Empire and the approaching French mandate.[22] In the minds of Syrian elite nationalists, World War I became a way to end both Ottoman Turk and European colonization of a largely Arab population that they intended to control and govern.

During the interwar years, Syrian nationalism tilted from a focus on Arabism to the defense of Syrian territorial integrity and demands of full independence from both the French and British mandates. European penetration into the Ottoman Empire proved to be catastrophic for Syrian national unity. Historic or Greater Syria consisted of what is now Syria, Jordan, Lebanon, Israel, the Palestinian territories, and a disputed piece of real estate currently held by Turkey. The Sykes-Picot Agreement (1916) by Western powers constituted a colonial land grab by the French and British. It divided Syria into four mini-states: Syria and Lebanon were ruled under a French mandate, and Jordan and Palestine were put under a British mandate. The Balfour Declaration (1917), a formal statement by the British government, supported Zionist plans for a national home for Jews in Palestine, along with the proviso that it must not prejudice the rights of existing communities there. In this manner, from the point of view of Arab and Syrian nationalism, Western powers subjugated the Arab East and dismembered Syria for the long term. Lebanon and Jordan were irreversibly lost and the colonization and eventual establishment of the state of Israel in Palestine placed a formidable enemy on Syria's doorstep.[23]

European penetration and territorial divisions of Syria exacerbated communal tensions in the country and caused conflicts to overlap surrounding countries. Ninety percent of the current Syrian population of 18 million people is Arab. Two-thirds of the eighteen million are Sunni Muslims, while another 16 percent are Arab members of various offshoots of Shi'a Islam—Alawis, Druze, and Ismaa'illi. Alawis dominate the numbers of non-Sunni Muslims with 11–12 percent of the overall population. Kurds, Sunni Muslims for the most part, constitute 8 percent of the population, and Christians roughly 11–12 percent.[24] During the time of growing European penetration in the region, Muslims developed economic and communal grievances against Christians connected to European political, economic, and missionary activity.[25] In addition, the French mandate initially divided greater Syria into six parts along sectarian lines, and created Lebanon largely as a Christian state by adjoining a heavily Christian area with surrounding Muslim communities.

Syria's elite was able to maintain their leadership of the nationalist movement in the early post–World War I years. The leader of the Arab revolt against Ottoman Turkey who fought alongside the British was Hussein bin Ali, King of Hejaz, Sharif and Emir of Mecca, and his three sons Ali, Abdullah, and Faisal. King Faisal led troops that occupied Damascus in 1918. During the Versailles treaty conference at the end of the war, Faisal demanded that British and other Western powers live up to promises of an independent Greater Syria. When Western support did not materialize, Faisal declared himself king of Syria in 1920. The

French utilized force to eject him from Damascus and then established their mandate over Syria and Lebanon.[26]

Under the French mandate, France governed in association with the Syrian economic and religious elite. In time, most of these elites became forces of opposition and voices for Syrian nationalism. However, in their hands, nationalism was constructed in a way that avoided issues of economic and social justice.[27] Instead they relied on the broad appeal of the independence of greater Syria, a romanticized vision of the Arab past, and religious solidarity. Their nationalism incorporated the language of constitutionalism, parliamentary forms, and personal freedoms, without touching on their country's basic internal economic and social conflicts.[28]

Syrian traditional elites dominated the nationalist movement between World War I and II, despite the eruption of a popular nationalist anticolonial revolt in the years between 1925 and 1927. Toward the end of the 1920s, the elite leadership of absentee landowners and the commercial bourgeoisie coalesced into a political organization known as the National Bloc, later transformed into the National Party, with its headquarters in Damascus. The National Bloc had active branches in Syria's other urban centers of Aleppo, Hama, and Homs.[29]

A split in the leadership of the National Party, partly based on tensions between wealthy landowners and capitalists, led to the formation of the People's Party just after independence in 1947. This new pro-business party pursued a cross-class social pact by considering policies to redistribute some large landholding and by proposing policies to improve workers' standards of living.[30] On their own behalf, the leaders of the People's Party called on government to enact stronger protectionist measures and grant more state support for industry, and legislative reforms to ease the regulatory burdens on small employers and craft workers.[31] The People's Party in coalition with other reformist parties, such as the Ba'th which was formed in 1947, was able to win elections and control parliament between 1948 and 1955. Ultimately, however, the People's Party's leadership was not able to implement a stabilizing social pact under its guidance. Instead, the political arena became more radicalized while more progressive forces, including the evolving Ba'th, grew more potent and demanded that popular sectors be integrated in the political arena independently, rather than as subordinate partners in a capitalist party.[32]

Beginning in the 1940s, political parties of the traditional elite in Syria began to be eclipsed by more ideological parties that were able to resonate with an emerging society struggling to find answers to fundamental questions such as "What are the boundaries of our homeland? To what nation do we belong? How can Arabs claim their rightful place in the world? But also, at home, how can the rule of the oppressive class be overturned?"[33] Three political parties gained mass support for the way in which they addressed these basic questions: the Syrian Communist Party (SCP), the Ba'th, and the Arab Socialist Party. A fourth organization, the Muslim Brothers, in alliance with city elites, battled all of the secular parties in the struggle to establish an Islamic state. The Ba'th would eventually triumph as Syria's hegemonic political party, and in 1963 Ba'thists in control of the state apparatus and the military outlawed all other political parties.

Ba'th means renaissance, and the Ba'th party referred to the renaissance of the Arabs to their ancient glories in the first few centuries of Islam. Three young teachers, educated at the Sorbonne in Paris—Zaqi al-Arsuzi, an Alawi; Michel 'Aflaq, a Greek Orthodox Christian; and Salah al-Din Bitar, a Sunni Muslim—provided the Ba'th's ideological moorings in pamphlets passed from hand to hand.[34] While schisms existed, core ideas of the Ba'th inspired a whole generation of Syrians, especially students, including long-time Syrian ruler Hafez al-Asad who was once the Ba'th's national student leader. Their ideas stressed the primacy of national revival and Arabism more generally (there were Ba'th organizations in Iraq, Palestine, and Jordan as well) and the universal values of Islam as the most sublime expression of Arabism. This formulation regarded Arabism and Islam as a culture that could attract Arab Christians and other minority groups to the Ba'th, and used socialist ideas to address the concentration of wealth and power in the hands of notables. It looked at exploitation and discrimination in Syrian society and addressed the issues of tribalism, sectarianism, and the oppression of women. By focusing on Syria and to an extent pan-Arabism, the Syrian Ba'th's socialism distinguished itself from the internationalism of the Syrian Communist Party.[35]

The Ba'th merged with the Arab Socialist Party (ASP) in 1952 in a move that gave the party more popular support.[36] In response to extreme agricultural land concentration in the region of Hama, a lawyer, Akram Hawrani, had formed the radical peasant-based political movement that became the ASP and later merged with the Ba'th. The ASP achieved much popular success, supporting direct parliamentary elections and a secret ballot to prevent landlords from intimidating peasant voters; it also used violence against landlords who abused sharecroppers.[37] The rise of the Ba'th was associated with minority groups in Syria hungry for Arab independence and social revolution. However, both the ASP and the Ba'th by extension took steps to garner support from Sunni Muslims from the same class as well.[38] In contrast, Ba'th support in the military took a more pronounced minority and especially Alawi character as the traditional elite avoided military service, which they regarded as a path for their social inferiors. This proved to be a fatal mistake for their rule.[39]

The United Nation's Palestine Partition Resolution of 1947 allocated more than half of Palestine to a Jewish state. That event contributed to the traditional elite's inability to muster a broad social pact in Syria that might have stabilized the country in the early post–World War II years. An encroaching enemy, vast social disparities, and widespread poverty also contributed to instability that led to a succession of conservative coups and military dictatorships in the years between 1949 and 1954. By this time, the Alawi and other minority officers favoring social revolution were numerous enough to make their presence known in the military. By the mid-1950s, Ba'th Party sympathizers had become the strongest single force in the military, just as they were in civilian society.[40]

Ba'thist party militants within the armed forces witnessed a chaotic and unstable period of democracy in the years 1955–1958. Syria was unstable both internally and externally. Externally, Israel was at its doorstep, and the Hashemite monarchy in Iraq had designs on Syria as did conservative Saudi Arabia.[41] Internally, destabilizing forces included the rapid succession of military coups in the post–World War II period, and gradually it became increasingly clear that the Ba'thist goal of social transformation would entail class warfare against the owners of land and capital.

While Syria wobbled under political strains in the 1950s, the charismatic Gamal Abdel Nasser had led the Free Officers' revolution in Egypt, dissolved the country's feudal agrarian structures, kicked out the British, and successfully stood up to Western powers and Israel over the Suez Canal. In addition, by making an alliance with the Soviet

Union, Nasser had also demonstrated that Arabs had options to Western arms and aid. These attributes made Nasser a powerful leader for followers of the pan-Arab nationalism preached by the Ba'th; as a result, Syrian Ba'thist military officers sought to form a union with Egypt and Nasser.[42] Their naive hopes and the excitement of the times was such that they believed that one great and charismatic Arab leader, Nasser, could realize all of their aims quickly. Forming a union with Egypt under Nasser could quickly fortify them against hostile regional and international powers and accelerate the social revolution within Syria.[43]

In 1958, at the request of Syrian military officers, Nasser agreed to a union between Egypt and Syria. The new country was named the United Arab Republic (UAR). However, the Ba'thist officers who sought the union soon learned that, contrary to their hopes, Nasser wanted to rule Syria with Egyptians largely, and wished to institute a form of Arab socialism without input from the Ba'th. Nasser's conditions for uniting with Syria included the dissolution of all political parties and a demand that the Syrian army withdraw from politics. The Ba'th's civilian leader, Michel 'Aflaq, obliged and announced the dissolution of the Ba'th.

As early as 1959, popular sentiment within Syria turned against the union due to its domination by Egyptians. Syria had lost control of its own affairs under Nasser. All major decisions taken by the United Arab Republic were made by Nasser and a small group of officers and security men in Cairo. Egyptian security agents spied on Syrians for the regime. Egyptian manufactured products were favored over their Syrian counterparts, and Egyptian peasants were favored over Syrian peasants in some land policies.[44]

Unhappy with the loss of their party and with the evolving conditions in Syria, five junior Ba'thist military officers stationed in Egypt during the UAR years formed a secret organization that they called the Military Committee.[45] The Military Committee in clandestine fashion began to rebuild the Ba'th. Their efforts were disrupted, however, in 1961 when a right-wing coup backed by Syria's disgruntled business community took power in Syria and dissolved the UAR.[46] This coup threatened to bring back the power of the traditional Sunni leadership and jeopardized hopes for socioeconomic justice and minority advancement. Two years later, in 1963, a Ba'thist countercoup led by members of the Military Committee brought the Ba'th to power. While pro-union and Nasser social forces remained in Syria, this time the Ba'th could begin to create its own version of an Arab socialist single-party regime.

In Algeria, socialism and single-party rule was established by the military after a bloody, eight-year war to achieve national independence from French forces that had conquered and settled Algeria more than a century earlier. The war (1954–1962) pushed military officers into the dominant role in the Algerian political system. They utilized the Front de libération nationale (FLN), a political party formed in the years just prior to the start of the war, and affiliated state corporatist organizations to link state and society. Military leaders ruled from behind the scenes during the consolidation of single-party Algerian Arab socialism.

The French invaded Algeria in 1830. It took forty-one more years to fully conquer the resistance of the population and implant a settler form of colonialism. Building on earlier transfers of Algerian land and other productive resources to European settlers, the French colonial system of 1871–1919 broke the backs of traditional elites, impoverished Algerians in general, reoriented the population's energies toward the needs of a colonial economy, and transformed social classes.[47] With military backing and a hunger to improve their standard of living, a minority of colons, French settlers in Algeria, forcibly placed themselves at the top of the Algerian socioeconomic and political pyramid and in a devastating display of colonial aggression annexed Algeria and made it an integral part of Metropolitan France. In 1848, the Second Republic in France declared Algeria to be French territory and transformed the provinces into *départements* as in the Metropole.[48]

The nationalist movement in Algeria blossomed between 1919 and 1954. There were several currents in the movement, and the future state party, the FLN, was organized in 1954 partly to move the nationalist movement past immobilizing factionalism. In the end, it took eight bloody years of a war of national independence (1954–1962), international pressure, and a French society brought to its heels by the war—the conflict led to the fall of the fourth republic and military coup attempts against De Gaulle—to achieve Algerian independence after more than five generations of French rule and settler colonialism.[49]

French colonization transferred the most valuable Algerian land and productive resources into European hands. This decimated the country's traditional elites' patrimony—the Turkish and indigenous

Table 3.1. European Population and Land Ownership in Algeria

YEAR	LAND IN HECTARES	POPULATION
1841	20,000	37,374
1851	115,000	131,283
1861	340,000	192,746
1872	765,000	279,691
1881	1,245,000	412,435
1891	1,635,000	530,924
1901	1,912,000	633,850
1921	2,581,000	791,370
1954	2,818,000	984,031

Source: John Ruedy, *Modern Algeria* (Bloomington: Indiana University Press, 1992), 69.

notables, absentee landlords, and small urban bourgeoisie—and impoverished virtually everyone else. The colon population that reached nearly one million acquired a monopoly over political and economic power and gained ownership of more than 2,800,000 hectares of the country's richest cultivable land.

French colonization largely destroyed the old social order and created a new one. A small number of the old elites survived in Algerian cities and emerged during colonialism to protect religious values. A newer Muslim bourgeoisie became evident during the 1890s. Over time, a gallicized middle class of small shopkeepers, agricultural wholesalers, small manufactures, and government officials learned to work and thrive to a degree in the new system. A small number of French-educated professionals and intellectuals also took their place in the new order that included subordinate Muslim governmental institutions, schools, and a torturous path to French citizenship that required a rejection of religious faith.[50] In the countryside, a small new land-owning class of Muslims took advantage of the progressive privatization of land under colonialism as the urban notables did in Syria. The rest of the indigenous population remained poor and largely uneducated.

Gradual recovery from colonial conquest eventually yielded new spurts of nationalism.[51] The reemerged religious leadership helped to guard and nourish national identity. Other movements of liberation against colonialism were drawn from the French-educated intellectuals, professionals, and successful business people. Called the *évolués* or Young Algerians, in the early part of the twentieth century they began to organize, publish periodicals and newspapers, articulate new social visions, and press for reforms, often using stated French values as their weapons. Their French orientation, however, hindered their mobilizational abilities among their countrymen and women. Finally, service in the French army provided a path of upward mobility for peasants and gave them a sense of power that would later foster self-assertion.

Between the two World Wars, members of the Young Algerian movement continued to press the French in the Metropole and at home to live up to their ideals of Liberty, Equality, and Brotherhood in Algeria. For the most part they were assimilationists who wanted French citizenship without renunciation of personal status as Muslims, until the vulgar celebration of the 100-year conquest of Algeria in 1930, and their failure over time to achieve their aims of equality. By the 1940s, a separatist position calling for full independence became the mainstream perspective.[52]

Including the Young Algerian movement, in the 1920s four nationalist movements developed to challenge the status quo in Algeria. The movements were of differing sizes and constituencies, and each mutated over the decades. Sometimes in competition and sometimes in collaboration they provided the framework that Algerians utilized in attempts to abolish the colonial system through political channels.[53] The Young Algerian movement morphed into the Fédération des élus indigènes. They pressed for an Algeria in which Algerians would have the same rights as Frenchmen and women. The initial detailed program of this gallicized Algerian elite called for native representation in parliament, equal pay for equal work in the bureaucracy, equality in length of military service, free travel between Algeria and France, abolition of the *indigénat* (set of laws that in practice discriminated against native Algerians), development of academic and vocational education, extension of metropolitan social legislation to Algeria, and reorganization of indigenous political institutions.[54] This movement found supporters but did not become the mass mobilizational instrument needed for the struggle against intransigent French colons.[55]

The Islamic reform movement was inspired by Muhammad 'Abdou and his pupil Rashid Rida. 'Abduh, a religious scholar, built on the liberal aspects of Islam and advocated interpreting Islamic morality and practice so that it could deal with the modern world and the challenge of the West. In the Algerian setting, the Islamic reform movement, Salafiyya, also sought to purify Islam and reform Maraboutism, rural folk Islam with practices considered heretical by the reformers, along more orthodox lines. Shaykh Abd al-Hamid Ben Badis led Algeria's Islamic reform movement. While never attracting a broad following, this movement helped in efforts to recover Algerian identity after the country was annexed by France. At a time when hopes for full and equal assimilation into France for all of Algeria's citizen still had some appeal, he was famous for his assertion that "Islam is my religion; Arabic is my language; Algeria is my fatherland."

The Communist Party in Algeria, an extension of the French Communist Party, provided some tactical and theoretical justification for Algerian challenges to the status quo, but their international orientation, secularism, and some internal racism limited the party's appeal on the ground. More successful in terms of mass mobilization was the organization and later political party inspired by an Algerian member of the French Communist Party living in France, Messali Hadj. Messali Hadj formed the Étoile Nord-Africaine, directing its focus away from the universal proletarian cause and toward the specific grievances of Algerians within colonial society. The Étoile Nord-Africaine served as a pre-revolutionary precursor to the eventually triumphant nationalist forces.[56]

The four nationalist movements in Algeria struggled to create a united opposition and a single party to guide their cause. After the Étoile Nord-Africaine was banned by the French, however, Messali Hadj formed the Parti du peuple algérien (PPA). This party became the most popular and active party in that country in the years just prior to World War II.[57] During the war, Ferhat Abbas and the Fédération des élus indigènes reorganized and founded first the Amis du manifeste et de la liberté (AML) and then a new party, the Union démocratique du manifeste algérien (UDMA), that also achieved significant popular support. Facing heavy repression, the PPA morphed into the Mouvement pour le triomphe des libertés démocratique (MTLD). By the time clandestine discussions about the necessity of removing the French by force became serious, the nationalist movement was split largely between two political parties, the UMDA and the MTLD.

The PPA-MTLD created the secret paramilitary structure, the

Organization spéciale (OS), which explored the options for revolutionary action and eventually launched the Algerian War of National Independence. PPA-MTLD and OS members created the Front de libération nationale (FLN) to represent all Algerians. The preponderance of power resided in the armed wing of the FLN, the Armée de libération nationale (ALN). After independence, the military rulers utilized the FLN as a tool to establish their version of Arab socialism, but remained involved in domestic politics from behind the scenes.

In Tunisia, a long gradual struggle for national liberation led by a single nationalist political party made for a relatively smooth transition to single-party rule and Arab socialism, after independence was achieved in 1956. The French Protectorate in Tunisia lasted seventy-five years, from 1881 to 1956. Before French colonization, Tunisia, nominally an Arab province of the Ottoman Empire, had been ruled by Turkish *beys* or governors. Beginning in 1881, the *beys* served as vassals of the French. Shortly after independence, the *beylik,* areas ruled by Turkish *beys,* was abolished by the country's nationalist leaders.

The beginning of modern nationalism in Tunisia emerged at about the time of World War I. Just after the war, the Destour (Constitution) Party was formed to challenge French colonial rule.[58] However, this was an elitist political party that never garnered mass support. The party's membership was comprised largely of the old pre-French Tunisian elite that included the religious leadership or *ulema;* the religious judicial leadership, or *muftis, caids,* and *aduls;* prominent merchants; leaders of the most respected crafts; old landowning notables, *mamluks,* military leaders of the Ottoman *bey;* and *baldi,* dynastic and wealthy families of the city of Tunis.[59]

Tunisia's traditional notables participated in the construction of a dual agricultural economy dividing rich from poor during the French colonial period. Reynold Dahl described the system in this way:

> At the time of independence in 1956, French and Italian "colon" farmers occupied 850,000 hectares of the best land, mostly in the North. . . . The modern sector consisted of 4,000 European families owning and operating farms of an average size of 200 hectares, and about 5,000 Tunisian families owning farms averaging 70 hectares each [who benefited from French land policies to develop modern private property]. The great bulk of the rural population, however, was in the traditional sector, which comprised 450,000 families owning an average of 7 hectares each.[60]

Table 3.2. Tunisia Land Tenure

FAMILY BACKGROUND AND NUMBER		HECTARES OF LAND	AVG. FARM SIZE	ROLE IN ECONOMY
European:	4,000 families	800,000	200 ha	Modern Sector
Tunisian:	5,000 families	350,000	70 ha	Modern Sector
Tunisian:	450,000 families	3,150,000	7 ha	Traditional Sector

Source: Reynold P. Dahl, "Agricultural Development Strategies in a Small Economy: The Case of Tunisia," staff paper, USAID (1971), 32–33.

The Destour and its aristocratic founders never gained widespread popular support, a robust broad-based coalition, or strong party organization. However, the Neo-Destour emerged from within the Destour Party in the 1930s to accomplish these tasks. The Neo-Destour was founded by men who were better able than their predecessors to capture the spirit of widespread aspirations, quicker to learn the value of organization and mass action, and bolder in attacking the status quo defined by colonial institutions.[61] Their version of the Destour led a mass movement against French colonial rule that culminated in Tunisian independence in 1956.

The leadership of the Neo-Destour was comprised of a new intelligentsia of modest, often rural origins that were educated in Franco-Arab schools, especially Sadiki College.[62] Founded by the Islamic reformer Kheireddine Pacha, who was prime minister of Tunisia from 1873 to 1877, the mission of Sadiki was to bring Western education to Tunisia in order to offset the challenge of the European powers. The college served as an important channel to elite status for bright young people from rural areas who mastered French, learned to negotiate the colonial administration, and frequently went to France for advanced education. The new party leaders were distinct because of the premium they placed on intellectuality in social leaders, organization, and activism in all sectors and areas of the country. They also hoped to organize social control in a centralized hierarchical structure.[63]

The most important Sadiki College graduate was Habib Bourguiba, the son of a low-ranking government functionary in the Sahel town of Monastir. Trained in political science and law in France, Bourguiba became the founding father of modern Tunisia and the charismatic leader of the nationalist movement. The Neo-Destour Party leaders aimed to guide a mass nationalist movement toward socioeconomic change that would nevertheless remain under their guidance and control.

As a national liberation movement, the Neo-Destour brought all Tunisian social forces into its sphere for the fight against the French. In rural areas, they helped to establish an agricultural union, the Union nationale des agriculteurs de Tunisie (UNAT), and deliberately organized a liberation army composed of peasants.[64] The party established branches in both rural and urban areas and incorporated into it one of the earliest and most powerful central trade unions in Africa, the Union générale de travailleurs tunisiens (UGTT). After World War II, 80 percent of the union members were also members of the Neo-Destour.[65] Other national organizations were founded on party directives and controlled by the party, including the national producer's association, Union tunisienne de l'artisanat et du commerce (UTAC; later, UTICA), and the national students' union, Union générale des étudiants tunisiens (UGET).

In sum, well before independence, the Neo-Destour Party had an imposing structure, with local branches throughout the country and allied organizations representing all functional groups in society, some of which the party created themselves.[66] Habib Bourguiba, rejecting the wishes of some of his comrades, even sought the support of the bourgeoisie in the Tunisian coalition against French colonial rule and included them in plans for rapid post-independence modernization. As one close associate wrote to him, "It is a delusion and great folly to pretend that our policy would attract the discontented bourgeoisie elements, which have been the allies if not the basis of colonization; it is to display an absence of political sense and a total incomprehensibility of the very essence of our movement."[67] Indeed, in the first five years of independence, 1956–1961, Bourguiba attempted a liberal economic transformation. The failure of that strategy contributed to the decision to implement a Tunisian version of single-party Arab socialism beginning in 1961.

Single-Party Arab Socialism in Egypt
Political Institutions

In contrast to the Tunisian case, Nasser and the Free Officers in Egypt did not emerge from a nationalist political party ready to fill the institutional and organizational vacuum left by their termination of the monarchy and the dismantlement of parliament. Their initial response to the demand to replace the previous set of institutions took the form of a political front known as the Liberation Rally (1953–1958), designed to replace the political parties it had outlawed.[68] The intent of this organization, however, did not include mobilizing supporting constituencies nor building party institutions at all levels of government to make that mobilization possible.

A second effort, more intensely focused on building a ruling party able to structure political life in support of the regime, was called the National Union (1958–1961). This party was formed in 1958 during the impulsive and short-lived union of Syria and Egypt known as the United Arab Republic (UAR). Nasser's charisma and symbolic leadership of pan-Arabism, which was spurred by his confrontation with Israel and the West during the Suez crisis, prompted leaders of Syrian Arab socialism to pursue a union with Egypt. As discussed, a rightist military coup in Syria in 1961 led to the dismantlement of the UAR and the National Union. This created a renewed need to design political institutions in Egypt.[69]

The next effort at political organization in Egypt, the Arab Socialist Union (ASU, 1962–1977), involved intensive attempts to build constituencies in support of the regime. It also entailed the building of political institutions within the ASU that would manage the regime's coalition of support and implement its more pronounced effort at socialist transformation. Nasser had ambitious goals for this version of a ruling party, as is stated by John Waterbury in *The Egypt of Nasser and Sadat:* "Nasser wanted the ASU to do everything: preempt all other political forces, contain the entire citizenry, and through a vanguard turn it into a mobilizational instrument with a cutting edge."[70]

The ASU was designed to represent the national alliance of working forces consisting of workers, peasants, intellectuals, soldiers, and national capitalists. National capitalists were contrasted with the exploitative ones, the latter presumably being those whose assets had been or were about to be expropriated. Those affected by land reform were also deemed to be enemies of the people and were therefore excluded from the emerging political structure. Each included sector of society or corporate body was granted representation within one over-arching political organization, the ASU.[71] In another populist step, the National Charter of July 1962 stipulated that at least 50 percent of all elected seats—national, local-cooperative, union—had to be reserved for workers and peasants. This policy reflected the regime's determination to mobilize constituencies that had always been on the margins of political life and that could be expected to support the regime against reaction as it undertook socialist transformation.[72]

Among other things, the ASU needed to incorporate organized labor under its auspices in order to progress toward Nasser's goal of a single party that could contain all citizens and preempt any opposition. This incorporation of labor into a unified front was a gradual process. The new regime's early relation to the labor movement was heavily influenced by a textile mill strike that broke out only a month after the 1952 coup. In Kafr al-Dawwar, four strikers were killed in clashes with police, ands several people from both sides were wounded. In a subsequent military tribunal, two workers were convicted of being communists, being hostile to the revolution, and holding responsibility for the strike. They were executed.[73]

After that inauspicious start, the regime began to negotiate with organized labor. To balance its repression of the Kafr al-Dawwar strikers, it enacted a number of beneficial labor laws.[74] One of the labor movement's aims was to establish a confederation on their own terms. However, partly due to the strike at Kafr al-Dawwar, the regime was apprehensive of such a prospect and initiated what would be the first of several efforts to purge communists from the unions while arguing for an "independent" confederation.

The establishment of the Egyptian Trade Union Federation in Egypt (ETUF) in 1957 represented a compromise, though one tilted toward the regime's viewpoint. A compromise was struck that the confederation should be formed strictly from the top down. A few unionists together with the authorities selected a list of people to be present at the founding convention, created by-laws, and formed the leadership. As Marsha

Pripstein Posusney wrote, "Thus a bargain was struck between the unionists and the state: the formation of a singular confederation in exchange for the government's right to choose its leaders."[75] From this point on, the unwritten bargain of the right of government interference in selecting confederation leadership continued.[76] The regime also centralized the labor movement more than the pre-coup labor activists desired, subjecting the locals to strict control and limiting their ability to respond to day-to-day issues affecting workers.[77] This subordination was brought about by the fact that the local level unions were in effect denied legal status, and thus were dependent on the federations. Likewise, restrictions of funding reinforced this dependence.[78]

Much of the additional government interference with labor organization came through the Arab Socialist Union and the "immersion of the confederation leaders in the intrigues of the ASU [which] served to detach them from other confederation matters, and to divorce them from the lower levels of the union movement where this dissatisfaction developed and grew."[79] However, the ASU also provided, for union leaders, an important vehicle for communication with policy makers and practical benefits for their constituencies.

While a ruling party and affiliated corporatist organizations helped link state to society, the executive branch and an alliance of the military and state technocrats ruled Egypt under Nasser. Even after the ASU developed organizational bite in society, the executive branch often operated outside of party parameters.[80] At the outset of the revolution in 1952, the Free Officers were governed by a fourteen-member Revolutionary Command Council (RCC).[81] Nasser was clearly the leader of this group of young military officers, though they initially chose an older general from outside their ranks, Muhammad Neguib, as the public face of the movement by electing him as president and commander and chief. General Neguib had been a hero in the 1948 war against the establishment of Israel.[82] Conflicts between Neguib and Nasser over how the country should be governed—Neguib wanted the restoration of parliamentary democracy—ended with Nasser taking over as both official and acting leader of Egypt in 1954. The RCC was disbanded.

The Suez Canal crisis contributed to the consolidation of Nasser's rule. Nasser negotiated the removal of lingering colonial influence over the zone with the British. The withdrawal was to occur over a twenty-month period and with caveats about reactivation of British power to defend Arab league members and Turkey. The Muslim Brotherhood demanded immediate withdrawal; members of the group attempted to assassinate Nasser in 1954. When the attempt failed, Nasser disbanded the organization and harshly cracked down on its membership base. In 1956, Nasser nationalized the Suez Canal and Egypt took full control over it and the routing of oil supplies through it. The Egyptian government under Nasser refused to accept international control over the canal and also struggled against British efforts to bring Egypt into the cold war against the Soviet Union. In retaliation for the Suez Canal nationalization, France, England, and Israel attacked Egypt. They failed in their attack partly because the United States would not support it, and the Soviet Union helped provide air power.

The Egyptian nationalist victory over the Suez Canal rebounded to Nasser's advantage. In 1956, a new constitution was promulgated that created a more powerful presidency to replace the leadership of the RCC. The presidency in form and substance now held tremendous power, especially given the uneven development of a state party. The president and his closest advisors, initially chosen from members of the RCC and other Free Officers but also including state technocrats, formed the inner core of the political elite that under Nasser's leadership made all of the country's most important decisions.[83] The president could appoint and dismiss the cabinet and all of the country's governors. He appointed the leadership of the ruling party. Nasser also took steps to civilianize this elite over time. In terms of state–society relations, Nasser's Arab socialism obliterated domestic alternatives to patronage that were not ultimately under the control of the president himself.[84]

Ruling Coalition and Policies

The policies that formed the basis of Arab socialism in Egypt led to two important and related results. First, they enabled workers and peasants to make important gains in the country's political economy. Second, state patronage established a rent-seeking context favorable to the lower classes.[85]

Arab socialism developed gradually in Egypt. However, once launched, its attacks on the interests of the private bourgeoisie and large landowners were aggressive. Nasser and the Free Officers made several revolutionary pledges when they took power in 1952. The promises included ending British imperialist control, removing the political and economic power of their allies among the feudal, cotton-growing landowners or parasitic industrial bourgeoisie, and ending the exploitation of landless peasants and sweatshop labor.[86] Over the course of a decade they went a long way toward attempting to implement these goals through various public policies that established the country's new dominant coalition of organized labor, peasants, the military, the public sector, and urban, white-collar interests.

The Revolutionary Command Council began with land reform. The essentially feudal structures that had been created by Khedive Muhammed 'Ali and his heirs between 1805 and 1952, coupled by the influence of British dispossessions, had created a powerful class of landowners that developed urban industrial interests while landlessness greatly increased.[87] This pre-1952 land-based power structure was stratified into an upper-class minority of rich landlords and cotton merchants and a mass of very low income and poor *fellaheen*.[88] Table 3.3 details the distribution of land ownership before the promulgation of Agrarian Reform Laws in 1952.

Egypt's land reform, enacted barely two months after the revolution of July 23, 1952, broke the economic and political power of the country's largest landholders. The law set a high ceiling of two hundred feddans on land ownership, which was gradually reduced to fifty feddans.[89] Some 864,521 feddans were distributed in the land reforms of 1952, 1961, and 1969, or about 12 percent to 14 percent of the cultivated area, and more than 346,469 families ($\frac{1}{10}$ of rural population composed of laborers, tenants, and small peasants) received land in two–five feddan plots. The pyramid of land ownership was truncated at the top and widened at the base: whereas large holdings were not entirely eliminated, the share of those owning fifty feddans or more dropped to 15 percent, and 95 percent of owners came to control 52 percent of the land instead of the 35 percent they had owned before the reforms.[90] In addition, royal estates were confiscated and foreign ownership of land disallowed. The *waqf* religious properties were confiscated by the state. Sharecropping laws were restricted to an even 50–50 percent split. Land concentration greatly decreased (see Tables 3.4 and 3.5). The land tenure changes were also designed to increase peasant participation in the political life of the country.

Agrarian reform in Egypt also included an agricultural minimum wage, tenancy reforms, and laws limiting agricultural rents to seven

Table 3.3. Distribution of Land Ownership
before Land Reform Laws Promulgated in 1952

FEDDANS	LAND OWNERS	HOLDING SIZE	LAND OWNERS PERCENT	AREA OWNED PERCENT
<5	2,642,000	2,122,000	94.3	35.4
5–	79,000	526,000	2.8	8.8
10–	47,000	638,000	1.7	10.7
20–	22,000	654,000	0.8	10.9
50–	6,000	430,000	0.2	7.2
100–	3,000	437,000	0.1	7.3
200–	2,000	1,177,000	0.1	19.7
TOTAL	2,801,000	5,984,000	100	100

Source: Ray Bush, "Mubarak's Legacy for Egypt's Rural Poor: Returning Land to the Landowners," UNDP Land, Poverty and Public Action Policy Paper No. 10 (August 2005), 4.

Table 3.4. Egypt Land Concentration Index—Gini Coefficent

1950	1965
0.61	0.38

Source: El-Ghonemy, M. Riad, *The Political Economy of Rural Poverty: The Case for Land Reform* (New York: Routledge, 1990), 30.

times the land tax. These changes contributed to raising peasants' standard of living.[91] Other issues had an impact on peasants' well-being during Egyptian Arab socialism as well. Small landholders created in the land reforms were required to join government-controlled cooperatives,[92] and the government also attempted to bring preexisting rural cooperatives, formed primarily around credit, under state supervision. These cooperatives were then used after 1965 as a means of generating state income when the state became a monopoly purchaser of rural products and then resold them.[93] By the early 1970s, some

Table 3.5. Distribution of Land Ownership after 1952–1961
Agrarian Reform (Upper Level of Holding Set at 100 Feddan)

FEDDANS	LAND OWNERS	HOLDING SIZE	LAND OWNERS PERCENT	AREA OWNED PERCENT
<5	2,919,000	3,172,000	94.1	52.1
5–	80,000	516,000	2.6	8.5
10–	65,000	648,000	2.1	10.6
20–	26,000	818,000	0.8	13.5
50–	6,000	430,000	0.2	7.1
100–	5,000	500,000	0.2	8.2
TOTAL	3,101,000	6,084,000	100	100

Source: Ray Bush, "Mubarak's Legacy for Egypt's Rural Poor: Returning land to the Landowners," UNDP Land, Poverty and Public Action Policy Paper No. 10 (August 2005), 5.

charged that the Free Officers' government was squeezing the countryside dry to finance their industrial ambitions. However, the government put nearly as much into the rural sector in the form of investment as it took out of it, and undoubtedly peasants under Nasser gained from land redistribution, new tenure relations, improved welfare security, and price and crop guarantees.[94] At the most fundamental level, the reforms were a success: they reduced rural poverty and promoted agricultural growth.[95]

The Free Officers' attack on the interests of the private sector bourgeoisie was more gradual. In 1955, the government sequestered the sugar factory of one of Egypt's most prominent entrepreneurs, Ahmad 'Abboud, in a dispute over sugar pricing. This was the country's first major leap into the transfer of assets in nonagricultural activities.[96] The Suez Canal crisis in 1956 precipitated the nationalization of virtually all foreign assets. In 1960, the government nationalized the interests of the Misr Group, an affiliation of Egyptian industrialists, along with the National Bank of Egypt, which had exercised many of the functions of a central bank in the country.[97]

In 1961 a welter of legislation, the "socialist decrees," put a considerable portion of the rest of the nonagricultural sector of the economy under public control. By 1962, the regime had confiscated assets from private hands and gained effective control of more of its economy than in virtually any country outside of the Soviet Union. The state controlled all banking and insurance, all foreign trade, all medium and heavy industries, all air transport and most maritime transport, all public utilities and mass transport, a limited portion of urban retail trade, major department stores, all newspapers and publishing houses, all reclaimed land, all agricultural credit and basic agricultural inputs, all major construction companies, and large infrastructural assets such as the Suez Canal.[98]

Egypt's socialist decrees and other economic policies created state-centered economic groups that provided political support for the regime.[99] At the top of the list were the administrative elite or higher echelon bureaucrats in the public sector and the military that designed and implemented the policies and ran the new state-owned enterprises. This group largely originated from the rural middle class.[100] In addition, masses of workers filled the positions created by SOEs (state-owned enterprises) under Egyptian Arab socialism. As Mark Cooper noted, "the expansion of an industrial labor force concentrated in the public sector and lower white-collar workers concentrated in the bureaucracy was unprecedented in Egyptian history."[101]

Labor received other concrete benefits in addition to jobs during the height of Egyptian Arab socialism. The 1956 constitution served as a harbinger for progressive labor legislation. Its preamble called for the achievement of social justice in a "democratic, socialist, cooperative" society. Article 53 of the constitution specified that the principle of social justice was to be applied to employer–employee relationships. Article 52 stated that work was a right of all Egyptians and guaranteed just treatment in jobs, hours of work, wages, vacations, and insurance against accidents. In article 21, the government promised to increase social insurance and improve public health, and affirmed the right of citizens to financial assistance in cases of old age, sickness, or disability.[102] This all came into effect in 1958. The 1959 Unified Labor Code then reduced the probation period for workers to three months, cut working hours to eight per day, and doubled the differential for shift work.[103]

The "1961 socialist decrees" led to both sweeping nationalizations and several more laws aimed at improving workers' living standards.[104] Law 133 of 1961 limited the work week in industrial establishments to forty-two hours. A compulsory social insurance scheme was introduced in the 1961 laws and modified in 1962, increasing the employers' contribution from 7 to 17 percent of salary. There was also the common pledge to provide employment to all university graduates. Laws concerning job security were strengthened. Under these policies, public sector managers could not fire workers at will but had to consult a tripartite committee consisting of representatives from the union, the ministry of labor, and management. Workers who felt that they were unjustly dismissed could appeal their cases to this committee before turning to the court system. Finally, the minimum wage was doubled to twenty-five piasters per day for many workers

A social contract was developed in Egypt under Nasser. Workers came to see their benefits as entitlements.[105] The state directly set prices and wages and manipulated access to basic consumer goods.[106] Beginning with a food subsidy system that at its peak included eighteen foods from bread and cooking oil to meat and fish, a broader set of consumer welfare programs emerged under Nasser to cover subsidized transport, housing, energy, electricity, water, health, education, and some nonfood consumer products such as soap and cigarettes.[107] In exchange for these benefits, workers and peasants were expected to provide political support for the regime and work harder. Strikes were forbidden.

Due in part to the need to focus on political survival, the leaders of Egyptian Arab socialism created a context for rent seeking. In addition to decapitating the power of traditional elites and attempting to live up to pledges of social justice and modernization, the administrative elite utilized its control over the state apparatus to build an alternative base of support among workers, peasants, and others that helped its ability to govern. This strategy produced a rent-seeking society by rendering the state's coalitional partners dependent on it for the conduct of economic activity. Economic policy became primarily redistributive in nature, and the leadership exchanged material advancement for political support. Financial income was not matched by corresponding labor or investment. Competitive pressure for productivity was lax. Actors had economic incentives to manipulate the economic and political environment in ways that were not advantageous for the economic system as a whole. Resources consumed in rent seeking were not available for productive activity. Resources were misallocated, leading to heavy social costs. Ultimately, despite the real material gains made by the masses, economic growth was hindered.

Legitimacy

A combination of material, social, and political gains for large underprivileged constituencies, along with their containment within ruling party structures and affiliated corporatist organizations, helped Egyptian Arab socialism under Nasser establish popular support and legitimacy. In addition, Gamal Abdel Nasser was a charismatic figure and symbol of both Egyptian and pan-Arab nationalism. This charisma helped sustain the regime when political institutions that supported it were lacking. As noted, pan-Arab socialism under Nasser took concrete form in the union with Syria between 1958 and 1961. Nasserism spread to other Arab countries as well.

Egypt under Nasser was a very repressive state that was willing to combat perceived enemies of the right and the left. Nasser built a vast network of intelligence agents and a formidable police apparatus to battle "reactionary feudal elements" that for obvious reasons opposed the sequestration of their properties.[108] Communists, striking factory workers, and Muslim Brotherhood members also faced the brunt of state repression. The Kafr al-Dawwar strike led to the arrest of 545 workers and the execution of two leaders. The sharp repression was partly linked to concerns that communists led the strikes; the regime wanted all social forces under its control.[109] Members of the Muslim Brotherhood were also frequent targets of police arrests in the 1950s and 1960s. On two occasions, in 1954 and in 1965, they faced especially harsh state repression. In 1954, this was linked to an assassination attempt on Nasser's life. Even though there were Free Officers sympathetic to the Muslim Brotherhood (MB), it was an organization that had its own vision for governance, especially the goal of an Islamic state, that did not always coincide with the regime's wishes, and as such they could not be tolerated. A general crackdown against the Muslim Brotherhood in 1965, based again on fears that they were plotting to bring down the regime, led to the arrest in some claims of 27,000 members in one day.[110] Torture and loss of life in jails became commonplace in Egypt under Nasser, though he sought to rein it in at the end of his life.[111]

Hassan Al-Banna's replacement as chief spokesman of the Muslim Brotherhood, Sayyid Qutb, was jailed and hanged in 1966.[112] Qutb, a theoretician of religious social criticism, developed the notion of a modern *jahilliya* (the period of ignorance before Islam). The modern *jahilliya* referred to un-Islamic, secular, and westernized governments such as Egypt under Nasser, which in his view posed dangerous threats to Islamic society that demanded confrontation. He argued that the same confrontation should be extended to the Western powers themselves. Qutb's political philosophy and writings have been very influential in a number of contemporary Islamist organizations within and outside of Egypt including al-Qaeda.

Single-Party Arab Socialism in Syria

Political Institutions

Single-party authoritarian regimes threatened by organized powerful opposition forces respond by building effective party institutions to mobilize their own constituencies. These early party-building efforts contribute to the long-term durability of single-party rule.[113] Few regimes on earth faced more powerful organized opposition than the Syrian Ba'thists of the 1960s. The reactionary military coup of 1961, backed by Syria's largely Sunni business community and landlords, made this point crystal clear by demonstrating that Syria's traditional elite represented still powerful class enemies that could topple hopes for distributive justice and social transformation. Once they regained power without Nasser in 1963, Ba'th party militants were determined to develop national and local party institutions that would fortify their rule.

Youth and student groups established around the country by 'Aflaq and Bitar in the 1940s and 1950s had provided the Ba'th with an early organizational foundation.[114] Hawrani's peasant movement contributed additional organizational resources in the countryside. After the 1963 coup, the Military Committee altered the party apparatus to better suit their needs. 'Aflaq had conceived of his party as a pyramid with a national command at its apex under a secretary general directing the party's affairs throughout the Arab nation. In each country, party matters were in the hands of a regional command, partly subordinate to the national command. Syria's new Ba'thist rulers made their regional command more autonomous from 'Aflaq and the national command.[115]

In a key innovation, Syrian Ba'thists in the Military Committee and regional command fused military and civilian vanguard sectors.[116] Hafez al-Asad was assigned the responsibility of making the army a Ba'th monopoly in an attempt to avoid the military factionalism and instability that had characterized the country since independence. Asad sought to build an ideological army along the lines of the civilian Ba'th. He built a hierarchical structure of party cells, divisions, sections, and branches throughout the country.

Seeking deeper roots in society, Ba'th Party leaders rebuilt corporatist organizations of labor, peasants, and business that had been initiated during the period of the UAR.[117] The Syrian labor movement, controlled and demobilized during the union with Egypt (1958–1961), had remobilized and reorganized during the 1961 secessionist coup, and an independent labor leadership existed in 1963 when the Ba'th took power. The labor movement spanned the political spectrum yet did not have close ties to the Ba'th Party. These leaders, some communists with a more international perspective, viewed the new regime with suspicion and resisted Ba'th efforts to impose their own cadres in leadership positions.[118] The regime's initial dependence on labor support was reflected in new legislation passed in 1964, which repealed previous anti-labor regulations and granted wide privileges to labor. In the constitution that same year, there was a call for an independent labor confederation.[119]

The years of Ba'thist consolidation of the state, 1965–1970, produced more effective corporatist controls over the Syrian labor movement.[120] Elizabeth Longuenesse noted that from the mid-1960s into the early 1970s unions that formerly had had rights began to speak of their duties."[121] In terms of labor representation, as the regime's hold on the labor movement became more secure, it gradually restored the electoral prerogatives of the workers within the labor movement. The party created a worker's bureau under the ministry of labor and social affairs to "rationalize" administrative relations between different levels of the organization and between the General Federation of Trade Unions (GFTU) and the government. The workers' production councils lost popular bite over time, but they established the new conception of trade unionism and the idea that the administration of public-sector firms could, as a matter of principle, work in the interests of the workers.[122]

A Peasant Union (PU) formed in 1964 and served as the mass organization representing peasant interests. It was later adjusted to merge with local cooperative organizations, and represented both owners and agricultural workers. The Ba'th had much better control of peasant organizations due to their membership base from the period of Hawrani, pro-land reform policies, and the rural origins of many leaders.

Women were favored in some new policies and became linked to the Ba'th organizationally as well. In addition, the Ba'th Vanguard Organization became compulsory for children aged six through eleven. Membership in the Revolutionary Youth (schoolchildren aged twelve through eighteen) was not compulsory but conferred considerable privileges. The Students' Union was reformed to stress ideological conformity.

In sum, national policy debates and decisions in this Ba'thist state occurred largely among the upper echelons of the party, army commanders, and security chiefs, with one powerful executive figure at its peak. Corporatist functional organizations affiliated with the Ba'th served social control purposes. These institutions allowed a limited degree of political activity and representation outside of elite circles, but more crucially they bolstered the party's ability to both mobilize and control core constituencies.

Ruling Coalition and Policies

The intense, perpetual, and often bloody conflicts in Syrian society during the rise of the Ba'th radicalized it by the time it took power from the leaders of the secessionist coup. Ba'thist leaders were determined to break the wealth and political power of Syria's traditional elites composed of primarily Sunni landowners, merchants, business people, and religious notables. To create constituencies of support, the Ba'th targeted workers and especially peasants in state policy. This political dimension of development policy created a rent-seeking environment (described in the conclusion of this section).

The power of the great landlords in Syria was weakened by land reforms undertaken under the UAR and the Ba'thist regime that took power in 1963. Peasants gained access or ownership of land that accompanied their growing political power. As noted, changes in land policies at the end of the Ottoman Empire and during the time of French colonization concentrated Syrian land in very few hands. The 1858 land code converted the peasant and communal land of hundreds of villages into private property owned by Sultan Abdul Hamid and a handful of powerful Syrian families.[123] In many cases, "tribal" chiefs were transformed into private owners while tribe members became their sharecroppers.[124] A small number of absentee landlords, merchants, the urban bourgeoisie, and conservative religious leaders took titles of private property as well. These new owners could also evict peasants from land that might have been farmed by generations of families. By the 1950s, owners of plots of more than 100 hectares constituted less than 1 percent of the agricultural population but held half the cultivable land, while 60 percent of the agricultural population owned no land at all.[125]

Under the UAR in 1958, the Agrarian Relations Law (no.134) regulated relations between landowners and tenants, and the Agrarian Reform Law (law no. 161) dealt with land reform, placing a ceiling on landholdings depending on rainfall and irrigation (Table 3.6). Previous owners were allowed to dispose of 8 percent of land prior to appropriation. In 1963, a new land reform law was promulgated by the Ba'th. Table 3.7 displays the amount of redistributed land by 1975.

Under the UAR and Nasser, in 1961 all banks and insurance companies were nationalized. Three industrial firms were fully nationalized and twenty-four others partially so. Some of these measures were reversed during the 1961–1963 conservative or secessionist countercoup.[126] In 1964, the Ba'th renationalized any changes made by the previous coup and greatly expanded nationalization to include sixty commercial enterprises, all cotton gins, and more than 130 industrial establishments and trading companies.[127]

The nature of concrete benefits to labor and peasants during Syrian Arab socialism resembled those granted in Egypt. Land was redistributed to peasants. There was the effective application of labor legislation, including regulation of working hours, social insurance schemes, employment in the new state-owned enterprises, and protection against firing. As in Egypt, the Syrian regime undertook measures to improve the purchasing power of both workers and peasants; it established an extensive subsidy system and price-control regime.[128] In Syria, real

Table 3.6. Ceiling on Land Holdings during Syrian Land Reforms

CEILING[1]	CRITERIA
80ha of in regions	Rainfed in regions receiving >500mm
120ha of rainfed	Rainfed in regions receiving 350–500mm
200ha (140ha)[2]	Rainfed in regions receiving < 350mm
300ha (200ha)[2]	In the Northwest (Muafazat Dayr al-Zawr, Hassakeh and Raqqah)
35–50ha	Orchard
15–45ha	Irrigated depending on region and type of irrigation

Source: Jonathan Rae, "Land Tenure Review of the Near East," Part II: Individual Country Profiles. Consultancy Report for FAO (Rome, 2001).

1. Landlord able to dispose of up to 8% of land to wife and children prior to appropriation.

2. May 14th, Decree No. 31, 1980.

Table 3.7. Land Redistributed in Syria by 1975

BENEFICIARY	LAND IN HECTARES
Landless Peasants and Small Farmers	446,000 (61,000 irrigated)
Co-Operatives, Ministries, and other Organizations	254,000
For Sale	330,000
Total Number of Persons Affected	300,000 Persons (50,000 Family Heads)

Source: Jonathan Rae, "Land Tenure Review of the Near East," Part II: Individual Country Profiles. Consultancy Report for FAO (Rome, 2001).

increases of workers' standards of living rose by 25 percent between 1965 and 1977.[129]

Once the economic and political power of the largely Sunni Muslim landed aristocracy and urban bourgeoisie was broken, a distributional coalition, described above, was formed to support the new Ba'thist regime. In contrast to our other cases, there was a sectarian aspect to Syria's populist coalition due to the pronounced presence of the minority Alawi within the state power structure. The degree of operative sectarianism in terms of coalitions of support as opposed to class cleavages has been hotly debated by scholars, with the weight of the evidence pointing to an Alawi military and security base and less sectarianism and more class warfare in terms of state policy in other areas. Nikolaos Van Dam, for instance, argued that in the late 1960s non-Alawi officers were swept from their top military positions, leaving Alawi domination of the state. These officers pursued policies that greatly favored their communal group.[130] In contrast, Raymond Hinnebusch and Volker Perthes suggested that Ba'thist policies favored certain classes and rural interests over urban interests, rather than purely focusing on primordial ties.[131] Hanna Batatu, while confirming the rural and Alawi identity of Syria's ruling elite, downplayed the extent to which Syria's Ba'thist ruling elite were motivated by sectarianism. He also argued that class background and rural social origin influenced their political behavior more than sectarianism.[132]

Either way, the ruling coalition during the ascent of populist authoritarian rule in Syria, from 1963 to 1970, certainly included a top stratum of senior Alawi military officers and other Alawis well placed among the state managerial class. Persons of Alawi background gained virtually exclusive control over command of the vital military and security apparatus in the 1960s.[133] The second core social base of support was the minority Alawi community as a whole (and, to an extent, other non-Sunni minorities). Alawi living conditions lagged far behind those of the majority Sunni population prior to the Ba'thist seizure of power and they were much improved relative to the Sunni Majority under Syrian Arab socialism. The third group of regime support was comprised of workers and professionals who relied upon public-sector employment. The fourth social constituency consisted of rural peasants, who benefited from land-reform measures undertaken by the Ba'thist regimes and became dependent on the state for access to credit and input subsidies.[134] The new regime, as noted, also provided education, social services, and employment opportunities in rural areas to build up a base of support in the countryside.[135]

In sum, the leaders of Syrian Arab socialism had laudable development goals, and they achieved some of them. Workers, peasants, and women (the majority of the population) made important economic and political gains. Syrian Ba'thist policies made Syria a much more industrialized country than it had ever been.[136] In some years good economic growth was attained. However, the political dimension of their development policies created a rent-seeking context that harmed economic productivity in the long term. The regime's core constituencies of workers and peasants became oriented to struggles over the distribution of income and wealth—subsidies, support prices, job security and benefits, social programs—rather than the production of additional output.

Legitimacy

The Ba'th Party that took power in Syria in 1963 was more ideological than the Arab Socialist Union in Egypt. They also took power after a reactionary coup that threatened previous gains by the party and its allies. That experience radicalized the party even more once they regained state power. Ba'thist ideas, as articulated by one of its founders, Michel 'Aflaq, emphasized Arab nationalism or a national "revival" and appreciation of the glorious historical achievements of the Arab nation stretching back to the founding of Islam. It also emphasized freedom from foreign military, political, or cultural domination. The separation of Lebanon, Jordan, and Palestine from Greater Syria and the founding of Israel next door increased the feeling of foreign domination in the country. Over time, Syrian Ba'thists focused more on a Syrian nationalism than on pan-Arab nationalism. Party leaders could also tap into nationalistic legitimacy by taking up the role of frontline state in the Arab–Israeli conflict. A third core idea of the Ba'thists was that nationalistic socialism was needed to end the concentration of wealth and power in the hands of notables in Syria.[137] These ideas resonated powerfully in Syria and contributed to the legitimation of the regime.

How coercively authoritarian regimes deal with their various opponents offers insight into their legitimacy. In those terms, the Ba'th in Syria has not fared well, though part of that is linked to a minority group controlling the state. Alawi and other minority offshoots of Shi'a Islam from rural areas in Syria turned the tables on the country's Sunni and urban traditional elite. The society this minority group is now leading is predominately Sunni. This gave the regime a major Sunni problem that became apparent soon after they took power in the mid-1960s and made the state fierce, creating a state so in opposition to society that it often dealt with opponents by using coercion and raw violence.[138]

The Alawi–Sunni split and class factors have been in play in the strongest challenge to the regime, its struggle with the Muslim Brotherhood. The Muslim Brothers in Syria, an offshoot of that founded in Egypt by Hassan Al-Banna, drew popular support from the Sunni traditional notables formed by an amalgamation of landlords, the bourgeoisie, and Sunni religious leaders. The Muslim Brothers also were implacable enemies of the Ba'th because of the party's secularism and pan-Arab rather than pan-Islamic orientation. Confrontations between the Muslim Brotherhood and the Ba'thist regime began in 1964 in Syrian cities, especially Hama, a conservative city dominated by traditional notables reeling from regime efforts to break down their social, political, and economic power. For Ba'thists Hama also was the main symbol of the rural poverty from which many had recently escaped.[139]

In the spring of 1964, prayer leaders across Syria preached inflammatory sermons against the secular, socialist Ba'th, whipped up street riots, closed the souks (markets), and attacked party leaders in the streets. In Hama, the National Guard was called up to battle the city's Muslim Brothers who were barricaded with arm supplies in the Sultan Mosque. The mosque was shelled and some seventy Muslim Brothers were killed.[140] The battle made the regime aware that small groups of Islamic militants had been underground organizing armed resistance. These guerrilla groups began a campaign of assassinations, drew ideological support from Muslim Brotherhood leaders in Syria and other countries, and challenged Ba'thist efforts to consolidate their rule. The regime responded with a ferocity that set the tone for state–society relations in Syrian Arab socialism that partly offset legitimacy based on ideology, policies, nationalism, and the benefits and gains made by workers and peasants under the Ba'th in the 1960s.

The evolution of Ba'th Syrian Arab socialism under the leadership of the Military Committee was marked by bloody infighting and a succession of coups by members of the committee, partly due to conflicts over the degree of radicalism and force needed to secure the revolution. The country and the region were also rocked by the catastrophic, from the point of view of the Arab regimes, Six Day War in 1967, a war in which Israel rapidly defeated a group of Arab countries and occupied Arab territory including the Gaza Strip and West Bank in former Palestine, and the Golan Heights in Syria. In 1966, General Salah Jadid launched a coup-d'etat and upon taking power led the country in the direction of radical social transformation that included nationalizations and fierce struggles to decapitate the economic and political power of Syria's notables once and for all. In 1970, General Hafez Al-Asad launched a coup and what he called the corrective movement that moderated some of Jadid's policies. Asad was the ruler of the Ba'th and Syria from 1970 until his death in 2000.

Single-Party Algerian Arab Socialism

Political Institutions

On November 1, 1954, members of the Organisation spéciale (OS) launched the Algerian revolution with their first guerrilla military action. They initially formed the Revolutionary Committee of Unity and Action (CRUA), and then, piggybacking on earlier political parties, they established a new political party or front called the Front de libération nationale (FLN). During its first two years of existence, the FLN managed to become the sole nationalist party able to overcome divisions and present a unified front for the nationalist struggle. Their tactics included violent ones: liquidating Muslim collaborators to the French establishment; battling rival militias created by other Algerian political parties, including a new one set up by Messali Hadj, who did not back their military action initially. Eventually other political parties capitulated and many of their members joined the FLN. The major reason they became the hegemonic nationalist movement, however, is that the men and women of the FLN and OS were risking their lives for the common good and drew a widespread following.

During the war, the FLN organized a counter-system to French colonial rule. Within Algeria, they organized, in addition to military units, clandestine institutions that included judicial structures, civil and tax authority, pensions, and family assistance programs.[141] The FLN set up a government in exile as well, the Gouvernement provisoire de la République algérienne, (GPRA), to conduct diplomacy and recruit sympathetic governments to support the nationalist cause. The moderate Gaullist Ferhat Abbas, who had become radicalized during the war, became its first president.

The armed wing of the FLN became the Armée de Libération Nationale (ALN). The ALN was divided into internal guerrilla units fighting the French in the interior of the country and a stronger, more traditional army based in neighboring countries, especially Oujda in Morocco. The external army was led by Colonel Houari Boumédienne. The war of independence was exceptionally brutal; counting both civilians and soldiers, Algerian leaders claimed that more than one million Algerians died.[142] War and the long colonial interlude devastated a population that suffered from widespread poverty and was fractured and broken at independence in 1962.

Though the war was won, difficult issues confronted the victorious nationalist movement and its leaders. For the most part, the Algerian traditional elites had long since disappeared and the new middle classes were more brutalized and consequently less able than their counterparts in other former French colonies. The new rulers were destined to struggle in creating a new political order to replace French rule. However, they would not be without material resources as large reserves of oil and natural gas had been discovered during the war.

The ALN, the armed wing of the FLN, entered the post-independence era more powerful than their political party counterpart. The FLN struggled to fulfill the task of dependable tool to mobilize support for the regime's agenda. It also did not perform satisfactorily in other areas assigned to the state's sole party: policy formation, leadership recruitment, ideological coherence, and vehicle to transmit preferences from society to the state. After independence, the FLN provided numerous patronage posts and intermittently was reorganized in an effort to gain a greater sense of mass popular control and regime support against waves of popular discontent and displeasure over bureaucratic mismanagement or indifference.

The FLN utilized familiar tools to link state and society, most importantly affiliated state corporatist organizations. As in Syria and Egypt, state corporatism was utilized to incorporate labor and other social groups into the populist authoritarian regime. The Algerian labor movement, L'Union générale des travailleurs algériens (UGTA) did not play a central role in the struggle for independence, which gave the ALN–FLN a powerful position from which to incorporate organized labor on its own terms. The FLN simply did not need the UGTA to achieve its aims.[143] The latter's very creation, in fact, was due to the FLN and its desire to use it to undermine internal competitors. After incorporation, the FLN immediately imposed strict limits on union activities.[144] The UGTA had no bloc of deputies in the national assembly in the single-party state or seat on the political bureau. The heyday of Algerian labor and peasant participation in the policy process was the early phase when Algeria promoted self-management committees in the plants and farms taken over from the French immediately after independence in 1962. However, labor did not have the resources to control its own base.[145] In addition, "government officials were too pre-occupied by internal conflicts and by the monumental task of constructing a new state to feel that they could incorporate UGTA into the policy process."[146]

To exercise political control over peasants, the state party created the National Union of Algerian Peasants along with similar organizations for youth and women. Peasants dealt with state bureaucratic structures as well when working on the some 2,500 Agrarian Revolution Cooperatives and "Socialist Villages" that were at the center of agrarian reform efforts. Through their membership in the peasants' union and selection of representatives they were part of local government organized in popular communal assemblies.[147] The popular communal assemblies were dominated by middle peasants, who were allied with military and government civil servants and FLN party activists.[148] Regional government (*wiliya*) also was controlled by the national political elite. *Wiliya* executives were formed from a party person from the national commissariat of the FLN (a political party that became fused with the government over time); from the chief military officer of the ALN in the region, the *wali,* or governor of the region, who was appointed by the minister of the interior; and from a representative of the ministry of agriculture.[149]

In sum, the emerging Algerian single-party state sought to mobilize and control workers and peasants, though it was only partially successful. It exercised centralized control over local and regional government, and attempted to assert tight controls over plant- and farm-level union activity as well.[150] The FLN handpicked confederation leaders and the leaders of peak unions. When the regime felt threatened by self-management committees, it converted the enterprises and farms into state companies.[151]

With a ruling party and affiliated organizations as tools and a traditional elite decimated by French colonization, the military and its leaders became the most powerful social force in post-independence Algeria, and served as arbiter of disputes among political elites.[152] The cleavages among various types of leaders in the struggle against the French—liberals, radicals, revolutionaries, prewar elite, military, and intellectuals—revealed themselves when state power and resources along with the *biensvacants* (vacant property in Algeria left by the French after the War of Independence) of the departing French were at stake. Beyond the ideological divisions were close-knit political clans bound by personal ties.[153]

The early independence years were especially volatile. Frequently occurring intra-elite conflict and attempts to build broad coalitions among the various elite coalitions led first to the regime of Ben Balla (1962–1965) supported by the military leader of the ALN, Houari Boumédienne. However, when Ben Balla attempted to limit the power of the military, he was removed and replaced by Boumédienne, who built his own broad coalition and more successfully fended off other challengers.[154]

The powerful back-stage role of the military in Algerian politics earned them the sobriquet, *les decideurs*. After Boumédienne's death by natural causes in 1978, *les decideurs* moved more into the background but continued to demonstrate a willingness and capability to be the ultimate shapers of the Algerian political system.

There have been times in Algerian post-independence political history when the presidents played a pronounced and autonomous role. Students of Algerian politics describe a sultanic rule for Algerian presidents—a tightly closed circle of power around a single leader independent of all groups, with an autonomous base of power, whether institutional, political, administrative, or social. The sultan relies upon an apolitical technocratic elite.[155]

Ruling Coalition and Policies

Aspiring to build their revolution in the name of workers and peasants, the soldiers and politicians who implemented socialism in Algeria were not faced with nearly as powerful a set of traditional economic and political elite challengers as was the case in Egypt, and Syria. Large reserves of oil and natural gas discovered during the war against the French also provided the leaders of the post-independence state with resources to distribute to groups in society in exchange for political support, as well as gains in resources and wealth that they could capture for themselves.

During the Ben Balla years, the first three years of Algerian independence in 1962–1965, a self-management *auto-gestion* movement was attempted but stalled. Policies included democratic collective management over both industrial and agrarian production based on many of the former French properties. This experiment ultimately failed under the weight of conflicts between new and old elites and emerging attempts of bureaucratic control by the state.[156]

After his bloodless coup, Boumédienne moved policy away from *auto-gestion* and established a rent-seeking coalition similar to those that had been constructed in the other three countries, with the added dimension of Algeria becoming a rentier state that received huge profits from oil and natural gas largely unlinked to productive aspects of its economy. Beginning in 1967, the regime embarked upon a strategy of popular mobilization around a program of radical social policies, though these programs were more top-down and bureaucratic than during the self-management movement. In the 1960s, the regime nationalized one foreign sector after another—minerals, banking, insurance, manufacturing—culminating in 1971 with 51 percent of the oil sector and all of the national gas sector.[157] These industries, and newly created ones especially in the hydrocarbon sector, provided some but not enough jobs for the urban population that was rapidly growing due to population growth and a development strategy that favored industry over agriculture. The industries were also largely capital rather than labor intensive.

The concrete benefits won by labor in Algeria did not match those of Egypt and Syria. The regime called for worker sacrifices for the sake of national reconstruction, but labor was given little in return.[158] Indeed, the minimum wage was frozen in 1963. Violent strike waves first hit Algeria in 1964–1965, involving 4,000 workers and paralyzing ports, docks, and construction companies in the region of Algiers.[159] Overall, the labor movement was relatively weak in the sense of having less centralized control over the base and also having limited lines of communication with the regime, which had frozen access to the policy process in 1965.[160]

Land reform, after much discussion, finally took place in 1971. Land was distributed to poor peasants in tenures that did not include the right to sale. They shared equipment and participated in production cooperatives to achieve economies of scale. The land came from the public domain and from the largest private estates, in theory, but in practice little privately held land exchanged hands. Agrarian reforms were centered on socialist villages designed to bring urban amenities and services to the rural populations while improving productivity and food security.[161]

The objectives of the land reforms were threefold: 1) To eliminate large private farms larger than 110 hectares; 2) to abolish absentee ownership of lands and unearned incomes from ground rents; and 3) to avoid fragmentation of production units by organizing peasants into agrarian revolution cooperatives.[162] Approximately 80 percent of these large farms were redistributed to the poorest two categories of the small peasantry, peasants who possessed less than 1 hectare of land or from 1–5 hectares. The remaining 20 percent of large farms were distributed to allies or relatives of middle peasants.[163]

In addition to jobs in state-owned enterprises and progressive land reform, Algerian socialism included social welfare programs that benefited both workers and peasants. The state subsidized or made free of charge food, education, housing, health care, medicine, and energy. Economic activity for the masses became oriented toward the state rather than the market. The top-down nature of Algerian state-sponsored socialism also contributed to this rent-seeking context.

Legitimacy

For a generation, the successful war of national liberation in Algeria provided the post-independence regime with a significant amount of legitimacy and admiration both inside the country and around the developing world. The humble backgrounds and initially egalitarian ethos of the wartime leaders who became the new Algerian elite also contributed to legitimacy, not least because the egalitarian ethos matched the socialist ideology promulgated by the FLN. In addition, the country's pursuit of state-led industrialization founded on petrol and natural gas income during the boom in the 1970s certainly contributed to a sense of national strength. Writing in the mid-1980s, John Entelis concluded that efficiency, accountability, and productivity directed by the state were the hallmarks of the new Algeria.[164] Both rational legal legitimacy and eudaemonic legitimacy would flow from those achievements. However, the next decade did not sustain those claims at all. Perceptively, however, Entelis also argued at the time that neo-Islamic totalitarian movements composed of people who felt left out of or uncomfortable in the New Algeria formed the main opposition to the populist authoritarian Algerian state.[165]

In terms of opposition during the peak of Algerian socialism, the regime had to handle a population that was at least 20 percent Berber, and a majority that were probably Arabized Berbers. The Berber–Arab cleavage contributed to difficulties in fending off the French, mounting resistance under colonialism, organizing a nationalist movement, and stabilizing the post-independence regime. Even after the consolidation of the regime under Boumédienne, the Berber population could not be completely comfortable with the stress on Arabism in the state–party military establishment.

Single-Party Tunisian Arab Socialism

Political Institutions

At independence in 1956, a counter-system to French colonial rule led by the Neo-Destour had already long been in place.[166] Shortly after taking power, Bourguiba and other members of the Neo-Destour leadership attempted to create a new institutional order by modifying the party and the government. The electoral system was changed to make competition to the Neo-Destour impossible. They changed the constitution inherited from the French in order to restrict the activities of representative assemblies, to reduce the independence of the judiciary, and to give wide discretionary authority to the executive, forming what one analyst described as a presidential monarchy.[167]

In addition, the single-party state established administrative control over regional and local government. At the regional level, it created fourteen jurisdictions, each headed by a governor appointed by the president. At the local level, party branches replaced many traditional structures such as religious brotherhoods, and weakened kinship-based solidarity. The branches transmitted the demands and grievances of the people to the party apparatus, mobilized people in support of government projects, and served as an instrument of recruitment into the state party.

After independence, regime leaders continued to transform major voluntary associations into corporatist organs of the ruling party. As noted, the UGTT organized and sustained long waves of militancy primarily through strikes and demonstrations in support of the nationalist struggle. This meant that the UGTT was in a strong position when the time came for negotiations with Neo-Destour Party leaders upon independence. That role gave the Tunisian labor movement a degree of systematic access to policymaking. The secretary-general of the UGTT sat on the political bureau of the ruling party, and the UGTT automatically had a bloc of deputies in the National Assembly. In this sense, the Tunisian labor movement was incorporated into the policy process, although in a subordinate role.

The early years of independence demonstrated the subordinate status of the UGTT. After first accepting numerous UGTT-drafted motions on socioeconomic issues and socialist arrangements, Bourguiba defected on these promises and Tunisia followed a liberal economic policy in the years 1956–1961. It was only in the 1960s, after the failure of liberal economic policies, that Bourguiba made the head of the UGTT, Ben Salah, economic czar and architect of Tunisian Arab socialism.

Even with one of their own in charge of economic policy the regime kept tight controls over labor, though they did begin to favor them in policy. Over the course of the development of Arab socialism in Tunisia the labor union was increasingly centralized, and its leadership grew more isolated from the rank and file. Previously powerful regional unions lost influence.[168] Party leaders also utilized finance regulations and other labor legislation to control the labor movement. In addition, the UGTT leadership was kept in check through co-optation and manipulation of rival elite blocs.[169] This corporatist institutional framework became an arm of the regime's struggle to eliminate external opposition, limit class conflict, minimize the political impact of wide wealth disparities, and enable the country to act as a single unit in the struggle for rapid national socioeconomic development.[170] While the state party both mobilized and controlled workers and peasants, they were favored in policy and active in national and local state institutions.

In sum, a combination of steps taken by the Neo-Destour leadership amounted to a new institutional order characterized by a single ruling party, affiliated state corporatist organizations, and a powerful executive with wide discretionary power. The measures also rooted the Neo-Destour deep into Tunisian society and fortified the party state for the long term.

Ruling Coalition and Policies

In terms of policies after independence, Tunisia gradually moved toward state-guided, state-dominated economic growth, and populist policies to improve the material well-being of Tunisian workers and peasants. French civil servants were replaced by Tunisians, and many other public-sector jobs were created to alleviate urban unemployment and deliver on the promises of independence.[171] A ten-year development plan to create Tunisian socialism was adopted in 1961,[172] and in 1964 the Neo-Destour changed its named to the Socialist Destour. As mentioned, a trade union activist, Ahmad Ben Salah, was designated as head of an economic superministry assigned the task of implementing the plan.[173]

The core of Ben Salah's plan was in the agricultural sector. At independence, a large amount of the country's arable land was owned by French settlers and the Islamic private and religious *habous* system.[174] At independence, the state confiscated most of the land within that system for redistribution and as state domains. Some communal land was parceled out to individuals at this time as well.

Traditional Tunisian agriculture suffered from low productivity and the country depended on French and other foreign agricultural enterprises. The UN's Food and Agricultural Organization (FAO) estimated that in 1962 each of 4,000 French families held on average 240 hectares of land and each of 5,000 Tunisian families held 100 hectares. This means that 3 to 4 percent of all farmers possessed about half of the arable land.[175] At the same time, 57 percent of the total Tunisian workforce depended upon agriculture for employment. Within the agricultural sector, 25 percent of the population was unemployed, and almost half of the remaining 75 percent were landless laborers.[176]

Ben Salah made an effort to modernize agriculture, redistribute land under state auspices, reduce poverty among peasants, and help them participate in national development and national politics. The economic czar created agricultural production cooperatives from nationalized French farms. His plan also aimed to consolidate small private holdings not near to French farmland into agricultural production cooperatives in order to create holdings of almost 506 hectares each, a size believed optimal for the use of machinery and modern cultivation methods.[177] The state also invested in inputs and technology to increase production. The small peasantry, those with limited access to land and work, were placed on the well-equipped properties with nearby smallholders. Thus Ben Salah boldly sought to utilize the most disadvantaged of Tunisians to modernize the agricultural sector and redistribute wealth where it was most needed.

In addition to Tunisia's experimentation in agricultural production cooperatives, Ben Salah's statism took over traditional crafts, monopolized external trade and retail shops, oversaw small businesses such as restaurants, monopolized trade in certain basic commodities, and controlled foreign trade, crops, and prices. Under Tunisian Arab socialism, the regime also started numerous state-owned enterprises and stepped in as the country's major industrial investor and employer at a time when few alternative investors existed.[178] The regime established more than four hundred state-owned enterprises producing everything from steel, ovens, clothing, and paper to chemicals, dairy foods, and cigarettes.[179] The state provided most of the capital formation in industry during the 1960s, contributing nearly 100 percent of gross capital formation in mining and utilities, 72 percent in agro-alimentary industries, 93 percent of metal, glass, and construction materials, 92 percent of electrical appliances and machinery, 62 percent of chemicals, and 83 percent of textiles.[180]

State patronage in Tunisia's socialist phase included providing services such as free education, subsidized transportation, housing, health care, and basic consumer goods including wheat, flour, milk, cooking oil, and sugar.[181] Peasants received access to land. Concrete material improvements for workers in Tunisia after independence also included social security benefits.[182] The 1966 labor code regulated the length of the working week, gave more power to inspectors, and established indemnities for workers who lost their jobs for economic reasons. It also provided regulations encouraging permanent work contracts.[183]

This discussion of coalitions and policies in Tunisia under Ahmad Ben Salah's economic management highlights state patronage to the benefit of lower economic classes. Such state interventionist populist policies, in the view of neoclassical political economy, create opportunities for nonproductive rent-seeking behavior. Thus, during the old authoritarianism in Tunisia rent-seeking activity was concentrated in the growing public sector and among groups that deliberately sought the benefits of jobs based on political rather than economic considerations. These groups also sought subsidies, tariffs, and regulations to maintain their claims to public resources. Over time, members of the domestic private sector understood, as well, that they could make "nonproductive gains" in the statist economies. The upcoming market reforms in theory were supposed to dissipate these opportunities for state patronage and rent seeking.[184]

Legitimacy

Legitimacy can be defined as political stability without the need for coercion. This definition emphasizes the belief in the validity of the exercise of power by both ruler and ruled.[185] In the Tunisian case, around the time of independence Bourguiba had to deal with a challenge that required state coercion: the 1950s saw a struggle between Habib Bourguiba and Salah Ben Youssef for leadership of the Neo-Destour and accession to control over the state in the post-independence era.[186] It was a battle of constituencies and for militancy within the party. Ben Youssef found support among Islamic religious authorities, traditional artisans and merchants, and the old commercial class of his native Djerba, an island off the coast of Tunisia. Bourguiba drew more support from merchants and landowners in the Sahel, the region that produced most of the Neo-Destour leadership. Just prior to independence Ben Youssef accused Bourguiba of being too Western and too slow to push for full independence from France. Once France granted Tunisia independence, Ben Youssef organized a private army in southern Tunisia. The French and Bourguiba's military men subdued the revolt and Ben Youssef fled into exile, leaving Habib Bourguiba as the uncontested head of the new single-party regime.[187]

In the first five years of independence, Bourguiba attacked the power strata that supported Ben Youssef. As noted, the religious establishment was dealt a blow to its independent financial base by the nationalization of public *habous* land, inalienable land under Islamic law utilized for religious or charitable purposes. Private *habous* property, which was to benefit the founders' families until the family line died out (at which time the property is converted into public *habous*) also came under pressure as the owners feared confiscation. Many sold their properties quickly. Owners of private *habous* were often members of the Tunis bourgeoisie; hence, these land tenure changes struck a blow against them as well.

With the Ben Youssef conflict behind him, Bourguiba and the Neo-Destour faced relatively limited opposition. The older generation of nationalists in the Destour had lost control of the nationalist movement for well over twenty years before independence in 1956. As noted, Bourguiba attempted to ease the concerns of the bourgeoisie and powerful landowners, some of whom had provided financing for the Neo-Destour during the long struggle against French colonial rule.[188] A homogenous country of Sunni Arabs or Arabized Berbers, the country lacked potential opposition built around ethnic or sectarian cleavages. The small size of the country and population, totaling less than four million at the time of independence, lent itself to the centralized control of the Neo-Destour.

During the early post-independence years in Tunisia, nationalist legitimacy drove support for the regime. The Neo-Destour and its predecessor the Destour had fought a long and difficult nationalist struggle against the French to end colonial rule that had lasted from 1881 to 1956. The party built a grand coalition against colonialism, attracting both mass and elite Tunisian support. The Neo-Destour leadership successfully tapped into nationalistic pride. By the time of independence, Habib Bourguiba, a strong leader and charismatic figure, had become the symbol of the nation much more than the discredited Bey, who was deposed in 1957.

It is noteworthy that Habib Bourguiba did not seek to gain legitimacy as a traditional Islamic ruler. Indeed he held a secular and modernizing view of political change, fighting against what he regarded as outdated Islamic traditions and discouraging the month-long holy fast of Ramadan because the nation needed all of its strength to participate in rapid modernization. He once drank a glass of orange juice on television during Ramadan to emphasize the point. As noted earlier, due partly to the religious establishment's support of his rival Ben Youssef, Bourguiba nationalized *habous* land and put religious institutions under state control.

The new government also pursued female emancipation from tradition.[189] Polygamy, for the first time in the Arab world, was outlawed, as was the tradition of male repudiation—the right of males to divorce by stating "I divorce thee" three times in front of witnesses. Before Bourguiba's rule, females seeking a divorce had to petition a religious court. Arranged marriages were abolished and women were granted the right to abortion, without regard to marital status. The government condemned the wearing of traditional garb, including the veil, which Bourguiba in some early speeches during his presidency called "a dishrag" unsuitable for school. Tunisian women were also granted the right to marry outside their faith.

Bourguiba was known for pragmatism more than ideological fervor, although the change of the Neo-Destour's name to the Socialist Destour in 1964 indicated a policy shift in the direction of Arab socialism. From a region-wide comparative perspective, the Tunisian state developed a high degree of rational legal legitimacy in terms of possessing conventional attributes of statehood: it had stable civilian administrations, well-organized military establishments, and adequate internal revenue services.[190] However, after the very early days of independence, eudaemonic legitimacy—promises to improve peoples' living standards and welfare—and delivery on those promises anchored noncoercive support for the regime.

Gradual Transition toward the New Authoritarianism

At the height of Arab socialism, regime leaders in Egypt, Syria, Algeria, and Tunisia implemented statist and redistributive economic policies. Populist and rent-seeking coalitions of workers and peasants helped regime leaders in their ability to rule. Institutionally, these new leaders favored single-party rule along corporatist lines backed by the military, and powerful presidencies. In different doses in different countries, various forms of legitimacy helped to consolidate the regimes. These included nationalism, developmentalism, eudaemonic legitimacy or legitimacy based on the distribution of material benefits, charismatic leaders, and rational legal legitimacy. Defining legitimacy as the ability to govern without coercion suggests that their legitimation efforts were at best just partially successful. Under Arab socialism, all four regimes were sharply coercive and repressive at times and built up effective military, police, and intelligence apparatuses to maintain social control.

Since the highpoint of authoritarian Arab socialism, these regimes have made a gradual transition toward the new authoritarianism. That topic will be the subject of the next chapter. These gradual transitions, however, did not include to any substantial degree the privatization of state-owned enterprises and land. Privatization and associated shifts in social relations, discussed in full in chapter 5, marked the definitive transition from the old to the new authoritarianism in the MENA single-party republics.

In terms of ruling coalition, the earliest movement toward a new authoritarianism was found in the small number of entrepreneurial bourgeoisie who instead of seeing menace or threat saw all the possibilities that a budding public sector and protectionism opened up to them. These members of the entrepreneurial bourgeoisie who survived nationalization policies adopted a parasitical relationship with the public sector.[191] They became secondary partners in the ruling coalitions under Arab socialism.

A question remains. Beyond the bourgeoisie that capitalized on the largesse of a malfunctioning public sector and gradually increased their power within the ruling coalitions, what explains the gradual changes in the policies of the old authoritarianism? In Egypt, Nasser's socialism was reasonably successful from 1952 until roughly 1965. The average real weekly wage for industrial workers rose dramatically[192] and the small peasantry's standard of living improved sharply. Gains were made in infrastructure and an industrial base was developed. Manufactured goods created by Egyptians filled store shelves. Nasser's regime addressed poverty, education, and a need for national pride. In the late 1960s, however, especially after the devastating defeat by Israel in the Six Day War of 1967, the costs of Nasser's socioeconomic development strategy became more apparent. The overstaffing of the public sector and civil service, and a constantly rising bill for subsidies led to macroeconomic imbalances.[193] The ISI strategy of closing the national market for manufactured goods to the international economy and maintaining largely noncompetitive domestic markets for goods and labor encountered significant snags.[194] Trade imbalances increased international debt. Nasser was considering ways to address these serious concerns when he died in 1970.

Economic reform in Egypt began in 1974 when Sadat's October Paper signaled to the public a shift toward the West and a capitalist path of development.[195] The international context in which reforms were considered included the economic strains in the Soviet Union, Egypt's main economic partner. In addition, Sadat's first government reached a consensus that the industrial sector needed technological overhauling, and foreign-exchange shortages had to be addressed.[196] Another major catalyst of the shift and economic reality check was the huge increase in fossil fuel prices after 1973. Sadat introduced such reforms after the partially successful 1973 war against Israel, which provided him with increased autonomy and political capital to embark on the new development strategy. Choosing economic reforms when he had political capital suggests a personal preference for the shift in strategy.

Sadat's *infitah,* or economic opening, took steps toward a market economy in Egypt. It included legislation that provided incentives for domestic and foreign private investment. It also opened foreign trade to private companies, and eliminated most controls on worker emigration.[197] Some of these new economic policies were met with resistance. Sadat cut subsidies on some consumer products and fuel in 1977, leading to street (bread) riots up and down the Nile Valley that threatened the regime. Adding to the tensions, unemployment rates reached a new high, economic growth had not broken the cycle of poverty and suffering, corruption seemed rampant, and the gap between rich and poor had spread.[198] The 1977 riots were violently suppressed and left hundreds dead. It was the first time since the 1952 revolution that the army had taken to the streets to take back the streets. To quell the demonstrations, Sadat reinstated the subsidies. The October Paper of 1974 encouraged privatization and public-sector reform as well, though little privatization occurred until the early 1990s.

A partial transition away from single-party rule occurred in Egypt along with economic liberalization. In 1974, Sadat formed a committee to reform the Arab Socialist Union and explore controlled multipartyism. He also pursued modest political liberalization, reflected in a more outspoken press and limited moves to provide opposition parties and interest groups with more influence on policy.[199] To explain these steps, analysts cited certain of Sadat's liberal principles, including a desire to shift Egypt toward constitutional rule and the rule of

law, along with a need to match economic reforms with political liberalization. Analysts noted Sadat's desire to impress his new Western
allies, especially the United States, whose aid and political patronage
Egypt required to address economic difficulties and recover the Sinai
oil fields from Israeli control. In addition, the reforms were aimed to
increase legitimacy, provide Sadat with a way to neutralize Nasserists
and build up support among the bourgeoisie, while creating a valve to
release political tensions caused by the rising inequality that economic
reforms had produced.[200] Summarizing most of these points, Moheb
Zaki has explained Sadat's shift to multiparty politics in this way:

> Sadat had envisaged a process of limited pluralization in terms
> of political parties as a means for channeling growing partici-
> patory demands, while still maintaining control. Besides lend-
> ing greater legitimacy to his regime and enhancing its stability, a
> multiparty system also served to improve his image in front of his
> Western friends. The political opening was not brought about as
> a consequence of mass pressure from below, but by a deliberate
> decision from above by the ruling elite, who believed that they
> could indefinitely maintain a monopoly on power by way of a
> hegemonic party. Consequently, the reintroduction of party poli-
> tics resulted not in the creation of a more or less evenly balanced
> multiparty system but in one overwhelmingly dominated by the
> regime's party.[201]

While more comfortable with political diversity than Nasser,
Sadat's political vision did not include mass mobilization of constituencies by political parties in opposition to the regime or any relaxing
of state corporatist controls. John Waterbury states that "Sadat continued the corporatist formula and through the introduction of corporate honor codes reinforced it, while allowing for open politics in the
interstices of the corporate edifice.[202] Sadat's "Listening Committee" on
political reform held hearings with most of the country's social forces
to discuss issues that included multipartyism. In the end, the ASU
National Congress gave permission for the formation of three platforms
(after the consolidation of two leftist groups), which developed into
three political parties that contested legislative elections in 1976. The
center party became the government party, the Socialist Democrats;
Sadat later changed its name to the National Democratic Party (NDP).
On the left was the National Progressive Unionist Party, or Tagammu,

and on the right stood the Socialist Liberals. In those first elections, the government party won 280 seats, the left won only two seats, and the right only twelve. Forty-eight Independents, not affiliated with any of the three tendencies, also won seats in the new parliament.[203]

The creation of three platforms from the ASU was designed to reinvigorate the government party, not to lead to multiparty democracy. The opposition parties were highly constrained by the regime. The official opposition party of the right was handpicked and the center party openly affiliated with the regime. No political activity outside of the three government designated political parties was permitted. The publication of political newspapers or journals was disallowed and parties representing religion and socioeconomic issues were forbidden, in a stroke placing the groups most able to mobilize the population outside the realm of legal political activity. Authorization of new parties was determined by a special committee that included ASU officials.[204] In announcing the conversion of the three platforms of the ASU into separate political parties, Sadat declared that the ASU (later changed to the NDP) would remain the dominant political force, controlling the budgets of the new parties and retaining its own supervisory power over the press and state corporatist functional organizations of peasants, workers, and others allied with the ASU.[205]

Regime leaders knew that the reintroduction of multiparty politics, banned since 1952, would result in an unbalanced multiparty system overwhelmingly dominated by the government's party. The ASU/NDP maintained authority in all branches of government and control over its vast patronage network and the electronic and print media.

Entrenched in power, whatever liberal sentiment that had existed among top officials under Sadat did not convince them to decisively alter their preference for the single-party regime they inherited.

Protests against cuts in food subsidies and increasing economic disparities, his own unpopular peace treaty with Israel, and rising, sometimes violent, Islamist movements, convinced Sadat to shut down his multiparty experiment shortly before he was assassinated by Islamic extremists in 1981. Mubarak's reigniting of political reforms in the 1980s and 1990s were accompanied by changes in policies and coalitions that marked a deeper transformation of the old authoritarianism in Egypt. In current times privatization marked the full transformation to the new authoritarianism.

Turning to Syria, when General Hafez Al-Asad took power and launched his "corrective" coup in 1970, he began changing the country's political institutions, policies, ruling coalition, and legitimacy strategies in the direction of the new authoritarianism postulated in this book. In terms of legitimacy, a pragmatic Asad tempered the ideological fervor of the Salah Jedid regime (1966–1970) that had been devoted to socialist revolution, populist policies, and breaking the economic power and political capacity of traditional rural and urban economic elites. He also began a gradual process of limited electoral legitimation. The policy direction he undertook began changing the ruling coalition of workers and peasants considered as the vanguard of economic and political transformation in Syria under Jedid, to a coalition that also made room for economic and social alliances with parts of the bourgeoisie and traditional landlords.[206]

Syria's cautious economic liberalization policies in the 1970s under Asad reflected his own economic beliefs and a desire to move away from the regime's strategy of socialist transformation, to reduce its reliance on the USSR and the Eastern bloc, to open up the private sector, and link up with conservative Arab states.[207] The policies were also designed to accommodate the bourgeoisie to his regime in order to broaden the political and economic base for the struggle against Israel.[208]

In the early 1970s, a known economic liberal, Abd Al-Halim Khaddam, was named Minister of Economy and Foreign Trade in one of Asad's first appointments.[209] Between 1971 and 1977, Asad implemented policies that increased the weight of the private sector and partially opened up the economy internationally, especially to non-Syrian Arabs and expatriates.[210] A mixed private–state sector was developed first in tourism and than in agriculture; it was private in all but name.[211] The private sector was also given advantageous opportunities to make money through credit facilities, by acting as intermediaries between the state and international companies, and by various linkages to the public sector. The boom time of oil export and remittances in the 1970s allowed the regime to broaden its social alliances to the private sector in this manner while largely maintaining its populist commitments.[212]

Syria's economic opening in the 1970s was accompanied by innovations in political institutions that began shortly after Asad took power. He promulgated a new constitution, established an elected parliament and the National Progressive Front (NPF), the latter being an institutionalized coalition of the Ba'th Party and a group of tolerated smaller socialist parties. Asad also brought popular organizations such as trade unions and the Peasants Union under greater Ba'th and state corporatist control. These institutional changes aimed to institutionalize and stabilize his regime, while broadening his base of support. Urban and rural traditional elites were permitted to run as independents in the new parliament.[213]

Syria's Hafez Al-Asad considered his introduction of an elected parliament and establishment of the Ba'th-led coalition of political parties called the National Progressive Front (NPF) evidence that Syria had institutionalized multiparty politics in the early 1970s.[214] That timid political transition ground to a complete halt during the confrontation between the regime and the Syrian Muslim Brotherhood in the late 1970s and early 1980s, culminating in the regime's full-scale military assault on armed Muslim Brothers in Hama in 1982 that killed tens of thousands of people.

As discussed, the Ba'thist regime had first become aware of small groups of Islamic militants organizing armed resistance to the regime soon after they began efforts to consolidate their rule in 1964. The National Guard attacked armed Muslim Brothers barricaded in the Sultan Mosque in Hama, killing more than seventy.[215] The Muslim Brothers' conflict with the regime was partly due to the latter's secular orientation. There was also a strong class dimension to this struggle. The Muslim Brotherhood drew popular support from Sunni traditional notables formed by the amalgamation of landlords, many absentee; the bourgeoisie; and Sunni religious leaders. Hama was an important base for this conservative group and the most visible symbol of the overturning of power and wealth between absentee landlords and the rural poor that the Ba'thist revolution represented.

This battle heated up again in the late 1970s and early 1980s. The Muslim Brothers accelerated assassinations and mounted urban demonstrations and attacks against Alawis, Ba'thists, military and police figures, and some civilians. Notably, in this struggle many Syrians chose the government side partly in reaction to the Muslim Brotherhood strikes in souks, bombs in schools, and the constant fears of death.[216] In 1982, the battle between Muslim Brothers and the Sunni establishment against the Ba'th reached a crescendo in Hama. Both sides gathered their forces in the battle for Hama; in the end, some twelve thousand government troops killed between five and ten thousand people and largely ended the Muslim Brotherhood uprising that had dragged on for nearly two decades.[217] After the Hama insurrection was crushed, state–society relations deteriorated to cynicism, some fear among the public, and mostly indifference toward Asad's political institutions that had been created in the corrective revolution of the early 1970s.[218]

Tunisia's old authoritarianism faltered in 1969. Low productivity and widespread disenchantment with state-run agricultural production cooperatives, the centerpiece of Tunisian Arab socialism, was compounded by the resistance of provincial elites who had funded the Neo-Destour Party in pre-independence days. Once their substantial holdings were threatened—privatizing large landholdings was necessary for the success of agricultural cooperatives—they revolted and as a group approached President Bourguiba to insist that he change directions.[219] Bourguiba chose their side, abruptly stopped the spread of the cooperative movement, ended its further expansion into commercial and manufacturing areas, and sacked Ahmed Ben Salah, the former trade union head and economic czar. State-led economic liberalization began at that time, although the government maintained cooperative, mixed, and private sectors throughout the 1970s and 1980s.

The collapse of the cooperative movement in 1969–1970 signaled the failure of the first major effort by the Tunisian government to deliver on the promises of independence. Disenchantment was widespread. Demands for political liberalization and democratization began within this context. Tunisia's most powerful Islamist movement, the Mouvement de la tendance Islamique (MTI), emerged at that time as well.[220]

After high growth rates in the early 1970s, stagnant growth and increasing inequality characterized the end of the decade. A national strike led by Tunisia's national trade union federation, the UGTT, in 1978 spiraled into calls for democratization and economic liberalization at the ballot box. Spinoff parties from the Neo-Destour emerged to demand political liberalization to go along with economic liberalization.

In response to the widespread discontent, Bourguiba authorized multiparty elections for the National Assembly to be held in November 1981. The Neo-Destour and the UGTT ran joint lists in a national front, and three other groups were permitted to present candidates. When the Neo-Destour won every seat, there were widespread allegations of fraud. At the last minute, the regime had aborted its experiment in competitive multiparty politics.[221]

Unlike the other three cases, Algeria's transition toward the new authoritarianism was more abrupt than gradual. Algeria did implement modest economic reforms in the early 1980s, but in the late 1980s President Chadli Benjedid pursued rapid economic liberalization, while implementing the most convincing steps toward democracy ever taken in the Arab world. The results were a disaster for the country due to violence that erupted after the military takeover to prevent Islamists from taking power. The new authoritarianism in Algeria has been built with the recent memory and lingering effects of waves of bloodshed caused by the conflict between the state and Islamist forces, especially the Front Islamique du Salut (FIS). The full transition to the new authoritarianism in Egypt, Syria, Tunisia, and Algeria, triggered by the widespread privatization of state-owned enterprises and land, is the subject of the next chapter.

FOUR

The New Authoritarianism

The present volume deals with transitions from certain authoritarian regimes toward an uncertain "something else." That "something" can be the instauration of a political democracy or the restoration of a new, and possibly more severe form of authoritarian rule. The outcome can also be simply confusion, that is, the rotation in power of successive governments, which fail to provide any enduring or predictable solution to the problem of institutionalizing political power. Transitions can also develop into widespread, violent confrontations, eventually giving way to revolutionary regimes, which promote changes going far beyond the political realm.

—GUILLERMO O'DONNELL and PHILIPPE C. SCHMITTER, *Transitions from Authoritarian Rule,* 3.

What determines the outcome of transitions away from certain authoritarian regimes toward an uncertain alternative "something else" in the Middle East and North Africa? If the outcomes are new forms of authoritarian rule, what are the salient traits of these new autocracies? This chapter has three related goals. First, it argues that the authoritarian leadership in Egypt, Syria, Algeria, and Tunisia made timid turns to democratization in the 1980s and 1990s. The leadership then utilized single-party institutional structures and new patronage opportunities generated by privatization to subvert full transitions to democracy and to reinforce control over a new form of authoritarian rule that can be characterized as a crony capitalist and landlord spoils system cloaked in a multiparty democratic façade.

Second, by showing the transformation in the substance of authoritarianism in this period in a subset of Middle Eastern states—the single-party Arab republics—it argues that authoritarianism in the Middle East and North Africa is both persistent and dynamic; and emphasizes that the shifting social relations, policies, and legitimacy strategies embodied in the new MENA authoritarianism have immediate effects on the welfare of millions of Egyptians, Syrians, Algerians, and Tunisians.

Third, the chapter calls into question assumptions in the neoclassical political economy literature by demonstrating that instead of dismantling rents, economic liberalization in the Arab single-party socialist republics reorganized opportunities for rent seeking,[1] and did so in a manner that benefited different social groups. Rent-seeking coalitions have been transformed in Egypt, Syria, Algeria, and Tunisia from the broad populist coalitions that sought rents created by public-sector jobs, access to state-owned land, welfare outlays, protectionism, subsidies, and tariffs to the urban- and rural-elite distributional coalitions of the more market-oriented environment that pursue rents generated by the privatization of state-owned enterprises and land.

Explaining the Authoritarian Outcomes of the Political Openings of the 1980s and 1990s: A Funnel Approach

After the gradual move toward the new authoritarianism (discussed at the end of chapter 3), Egypt, Syria, Algeria, and Tunisia introduced new multiparty experiments in the 1980s and 1990s and accelerated economic liberalization by taking crucial steps toward privatizing their economies. Once these transitions from a certain authoritarianism to an uncertain something else began. a range of factors influenced the authoritarian outcomes of the countries' political openings. In the funnel approach presented in chapter 2, variables at a particular level of analysis are understood to explain part of a regime outcome; hence, one must consider variables from all levels to approximate a full explanation. At the outset here, I highlight factors that contributed to authoritarian outcomes in the Arab republics but that could not serve as full explanations if we failed to consider how autocrats utilized patronage-based economic liberalization and the dominance of ruling parties and affiliated corporatist organizations to subvert impulses toward democratic politics. Or, in the language of the funnel approach, domestic structural changes and an institutional legacy were particularly important factors that enabled authoritarian incumbents to transform authoritarian rule without losing power and control.

In terms of macro-structural factors, international political trends and global economic changes worked against democratization during the Arab republics' political openings in the 1980s and 1990s. Even before September 11, 2001 and the rise of international Islamist terrorism, global powers had been more willing to accept authoritarianism in the Middle East and North Africa than elsewhere in the developing world.[2] Globalization, which favored capital over labor, weakened the economic power and political clout of workers and peasants who felt increasingly alienated from the authoritarian regimes in Egypt, Syria, Algeria, and Tunisia . In terms of national culture, claims that Arab and Islamist societies were impervious to democracy did not fit the reality of democratic impulses in the region nor its diversity. Nonetheless, patronage politics did act as a historically specific cultural factor that contributed to sustained authoritarian rule.

In addition to single-party legacies, other institutional arrangements influenced the choices of political activists and elites that served to perpetuate authoritarian rule in the four countries discussed here.[3] Autocratic rulers became adept at divide-and-rule tactics to prevent a broad coalition of parties from overtaking the ruling party, including allowing some to compete while outlawing others. Electoral and political party laws were designed to subvert democracy; electoral fraud was common. Freedoms of association and press were limited when deemed necessary by autocratic leaders. State parties received the bulk of government campaign funding and perpetuated their amalgamation with the state. Opposition parties could not find private money because those with resources did not want to back losers. To prevent political parties from gaining support, the regimes favored independent candidacies and funneled political participation toward other civil society organizations. To weaken the power of "popularly elected" parliaments, rulers installed or gave more power to unelected upper houses.

The resort to sheer repression and the security state served as the bluntest incumbent strategies for utilizing institutions as resources to sustain authoritarianism. More favorably endowed in the areas of military, security, and police capabilities than other developing countries, rulers proved willing to unleash these powers when threatened.

Islamism, the most powerful social movement in the Middle East and North Africa, fostered authoritarian trends. Regime leaders in all four cases utilized the threat of Islamists to turn authoritarian after soft political openings. The domestic violence of militant Islamists persuaded many citizens of the four countries to accept their rulers' explanations for limiting democratic progress or for making sharp authoritarian turns. Yet while not in the majority, moderate Islamists who adopted expressions of Islam compatible with democracy and human rights offered the potential for Islamism to contribute to democratic rule.

At the leadership level, rulers in the region over time demonstrated personal preferences for authoritarianism even when the prevailing structural and cultural conditions provided them with small openings to shift their countries' political systems in a more democratic direction. All of these factors were necessary but insufficient explanations for the authoritarian outcomes of transitions away from the old authoritarianism in Egypt, Syria, Algeria, and Tunisia.

In addition to the above factors, economic reform in the Arab socialist republics created and favored a rent-seeking urban and rural elite favoring authoritarian rule. Resources were increasingly taken away from the workers and peasants; they were the groups with the most to gain from democratization. The changes in the domestic structural conditions, in conjunction with the social-control powers of state party institutions and their affiliated corporatist organizations, drove the outcomes of political openings in an authoritarian direction.

Given their economic gains, landlords and capitalists showed little inclination to struggle for democracy and transparency at a time in which their countries were experiencing political openings. Instead they rallied in support of the ruling parties during the various multiparty experiments. The losers of economic reform, workers and peasants, had increasingly good reason to be advocates of democratization, but they found themselves confronting state elites in control of a ruling party that was amalgamated with the state. In addition, they confronted the state parties' affiliated corporatist organizations, which had been designed to incorporate and demobilize worker and peasant political power. Their narrow choices remained as follows: to accept their vastly diminished role in the coalition of the ruling party and whatever state patronage remained for them; to support the weak secular or liberal Islamist opposition parties that were unlikely ever to obtain patronage to distribute; to turn to radical Islamists if especially aggrieved; or simply to withdraw from politics and ignore the multiparty elections that had become part of the political landscape. Overall, these new social relations and policies reflected how authoritarian incumbents utilized ruling-party institutions and new sources of economic patronage generated by privatization to undermine the development of competitive multiparty politics during the political openings of the 1980s and 1990s in Egypt, Syria, Algeria, and Tunisia.

The New Authoritarianism in Egypt

As the previous chapter recounts, in the immediate aftermath of Nasser and the Free Officers' military coup in 1952, the emerging regime staked its legitimacy on statist and populist policies that enabled workers and peasants to make important gains in Egypt's domestic political economy. However, the gradual economic and political liberalization that began in the mid-1970s eroded those gains. The full transformation to the new authoritarianism, ushered in decisively by politicized privatization policies to the benefit of economic elites, included changes in political institutions, policies, ruling coalitions, and legitimacy strategies; and can be dated from Mubarak's political opening in 1984.

Political Institutions

A number of institutional changes have occurred in Egypt since Mubarak took power after the assassination of President Anwar Sadat in 1981. Most prominently, he has presided over the development, or reemergence, of a façade of multiparty politics, under the continued domination of the state party, the NDP. The NDP itself has been transformed from a populist party to one that caters to economic elites, increasing a trend that began in the 1970s under Sadat. An Islamist party, the Muslim Brotherhood, has emerged as the main opposition social force and the only real threat to single-party rule in a nominally multiparty political system. State corporatist mechanisms of social control in Egypt under Mubarak have been frayed, with significant splits resulting between the base and leadership due to Egypt's economic reforms, especially privatization. Presidential power has increased.

This section highlights the capacity of single-party regimes to orchestrate changes in ruling coalitions, control elite fragmentation during difficult times, and deliver the votes of alienated constituencies in multiparty contests. We also analyze the decision-making process behind Egypt's various steps to implement and backtrack from political and economic reforms under Mubarak. While discussing a number of structural considerations that impinge on elite decision making for political and economic reform, it emphasizes how Mubarak and other Egyptian leaders have utilized state party and state assets as resources to sustain authoritarian rule while publicly claiming to be committed to a transition to democracy.

Three years after coming to power in 1981, Mubarak relaunched Egypt's embryonic multiparty political system. A number of themes emerge from the controlled multiparty elections that have been held in Egypt under his rule. First, no opposition party that represents the interests of the bourgeoisie, labor, or peasants has been able to gain traction against the state party. Instead, economic elites have supported the NDP while workers and peasants have signaled their discontent with the regime largely through strikes and struggles against the regime-controlled leadership of the national trade union federation. Second, the Muslim Brotherhood emerged as the strongest opposition social force in Egypt. Third, both state patronage and NDP institutional resources, including ancillary corporatist organizations, have been mobilized to prevent Egypt's timid political openings from spiraling out of regime control.

During the era of multipartyism under Mubarak, Egypt's state party has proven to be adept at creating a new social base of support among economic elites. The natural party of traditional economic and political elites in Egypt, the Wafd (an updated version of the nationalist party during Egypt's pre-1952 liberal era) began well in Egypt's multiparty legislative elections by garnering fifty seats in the 1984 elections. Their number of seats in parliament dwindled, however, in successive elections, to thirty-five in 1987, a boycott in 1990, six in 1995, seven in 2000, and six in 2005 (see election results in tables 4.1–4.3, at the end of this section). For the most part, landlords and the private-sector bourgeoisie have supported the NDP in Egypt's multiparty legislative elections.

The number of businessmen in parliament increased during the 1980s and 1990s. These new parliamentarians overwhelmingly supported the long-dominant NDP. The electoral laws of 1986 and 1990 allowed independent individuals—those not affiliated with any political party—to run for elections. This law resulted in the election to parliament of a number of prominent businessmen who ran as independents only to join the NDP after being elected.

The higher numbers of businessmen and landlords in parliament became noticeable in the 1995 elections when they comprised 16 percent of the new parliament. The total number of members included 66 businessmen, 59 of whom belonged to the NDP.[4] In the 2000 elections 120 prominent economic elites took office as representatives of the NDP.[5] From 2000 on, businessmen rose sharply in prominence in that party. The policies committee, the most powerful group in parliament was formed by Gamal Mubarak, son of President Hosni Mubarak, and included powerful businessmen such as Ahmad Ezz, Husam Badrawi, Ibrahim Kamil, and Jamal al-Nizar. The local NDP cells also began to include more businessmen.[6]

In addition to the capacity to create a new core base of support, the NDP has been able to prevent elite fragmentation. This capacity was strikingly put to the test at the end of the 1990s. As noted by Jason Brownlee, an internal split roughly along generational lines led a younger leadership within the NDP to consider breaking away to form their own political party, the Future Party. The new generation consisted of men, largely educated in the United States and Great Britain, who had close ties with the business community and wanted to accelerate economic and social reforms.[7] The conflict was resolved when the younger group, headed by Gamal Mubarak, was enabled to take more control within the party. Plans for the Future Party were dropped after its core members took over leadership of the NDP;[8] the government formed by Ahmed Nazif in 2004 represents this group.

The NDP was able to maintain electoral control during the shift to multiparty politics partly by blocking the emergence of a labor- or peasant-based political party capable of challenging its hold on power. The nexus of political, economic, and security power that the ruling party can deploy in "contested elections" has successfully stunted the growth of secular opposition parties.[9] The leftist Tagammu and Nasserist parties lack a strong popular base, and no leftist party has garnered more than twenty-seven seats in any election. Indeed, that number was reached only once, while their highest share of votes beyond that total in any election has been just six. Their poor showing is largely due to the NDP's monopoly of state patronage and government controls on labor-organizing that restrict the parties' outreach to their natural constituencies—Egyptian workers and peasants. Even though the NDP has sharply curtailed the Nasserist era's job security, subsidies, benefits, and welfare provisions, it has continued to turn a sufficient number of public resources into patronage goods that benefit popular sectors to bias electoral competition in its favor. More significantly perhaps, the NDP has utilized its roots in society and the party machine throughout the country to deliver the peasant and labor vote.

With Egypt's multiparty elections under Mubarak, the votes of workers and peasants have been delivered by the NDP party machine and security agencies, even when the political programs of other parties were more suited to their interests.[10] Monitors of the 2005 presidential and legislative elections claimed that the state collectively transported workers from industrial areas to vote. During the voting process they were watched by NDP deputies to insure votes for the state party. Six months prior to holding elections, the state bolstered support for its party by opening up slots for seasonal and part-time employment in state institutions.[11] A study of parliamentary elections between 1981 and 2005 revealed that public expenditures flowed to the urban poor, small farmers, and state bureaucrats in the months preceding each election. These expenditures increased inflation and reduced the state's fiscal reserves.[12]

The Egyptian Trade Union Federation was also used to deliver the votes of workers.[13] In some cases, there were threats to deprive workers of social security benefits provided by the ministry of social affairs.[14] Some powerful businessmen who own factories collected thousands of workers' votes for themselves as NDP candidates, by busing the workers in from their factories to vote. Ahmad Ezz, a wealthy and powerful member of the NDP, collected significant numbers of votes in this manner.[15]

Peasant votes were also delivered to the state party. The NDP typically co-opted its candidates from local notables who in turn were used to distribute patronage: "Patronage could range from the distribution of chickens at election time, to the promise of government jobs or the delivery of roads and utilities to a village, to the refurbishing of the local mosque."[16] For most peasants, issues and ideologies rarely played a role in voting behaviors; many voters either lacked political consciousness or were unconvinced of the efficacy of voting in an authoritarian regime.[17] In rural areas, most people cast their votes for the notables for whom they worked or for those who had the government connections to deliver favors. The government could thus offset the votes of the more politically conscious with a mass of rural votes delivered on a clientage basis.[18] The efficiency of the NDP machine in local areas delivered a high percentage of rural voters, often up to 40 percent, that made up for very low urban turnout.[19]

In villages in upper and lower Egypt, NDP members used microphones to get out the vote and charged fines to those who did not vote. Government officials took peasants to the polls in groups.[20] NDP deputies kept a close-enough watch on the proceedings to violate any secrecy of the ballot. Bribery, threats, and mobilization of the collective votes of peasants were accompanied by government officials providing peasants with ad hoc services and goods in order to win NDP votes.[21] In towns and villages, government officials erected new buildings, amended laws to benefit certain areas economically, and improved public services around election time to deliver votes to the NDP.[22]

In addition to the obstacles to electoral competitiveness posed by the government party, including their capacity to turn public resources into state patronage under the NDP banner, the opposition parties have their own weaknesses. In the 2005 elections, none of the opposition political parties was able to position a new dynamic leadership with persuasive, concrete plans of action and a suitable nationwide organizational framework.[23] The parties in most instances lacked internal democracy and were unable to connect with popular constituencies.[24] Added to or as a result of ruling party machinations and opposition party impotence is a disengaged electorate—voting in urban areas is as low as 10 percent—largely uninterested in multiparty elections because of the nature of the political arena that the government has imposed.[25] In the 2005 historic multicandidate presidential election, less than 10 percent of the country's thirty-two million registered voters turned up to vote.[26]

Political parties often play a minor role in a popular upsurge's mobilizations and pressures. Most of the effort is often borne by unions, professional associations, human rights organizations, religious groups, intellectuals, and artists.[27] As just discussed, opposition parties are frequently in too great a disarray, due to steps taken by the state party and their own weaknesses, to accomplish this task. Instead of taking a stand in Egypt's controlled multiparty elections, the popular mobilization and pressure against economic reform and political reform has often been centered in the base of unions that are frequently at odds with the leadership of the country's peak federations, and by peasant insurrection and violence in the countryside.

The only legal labor unions in Egypt are still part of the Egyptian Trade Union Federation (ETUF), the national confederation of unions that became a part of the state apparatus under Nasser. After the Egyptian government tangibly began privatizing in 1991 with the implementation of law 203, the ETUF leadership endorsed the legislation.[28] This step severely strained state corporatist mechanisms of control in Egypt, as workers resisted the privatization policies that their national leadership adopted. The implementation of law 96 in 1992 that resulted in upward land redistribution and the reversal of Nasser's agrarian reforms mobilized peasants in a similar manner.

Despite laws forbidding strikes, strikes against privatization in Egypt occurred in the early and mid-1990s.[29] The textile industry led the way with major strikes at Misr Fine Spinning and Weaving in Kafr al-Dawar in November 1994 and Misr Helwan Spinning and Weaving in August 1998.[30]

Since 2004, Egypt has been experiencing its longest wave of worker protests and strikes since World War II.[31] Wildcat strikes have flared across the country, hitting everything from small processing factories to massive state-owned enterprises.[32] In addition to new strikes in the textile industry, demonstrations and strikes have occurred among food processing workers, garbage collectors, Cairo subway workers, and others.[33] In 2006 alone no fewer than 222 sit-in strikes, worker stoppages, hunger strikes, and demonstrations occurred in Egypt.[34] There were more than 200 worker protests in 2005 as well.[35] To respond to this substantial and broad-based kind of resistance to the regime, government authorities have been using proceeds from high oil prices and the sales of state-owned enterprises (SOEs) to quickly, if often only partially, respond to striking workers' demands for unpaid bonuses, benefits, salaries, and compensation for lost jobs and arbitrary dismissals resulting from privatization.[36] However, the government has utilized the stick as well as the carrot. In late April 2007, it closed down the headquarters of the Center for Trade Union and Workers' Services (CTUWS) and shut down its local offices. CTUWS offers legal aid to Egyptian factory workers, and educates workers and the public about Egyptian labor law. In reaction to government repressive measures toward the CTUWS, members of various civil society organizations began a sit-in to express solidarity with the organization.[37] The CTUWS also aroused government repression by reporting that the government interfered in the 2006 union elections of the ETUF. Strikers complained that the government should address the causes of the widespread labor unrest instead of going after workers' rights groups.[38]

The current strike wave began at the same time as the emergence of the Kifaya (Enough) protest movement, and during a period when the Muslim Brotherhood demonstrated broad popular support. Since 2004, both of these movements, along with leftists and secular nationalists, have been behind the strongest pro-democracy street protests in Egypt in years. The Egyptian government clamped down on Kifaya and the Muslim Brotherhood recently, and now are doing the same against the workers' movement. Government repression has ramped up as activist workers shift their focus from wages and benefits to the explicitly political question of their relation, through the ETUF, to the state.[39] The government is aware that there is a new movement afoot to replace the ETUF with an independent trade union federation; the regime intends to thwart it.[40]

To appease workers as they dismantle the old social contract, the Egyptian government has implemented different projects for financial compensation. In 2005 compensatory plans were put in place before 41 state companies were privatized. The 41 companies raised the number of privatized state enterprises to 234 out of the 314 SOEs affected by law 203 of 1991. Compensatory strategies included early retirement programs for workers in SOEs funded by foreign donors and privatization proceeds. Workers were offered upfront cash payments based on their anticipated salary losses, along with a monthly stipend.[41] Critics complained that the pensions were less than half of what the workers would have received under the old plan, and alternative job opportunities were nonexistent. Workers often accepted out of fear that their alternative was not receiving compensation at all.[42] Implicitly acknowledging the issues in a recent Labor Day speech, President Mubarak asserted that the state is committed to maintaining the hard-earned gains of workers. He claimed that he gave rigid directions to the government to protect workers' rights during the application of the privatization program and also made unions partners, in bargaining and evaluation to obtain the best terms, in the process of selling state-owned enterprises. He pledged that the state would expand its social security system by one million families and would raise the level of pensions.[43]

Peasant reaction to economic and political reform in Egypt has been just as volatile as the reaction of workers. Law 96 of 1992 reversed Nasser's land reforms and returned land to large landowners and landlords. The changed law increased levels of tenant impoverishment and led to systematic violence.[44] Its full implementation occurred in 1997 with fear, in some quarters, of social revolution. While revolution did not occur, the level of violence in rural politics in the wake of the reforms has been sometimes intense, and has been minimally reported by the Egyptian government. With little result, tenant farmers have also pursued legal channels to retain their land rights; thousands have gone to courts and have filed lawsuits through organizations such as the Land Center on Human Rights (LCHR).[45]

The LCHR in Egypt documented 32 deaths, 751 injuries, and 2,410 arrests between January 1997 and May 1998 in the Egyptian countryside, related to the implementation of law 96. There were also violent clashes in about one hundred villages in Egypt that year, resulting in numerous incidents of intimidation, illegal detention, and torture of farmers on the part of the police and security forces.[46] Between January 1998 and December 2000 there were a total of 119 deaths, 846 injuries, and 1,409 arrests related to the law.[47]

The violence stemming from law 96 can be further cataloged. In February 1996, a tenant farmer was stabbed to death by his landlord after refusing to evacuate a plot of land.[48] In December of that year, organized resistance began when some three thousand tenant farmers in the town of Beni Suef, 150 kilometers south of Cairo, demonstrated against a branch of the Agricultural Credit and Development Bank which refused to offer the farmers' annual loans due to the impending implementation of law 96. The farmers marched to the governor's office to protest the law. The security forces ended the demonstration by arresting ten protestors.[49] The opposition newspapers *Al-Destour* and *Al-Sha'b* were shut down for reporting these and similar incidents.[50]

The dispute in Beni Suef marked the start of a series of protests denouncing the law in the Egyptian countryside; these took the form of meetings, demonstrations, signature collections, the raising of black flags over rooftops and in fields, and the display of signs in houses.[51] There were efforts to organize these protests. A group of opposition parties and NGOs organized the Farmers' Committees for Resistance to Law 96, and the Tagammu Party staged a rally in Cairo against the law on April 30, 1997. Seven thousand farmers gathered to protest. In response, the state used repressive measures designed to target armed Islamic groups against the tenant farmers and their supporters.[52] Many of the protests erupted into violence. In two southern villages, several thousand leaseholders gathered for a march and then blocked the main traffic thoroughfares and local railroad tracks. They set fire to several houses of local landlords and a bus, killing three people and injuring twenty. The next day in a Nile Delta village, tenant farmers set fire to the offices of the local branch of the ministry of agriculture in an attempt to destroy land tenure records. More than 160 people were arrested. In another delta village, a seventy-year-old tenant farmer and his wife were beaten to death by the owner and his son for refusing to pay a rent increase.[53]

There were other sparks of resistance to the new land policies. Farmers held meetings sometimes backed by NGOs and opposition political parties to discuss their rights under the law. These meetings were followed up by the police taking in many participants for questioning.[54] Farmers in a village in the Talka district designed and hung up banners condemning the law and were quickly arrested by security forces and prosecuted for inciting protests.[55] Similar arrests occurred in other villages in reaction to plans to hang black banners on the walls of agricultural cooperatives as a sign of mourning to protest the law.[56]

Formal political institutions have been too weak or too hostile to advance the interests of peasants during the revolution in rural social relations caused by law 96. State corporatist organizations and rural cooperatives are dominated by NDP members and large landowners.[57] Despite years of efforts by peasant activists and leftist intellectuals, it is illegal for peasants to form their own independent trade union.[58] The reconciliation committees created to resolve disputes have systematically favored landlords.[59] The security forces, police, and gangs of thugs hired by landlords and backed by the central government to enforce the law have suppressed resistance harshly and have created a new fierce view of the security state in the Egyptian countryside.[60] The secular opposition, Tagammu, Labor, and Nasserists organized opposition against the law, and the parties and tenant farmers collected 350,000 signatures petitioning the government to change the law. Asserting that opposition to the act could not be so strong, the minister of agriculture refused to accept the petition.[61] The compensation of distributing reclaimed desert land to some tenants was not accompanied by the resources needed to make farming in those areas viable.[62]

While workers and peasants strained against changes in the NDP state largely outside the electoral arena, the mobilizational force of political Islam challenged the regime's commitment to controlled pluralism at the ballot box, and at times with violence. In Egypt there currently are Islamic political movements that correspond to Neo-Islamic Totalitarianism, Liberal Islam, and movements somewhere in between. In this chapter I describe the activities of the Neo-Totalitarian, Jamaat al-Islamiyya (Islamic Group), the Wasat (Center) Party that represents a form of liberal Islam, and the Muslim Brotherhood, a movement that falls in the middle. The Muslim Brotherhood is Egypt's most powerful opposition force.

The Islamic group is Egypt's largest Islamist militant organization. The organization's roots began among students at Asyut University in Upper Egypt, led by Umar 'Abd al-Rahman and Karam Zuhdi. This group participated in theatrical acts of violence designed to bring down the regime in Egypt in 1974–1981, culminating in the assassination of Anwar al-Sadat in 1981.[63] Some of its radical leaders were former Muslim Brothers. The group began a new wave of violence in 1992 that largely ended in the late 1990s due to a combination of repression and the loss of public credibility.[64] The armed offensive included the assassination of the secularist journalist Farag Fuda in June 1992, the intensification of armed struggle in Upper Egypt spurred by the arrest of Umar 'Abd al-Rahman in the United States in 1993, and the massacre of fifty-eight foreigners and four Egyptian tourists in Luxor in November 1997. A faction of the Islamic Group with a global perspective sought to engage the "greater enemy" in Afghanistan and elsewhere; that group includes al-Qaeda's number two man, Ayman al-Zawahiri.[65] Around the turn of the twenty-first century, the Islamic Group within Egypt, including Sheikh Umar 'Abd al-Rahman, made a firm commitment to nonviolence in statements sent to newspapers and other outlets.

The Wasat political party began as a splinter group from the Muslim Brotherhood in 1996. It claims to represent the middle (*wasat* means middle) position between those who subscribe to a rigid defense of Islamic tradition and those ready to jettison that tradition in its entirety in favor of values and institutions imported from the West.[66] Unlike the Muslim Brotherhood, and in the spirit of Liberal Islam, it disagrees with approaching the *shari'a* (Islamic law) as a fixed and unchanging set of rules hostile to Western values and institutions. Instead, it interprets *shari'a* as compatible with popular sovereignty, ideological and political pluralism, and equal citizenship rights.[67] The Wasat Party advocates opening up political office including the presidency to non-Muslims and calls for full citizenship rights for women and non-Muslims.[68] Like all religious parties, the Wasat Party is banned from the formal Egyptian political system. It has much less popular support than the Muslim Brotherhood.

The Muslim Brotherhood is Egypt's oldest and most influential Islamic political organization. Running as independent candidates and in alliance with secular political parties, the Muslim Brothers has the most popular support of any opposition social force, as the election results at the end of this section indicate. Like the Wasat political party, in recent years senior Brotherhood leaders have incorporated rhetorical support for democracy, pluralism, and human rights in their official statements, but their sincerity in this regard is doubted due to their insistence on rule according to strict enforcement of traditional legal rulings and traditional interpretations of *shari'a*.[69] Their support for popular sovereignty is undercut by their qualifying statements that insist that man is only allowed to rule according to principles of religion and strict enforcement of *shari'a* as traditionally understood.[70]

In the mid-1990s, during its counteroffensive against the wave of violence from the Islamic Group, the Egyptian government declared that in terms of using violence there was no substantial difference between the Muslim Brothers and the Islamic group. Hence, the government cracked down on both.[71] Publicly, the Muslim Brotherhood, occupying a grey zone between Neo-Islamic totalitarianism and Liberal Islam, continues to propagate a nonviolent Islamist message and continues to organize to overtake Egypt's controlled multiparty political system by winning majority representation in both civil society and the parliament. After the Muslim Brotherhood's success in the 2005 elections, in which they won a historically high number of opposition seats and demonstrated that they are the main opposition to the status quo, the Mubarak regime intensified measures to drive them out of the formal political system. A national referendum championed by Mubarak gave limited legislative authority to parliament's upper house, which was previously an advisory body. The Muslim Brotherhood was ousted from the electoral competition for seats in the Shura Council (the upper house created to provide secure support for the regime) by the regime, thus enshrining the prohibition of political activity informed by religion.

The oscillation between opening and closing of political space in Egypt under Mubarak raises the question of how structural factors such as the balance of class power, cultural influences, and historical institutional arrangements influenced his political formation of preferences and power. In terms of decisions about political and economic reforms, the evidence indicates that Mubarak and other Egyptian leaders believed that they could increase regime legitimacy by conducting multiparty elections while utilizing the state party to maintain power and control and state patronage to rebuild a coalition of support. While leadership choices regarding political and economic reforms in Egypt as elsewhere are often connected, for analytical purposes this section will discuss political reforms and the next section will discuss decision making with regard to economic reform.

Observing the Egyptian legislative elections of 1984 and 1987, one analyst argued that there were steps toward real democracy and that the steps were taken because Mubarak himself was a democrat. According to Derek Hopwood, writing in the early 1990s, Mubarak "genuinely wishes to see a wider democratic system which is introduced by consensus and responsibility."[72] Other analysts have been less convinced and for good reason. Based on an analysis of Mubarak's speeches, Roger Owen has argued that Mubarak wanted democratic legitimacy but continued authoritarian single-party rule:

To begin with, his speeches have consistently made the point that Egypt's pre-1952 exercise in pluralism was a total failure, with the parties of those days occupied with their own disputes and incapable of uniting their efforts to confront the demands of national independence. He has been equally insistent that the introduction of democracy is a difficult business and can only be properly achieved over a long period of time.[73]

Owen puts the preference for single-party rule into historical perspective; one can infer that justifications for this form of authoritarianism are part of the socialization process within the NDP leadership. To explain the measured political reform steps that Mubarak took, Owen points to their role in building up support and helping to defuse some of the tensions of economic liberalization exacerbated by growing international debt.[74] It is important to note that between the 1984 and 1987 elections, Egypt experienced a second dose of volatile bread riots linked to new cuts in consumer subsidies, along with a violent mutiny among the Central Security Force, and strikes over workers' pay. Mubarak and his ties with Washington were blamed. The army quickly contained the situation.[75]

In 1990, Egypt's Supreme Constitutional Court ruled that the 1986 election law, prepared for the 1987 elections, was invalid because it discriminated against independent candidates, and declared that the parliament elected under that law to be null and void. Again, Mubarak suspended parliament early, this time by two years, and new elections under different electoral laws were held in 1990.[76] While nominally more competitive, the NDP won those elections in a landslide as well. Mubarak was again able to claim some democratic legitimacy without the threat of losing power.

The legislative elections of 1995 were widely viewed as a setback in terms of political reforms. The context contributed to the backtracking. In 1992, the Islamic Group launched a broadside-armed offensive against the government. When the United States arrested Umar 'Abd al-Rahman in the United States in 1993, armed conflict intensified between the security services and the Islamic Group.[77] The government was also aware of the civil war in Algeria that began after the Islamist FIS won parliamentary elections and were not allowed to take power in early 1992. The Egyptian government responded with harsh repression against its own Islamists, lumping the Islamic Group and the Muslim Brotherhood together, though the latter renounced violence officially. The dialogue between Islamists and the government was, to put it mildly, strained. In his version of Egyptian–Islamists relations, Mubarak summarized the situation at that time in this way:

> The Illegal Muslim Brothers and the so-called Islamic Groups are all the same. They say they are moderates. There are no moderates. . . . Since the 1970s there was some kind of dialogue. It continued to some extent until 1992 in hopes that these people could be persuaded to give up violence. But then [militants] came back from Afghanistan and started using machine guns and killing people here. . . . When they killed the speaker of the Parliament and a famous writer, and started to attack tourists—just anybody on the street, we said "enough!" . . . Look we understand this area very well. [In response to U.S. pressure to engage with Islamists:] Your media said that Americans were "advising Egypt with their dialogue." Never. And whoever says to me "dialogue," I tell him, "No. Go have a dialogue in your own country. We know our people, and how to deal with them."[78]

Repression in the mid-1990s in Egypt was also increased to stifle resistance to economic reform policies that were leading to readily apparent gross inequalities.[79] The legislative elections of 1995 reflected these societal strains; indeed, the Egyptian government utilized its entire "menu of manipulations" and coercion to engineer a parliament in which all but 14 of 444 seats went to the NDP.[80] At that point, the support of economic elites was vital due to the regime's need for allies, within a mass of discontent; and by that time landlord and capitalist support of the NDP was already growing within parliament. The government also had to gamble that state control over unions could contain dissent.

In contradiction to the results of the 1995 elections, President Mubarak told reporters that high voter turnout was a "clear sign of the impartiality and fairness of the electoral process, and an indication of the progress of democracy in Egypt." Yet when asked whether he intended to make changes to accompany the installation of the new parliament he seemed irritated by the suggestion, "What change?" In response, he asked,

> What will we gain from making unnecessary changes? . . . the present government could remain for several years and could be changed in three months. But there is no need to change the

government completely and bring in one, which knows nothing about how to run the country's affairs and starts studying things anew and saying this or that was wrong. That would create a period of paralysis for the country. I have no time for paralysis. The processes of political reform and development are going ahead, so I am not going to stop them.[81]

In its clashes with the government in the 1990s, the Islamic group targeted the tourist industry in particular, culminating in a massacre of fifty-eight foreigners and four Egyptians in Luxur on November 17, 1997. According to one analyst, the combination of repression and loss of credibility following the incident ended the viability of the jihad option in Egypt.[82] The quelling of Islamist violence in the late 1990s set the stage for new political reforms. The Supreme Constitutional Court (SCC) ruled that the 1990 and 1995 parliamentary elections were unconstitutional because they did not permit judicial oversight. Instead, the status quo was enforced when the ministry of the interior began to supervise the elections.

The 2000 elections were the first elections supervised by the judiciary, a long-time opposition demand. The elections took place in three stages due to the limited number of judiciary members. These elections, which were moderately more favorable to the opposition parties, countered the trend in which the NDP had steadily received increasing shares of parliamentary seats: 68 percent in 1987, 86 percent in 1990, and 94 percent in 1995. The NDP's share fell to 87.8 percent of the 2000 parliamentary seats.[83] The elections, however, were also marked by broad repression of the Muslim Brotherhood, which appeared to be growing in popularity (17 new members of parliament out of 454 were members of the Muslim Brotherhood running as independents), a stifling of civil society organizations, and new tactics to prevent judicial oversight by requiring that judges stay inside the polling station while regime intimidation occurred outside, and by naming state attorneys as judicial observers.

The tepid step toward political reform in Egypt in 2000—allowing electoral supervision by the judiciary as required in the Egyptian constitution—was attributed by one analyst to an economic crisis in the summer before the November elections that fostered the consideration of political reform to relieve political tensions. Due to a liquidity crisis, the Central Bank devalued the Egyptian pound, the price of many goods rose, and several parliamentary deputies were convicted of corruption.[84] The decision by the Supreme Constitutional Council to declare the 1990 and 1995 elections unconstitutional and provide for supervision of voting by the judiciary was also a response to charges of electoral fraud and corruption in the previous two legislative elections.

The Egyptian government allowed the SCC decision to stand in order to refurbish its own democratic credentials.[85] A government supporter noted President Mubarak's personal dedication to democratization and called the electoral reforms "the single most important political development of 2000 in Egypt . . . the president has acted rapidly and energetically to bring the ruling into effect, as a result of which legislative reform this year ensured full judicial supervision over the legislative elections for the first time in Egyptian history."[86] Mubarak's decision to allow judicial supervision also was aimed at the international community. In a speech given at the time, Mubarak asserted that the step "shows clearly that Egypt is a democratic country . . . which has a democratic system based on multiple parties and seeks to strengthen [its multiparty democracy] in conformity with the genuine nature of [Egyptian] society . . . and [its][87] values, customs, and traditions." Regionally, some speculated that elections in Iran, considered more democratic than those in Egypt, prompted a step toward democracy in Egypt in order to place Egypt at the forefront of political reforms in the Middle East.[88]

To explain the 2000 political reforms, other analysts pointed to a revival of street politics, regime unpopularity due to the country's ties with Israel, and weak Egyptian support for the second Palestinian Intifada. The regime calculated that opposition could be dampened by a democratic step to allow discontent to be registered within the system.[89] Again, this calculation also had to take into account the social control capacities of the NDP–Egyptian Trade Union Federation alliance.

A new phase of political reforms was launched in 2005. In a move that startled both Egyptians and foreign observers, Hosni Mubarak announced in February 2005 that the country's election laws would be changed to allow multiple candidates in direct elections for the Egyptian presidency. Previously, the Egyptian president had been elected by a two-thirds majority of the People's Assembly, and then, in a second stage, was confirmed by public referendum.

A range of explanations has been proffered to explain the leap to what turned out to be nominally competitive presidential elections in Egypt. Mubarak won in a landslide capturing 88 percent of the vote. To the cynical, the multicandidate presidential election was engineered to smooth the transition from Hosni Mubarak to his son, Gamal.[90] Others argued that domestic tensions had increased pressure for political reform.[91] Economic woes and social frustration had led for the first time to widespread public calls for alternatives to Mubarak: "While Egyptians have long sanctified or loathed the persons of their presidents, it is only during Mubarak's tenure that specific demands to trim presidential powers have migrated from the pages of law journals into everyday conversation."[92] At the time, the economy was beset by recession, double-digit unemployment, and glaring inequality. Police brutality between 2003 and 2004 caused further anger and disenchantment in Egyptian society.

A cabinet reshuffle in 2004 brought in a group of ministers committed to more rapid and unpopular economic reforms. The ministers of investment, finance, industry, and trade all were linked to a new market-oriented generation led by Gamal Mubarak.[93] That cabinet reshuffle led to the first ever public rally calling for Mubarak to step down. The demonstration was led by a group organized within days of the July 2004 reshuffle to protest what they viewed as a cosmetic change when the country required fundamental constitutional and economic reforms. The protestors wore stickers over their mouth with the slogan *Kifaya* (Enough).[94] The Kifaya movement went on to gather signatures supporting contested presidential elections.

International and regional factors also contributed to Mubarak taking the 2005 political reform step to hold multicandidate presidential elections. Between 2003 and 2004, the U.S. administration under George Bush introduced various plans to democratize the Middle East: the U.S.–Middle East Partnership Initiative (MEPI), the Greater Middle East Initiative, and a watered-down version of these two, the Broader Middle East and North Africa Initiative (BMENAI).[95] Because Egypt was a major regional ally and recipient of U.S. aid, the Bush administration expected Egypt to lead the way for freedom in the wider region.[96] The Egyptian government was publicly chastised by the U.S. Secretary of State, Condoleeza Rice, for its treatment of jailed democracy activist and respected researcher Saad Eddine Ibrahim, the direc-

tor of the Ibn Khaldun Center for Development Studies. A G-8 statement of principles supporting Middle East democratization and desire
for a U.S.–Egypt economic partnership initiative also figured into the
regime's calculation.[97]

There were also regional pressures for political reforms, sometimes linked to the same pressure applied by the Bush administration
on Egypt. The Palestinian presidential elections of 2005 were widely
judged to have been free and fair. In Saudi Arabia, Crown Prince
Abdullah pledged to hold the kingdom's first ever municipal elections.
In Libya, Muammar Qaddafi pledged to cancel his country's emergency
law. Speaking in 2004, Jordanian foreign minister Marwan Muasher
stated that "A year ago, reform was not even on the radar screen of
most Arab countries. . . . Today the debate has moved from defining
the elements of reform to how to implement it."[98]

Reacting to the international and domestic pressure, Mubarak
informed the public in a series of interviews that "ruling Egypt is no
picnic" and that he was "compelled by presidential duty to sacrifice
creature comforts such as dining out or frequenting the cinema."[99]
Even as the regime was preparing for presidential elections, Gamal
Mubarak remarked, in reference to ending twenty-three years of emergency rule and undertaking constitutional reform, that "it is not wise
to broach issues affecting domestic stability, and it is not possible to
follow the wishes of the man on the street on everything and make
them a reason for fundamental change."[100]

After Mubarak's landslide victory in the 2005 presidential elections, parliamentary elections were held and were judged to be as free
as any ever held in the recent multiparty era.[101] In the 2005 legislative elections, the Muslim Brotherhood gained the most. More secure
about having stamped out radical Islamists, the government had shifted
from a position of absolute repression to limited accommodation of
the Muslim Brotherhood.[102] Running as independents, the Muslim
Brotherhood won 88 seats or nearly 20 percent of the vote; The NDP
won 311 seats or 68 percent. The secular opposition parties had formed
the United National Front for Change and faired miserably. Tagammu
received 2 seats and the New Wafd, 6. The Nasserist party did not
win any seats, nor did the Liberal party, the right platform of Sadat's
platform with Islamist tendencies.

After the 2005 elections, the Egyptian government sharply

backtracked on political reform. A national referendum championed by Mubarak gave limited legislative authority to parliament's upper house, which had previously been an advisory body. In addition, constitutional changes removed requirements that judges supervise elections, enshrined the prohibition of political activity informed by religion, and allowed for the suspension of constitutional civil liberties in cases deemed by the government to involve terrorism.[103] Mubarak also canceled local elections scheduled for April 2007 and sentenced one of his presidential opponents, Ayman Nour, to five years in prison on trumped-up charges, and began criminal investigations on those in the judiciary who questioned his electoral cancelation decision.[104] Repression of the Muslim Brotherhood was stepped up by the regime as well. After their advances in the 2005 parliamentary elections, "Mubarak, who had never truly embraced democracy, reverted to his old autocratic practices."[105]

Other than dislike for the results of the 2005 elections and Mubarak's authoritarian ways, foreign influence had a role in the Egyptian government's backtracking. The U.S. pressure for political reforms weakened because of its preoccupation with Iraq and fear of Islamist takeovers across the region, including Hamas's victory in the free and fair 2006 legislative elections to the Palestinian Authority.[106]

At the time of this writing, March 2009, every multiparty parliamentary election in Egypt since their relaunch in 1976 by Sadat has delivered at least a two-thirds majority to the state party. That total is needed to pass legislation; such a landslide is always delivered in Egyptian elections, including the recent multicandidate presidential one. The top leadership in Egypt has clearly decided that limited reform can be managed by the NDP and its affiliated corporatist organizations, and that controlled multiparty politics is less costly than the social strains caused by a completely closed political economy enduring hard times and undergoing fundamental transformations.

In addition to experiments in multiparty competition and the weakening of state corporatist organizations, changes in political institutions that characterize a new authoritarianism in Egypt include increasing presidential power. Economic reforms globally have been accompanied by a shift in the policy-making process to privilege-insulated technocratic change teams under presidential auspices. This insulation of technocrats and the presidents' closest advisors has even

Table 4.1. Egyptian Legislative Elections

PARTY	1984	1987	1990	1995	2000	2005
NDP	390	348	360	417	388	311
Muslim Brotherhood	8	30	Boycott	1	17	88
New Wafd	50	35	Boycott	6	7	6
Socialist Labor Party		27	Boycott			
Liberal Party		3	Boycott	1	1	0
Progressive Unionist Party			5	5	6	2
Arab Democratic Nasserist Party					2	0
Nasserists						5
Independents			79	13	16	24
TOTAL	448	413	448	444	444	444

Source: Daniel Brumberg, "Liberalization Versus Democracy: Understanding Arab Political Reform," working paper, Carnegie Endowment for International Peace (Washington, D.C., 2003); Wikipedia 2005 results, accessed February 8, 2006.

been recommended by the international financial institutions pressing to advance market-oriented policies in the Arab world.[107] Multiparty politics weaken state parties in relationship to executive branch elites. In such circumstances, historic ruling parties to some degree have to compete with other parties for privileged access to presidential power. The new institutional arrangements reduce structural resistance to policies, which transfer economic management from the state–single-party alliance to the new state–bourgeoisie–private sector alliance.[108]

In sum, president Hosni Mubarak and presidents in the other former Arab socialist single-party regimes probably calculate that the new multiparty systems weaken the single party, the national trade union federation, the bureaucracy, and potentially the judiciary relative to themselves while retaining their social control capacities. Writing about Egypt under Mubarak, Jason Brownlee asserted that

Table 4.2. Egyptian Electoral Elections, Shura Council

PARTY	1980	1983	1986	1989	1992	1995	1998	2001	2004	2007
National Democratic Party										84
Independents										3
National Progressive Unionist Party										1
TOTAL										88

Source: Wikipedia 2007 results, accessed September 1, 2007.

> After a tenuous period of political opening in the 1980s and very early 1990s, the regime has progressively limited opportunities for the dispersal of power beyond the president, let alone for an actual alternation in power. If any form of "freedom" has been expanded in Egypt, meanwhile, it has been the freedom of the presidency from the informal constraints that earlier limited his authority. . . . Overall, pluralism has declined markedly since the outset of his rule. And unless domestic—perhaps more importantly—international actors compel the Egyptian president to cede power to other branches of government and to allow civil society organizations to operate independently, the outlook for organized political contestation in Egypt will only continue to dim.[109]

Perhaps to compensate for increasing presidentialism and partly due to the external pressures and domestic unrest just discussed, Mubarak implemented directly elected "contested" presidential elections in September 2005. Typical measures were taken to prevent any chance of an alteration in power, and Mubarak won by a typical landslide margin as indicated in Table 4.3.

Table 4.3. September 7, 2005, Presidential Election Results

CANDIDATES, NOMINATING PARTIES	VOTES	%
Hosni Mubarak, National Democratic Party	6,316,714	88.6
Ayman Nour, Tomorrow Party	540,405	7.3
Numan Gomaa, New Wafd Party	201,891	2.8
TOTAL	7,059,010	

Source: 2005 Election Data provided by Wikipedia, accessed September 16, 2007.

Ruling Coalition and Policies

The argument in this section is that the Egyptian government has utilized privatization policies to shape a new authoritarian ruling coalition among a rent-seeking urban and rural economic elite. The policies also deprived the Egyptian political system of an opportunity to foster democracy by distributing stock more broadly, thereby taking resources away from workers and peasants who increasingly have the most to gain from democratization. The results of Egypt's privatization policies (crony capitalism) and an analysis of Egyptian leaders' decisions to adopt economic reforms support this argument.

In 1984, when Mubarak relaunched multiparty political elections after the 1981 assassination of Anwar Sadat, the regime, through its economic policies, still maintained a multiclass ruling coalition and credible claims to populist legitimacy due to the extensive state sector employing organized labor, welfare policies, and Nasser's land reforms that continued to benefit peasants. In the course of the controlled multiparty elections in Egypt between 1984 and 2005, however, state-led economic liberalization, especially privatization, signaled a shift to a ruling coalition anchored by a rent-seeking urban and rural elite.

Privatizations of state-owned enterprises and land have been the most important economic reforms implemented by the Egyptian government. Theoretically, privatization policies should decrease rent seeking in the economy and should limit corruption. The general debates about implementing all aspects of an orthodox economic reform program have been driven by the proponents of the tenets of neoclassical theory, which assume that divestiture programs and other economic reform policies act to overcome rent seeking.[110] However, recent experience has demonstrated that economic liberalization is a process that reorganizes opportunities for rent seeking.[111]

There are a variety of methods by which ownership of State-Owned Enterprises (SOEs) can be transferred to the private sector. Firms can be sold to another company (anchor firm) or to a strategic investor after competitive bidding. The state can also liquidate public firms and sell their assets to the highest bidder. Other methods distribute stock more broadly. Voucher programs allocate shares of stock to all adult citizens on an equal basis, who may then choose either to hold their shares or sell them. Finally, employee stock ownership plans allow workers to purchase stakes in the firms that employ them in Employee Shareholder Associations (ESAs).[112]

Most economists and lending agencies tend to prefer sales to anchor firms or strategic investors because they assume that capitalist firms and strategic or wealthy investors will operate the enterprises according to efficient market principles and will infuse the firms with new capital to modernize equipment and production techniques.[113] But Egypt's privatization process has lacked the regulatory framework necessary to prevent the sale of the majority of its SOEs at below market value to a small group of investors. The result has been the creation of a series of privately owned monopolies or near monopolies. Ultimately, privatization in Egypt has been less about generating economic efficiency than about picking winners and losers.[114]

Privatization in Egypt began in earnest with the passage of law 203 in June 1991. The program aimed to privatize 314 public sector companies.[115] Out of the 190 companies privatized by 2002, a total of 34 were sold to Employee Shareholder Associations. The ESAs struggled. The 34 companies were sold in installments that were to be funded out of dividends, with the ESAs granted five to ten years to pay the holding companies. However, many of the companies failed to prosper and were unable to make the payments.[116] Most of the remainder of the companies were sold to anchor firms and strategic investors.

The Arabic press and Egyptian social science research centers have emphasized the prevalence of rent seeking in Egyptian privatization programs. Hassan Tawfiq Ibrahim argued that privatization led to state bureaucrats colluding with businessmen to purchase state-owned enterprises at lower-than-market prices. He noted that while corruption had existed before, privatization opened the door wider due to the lack of transparency and accountability in the process of selling SOEs.[117] According to newspaper reports, the Egyptian government does not provide accurate figures about the total sum of money gained by the state treasury through the selling of public sector companies.[118] They assert that former Prime Minister 'Atif 'Ubayid presented contradictory figures that seem much lower than the actual market value of the companies sold. By 2000 the government declared that it sold 138 SOEs for less than $8 billion. In addition, the reports argue that profits from the sale of the enterprises that were supposed to be used to create new jobs never for the most part materialized. The unemployment rate in Egypt increased sharply in 2001.[119]

Ahmad al-Sayyid al-Najjar identified several companies that were sold by the government at prices so low that at times the price paid was lower than the value of the land on which the companies stood. These companies included an Egyptian state-run Pepsi Cola company, al-Nasr Boilers, al-Ahram Beverage, Asyut Cement, and the Meridien hotel. According to the author, all of these companies were profitable at the time that they were sold.[120]

The 2004 Human development report in Egypt unveiled more cases of rampant rent seeking,[121] declaring that the state sold profitable companies and kept failing ones. The central bureau of accounting, according to this report, is excluded from the privatization process, and parliament and its councils are not consulted about the selling procedures. The overall privatization process in Egypt has lacked transparency. In one case described in the report, an investor bought the Qaha Company for Preserved Food with a loan backed by fake guarantees and then kept the company even after failing to make installment payments.

The current Egyptian privatization policy of selling assets to strategic investors, small groups of investors, or anchor firms led to monopolies or near monopolies in many sectors of the increasingly marketized economy. These included cement, iron, food, telecommunications, and beverages.[122] For example, Ahmad Ezz, a powerful businessman and personal friend of President Mubarak, controlled more than 50 percent of the iron market, and Ahmed Baghat controlled more than 31 percent of the television market after such purchases.[123] Evolving monopolies and corruption have been reported in specific companies such as the Iron and Steel Company, Telemisr,[124] Nasir for Iron Pipes,[125] The Egyptian Company for Chemicals and Metals Trade, and the Holding Company of Tourism, Habitation, and Cinema.[126]

According to the opposition organization the Free Egyptians,[127] the president's son Gamal Mubarak has been linked to numerous rent-seeking arrangements via several organizations: the Policies Committee, the Future Generation Foundation, the Social Fund for Development, the U.S.-Egypt Business Council, and the Egyptian Center for Economic Studies. Prominent business partners of the Mubaraks in these endeavors include Ahmed Bahgat, Ahmed Al Bardai, Ahmed Zayat, Ahmad Ezz, Galal Abdel Maksoud Al Zorba, Hosna Rachid, Hossam H. Badrawi, Ibrahim, AL Alfi, Mahamed Farid Khamis, Mahamed L. Mansour, Mohammed Abou-Al-Enein, Raouf Ghabbour, Sarwat Sabet Bassily, Yaseen I. Loutfy Mansour, Yasser Al Mallawany, and Youssef Loutfy Mansour. The president's family gained stakes in numerous products, franchises, and companies including Sofitel, Hundai, Nissan, KFC, Skoda, Stella Beer, and Marlboro. The Mubaraks' partners acquired the most lucrative franchises and companies by utilizing supporting loans from state-associated banks attained without proper collateral.

Comprehensive data on the concentration of ownership in various industries would be one indicator of the overall amount of crony capitalism in Egypt. Unfortunately, this data does not exist.[128] Absent that, anecdotal evidence on conspicuous consumption indicates levels of cronyism in the privatization of Egyptian industries.[129] In the mid-1990s conspicuous consumption rather than productive investment increased, according to Egyptian economists:

> Between the Nile and the Cairo zoo, workers are constructing the First Residence, an exclusive apartment complex offering units at more than $3 million each, a helipad, and separate villas equipped with swimming pools. On Cairo's streets even the most expensive Mercedes Benz cars—such as the $440,000 model S600—have become a common sight. And at the upscale World Trade Center mall, a growing number of ritzy shops sell fine French china and imported designer clothing.[130]

As the rich have grown richer, the poor have become poorer. Economic reform has meant rising prices and fewer job opportunities for Egypt's population of 60.6 million, striving to survive on $750 a year per capita. "The gap [between rich and poor] is certainly getting wider," said Galal Amin, an economics professor at the American University of Cairo. "In the '90s this disparity has become very obvious."[131] The structural-adjustment policies, which were applied in 1991, were much harsher than those applied in the 1970s, but wealthy entrepreneurs took advantage of the growing capitalist atmosphere.[132] On Egypt's north shore and the desert road from Cairo north to Alexandria, developments of million-dollar villas are sprouting. Shops sell designer clothing by Christian Dior and Donna Karan, Lalique crystal, and Cristofle silver.[133]

Another description of conspicuous consumption in Egypt concluded with the following:

> But five years of free-market economics have contributed to a surge of luxury spending in Egypt, at least by a privileged few. Like Moscow or Shanghai, Cairo is awash in the badges of new wealth, from $14 million penthouse apartments to gourmet bakeries selling cheesecakes for $50 each. In perhaps the ultimate testimonial to Egypt's new-found purchasing power, the German luxury-car maker BMW recently announced plans to open an assembly plant here. Mercedes-Benz is expected to follow.[134]

Moving beyond the discussion of crony capitalism and conspicuous consumption, land privatization policies in Egypt have also been more about choosing winners and losers than about generating economic efficiency. An analytical literature focuses on the relationship between farm size and productivity;[135] its central theme is that smaller holdings are more productive than larger ones per unit of land. The arguments supporting the superior productivity of smaller holdings highlight the reliance on cheaper family labor (instead of hired labor). Supervision costs of managing hired labor and enforcing effort are higher. Often large holdings are not cultivated entirely and some elites hold stretches of property for reasons of political power or prestige rather than undertaking active exploitation of full productive potential. Dangers of overproduction are low for smaller, family farms. Defenders of large farms contend that the use of farm machinery requires a minimum farm size. However, the literature asserts that capital is often scarce and labor abundant in developing countries, so costly machines should be avoided where possible. In addition, in those cases where large machinery is useful improved rental programs could easily make the necessary machines available to small farmers.

As discussed, recent land-tenure policies implemented in Egypt reversed Nasser's land reforms. The Egyptian agrarian reform of 1952 maintained the private property of the original owners, but beneficiaries received inheritable tenancy rights where the rent was fixed at seven times the land tax. Tenants could be evicted only if they did not pay the rent, and they were registered in agricultural cooperatives as holders, farming the land as if it were their own. Landowners were unable to sell their land because rents were not reevaluated and over time fell to levels that were much lower than market value, with the added burden of tenants who for the most part could not be evicted.[136]

Rent ceilings and secure tenancy led to the stagnation of agricultural production. Rents remained fixed much too far below market prices and frequently peasants did not have the resources to increase production. Through law 96 of 1992, the Egyptian government revoked Nasser's Agrarian Reform Law of 1952 that gave tenants rights of security of tenure and legal rights of tenancy. After a five-year transition period, on October 1, 1997 all owners were able to retake their land and charge tenants market-based prices. To explain the tenancy reforms, the Egyptian government stated that it was redressing an imbalance that had emerged over time between rental values and market rates for land.[137]

The solution to the conflict between tenants and landowners could have been resolved in a number of ways, including efforts to bolster small-scale ownership and production among former tenants in a more market-oriented environment. In the end, however, law 96 dramatically favored the interests of owners over those of tenants. Tenants were evicted en masse and compensation to them amounted to only one-fifth of the sum considered during the debates on the subject. In addition to these rent ceilings, the state chose to sell much of publicly owned lands to the highest bidder, causing a steep drop in the proportion of small landowners[138] By the end of the 1990s, 7 percent of the population owned 60 percent of agricultural land.[139] A close observer of rural politics in Egypt claimed, "In passing [law 96] the GOE managed a most careful slight of hand: they managed to mask the naked return of power, money and authority to [landlords] while insisting no change to the Nasserist revolutionary inheritance that secured tenant rights [had occurred]."[140] The Egyptian government chose winners and losers in this instance, weakly backed by claims of increasing productivity. By formulating Egypt's agricultural crisis as a crisis of ownership rather than access, security of property rights for owners rather than security of rights for tenants and employment opportunities for the landless and near landless, law 96 accelerated rural social differentiation, marginalized female-headed households, and promoted a return to indentured child and adult labor.[141]

Resistance against deepening economic reforms in Egypt slowed privatization during some years and helped achieve marginally better terms for workers, but by the time of this writing in 2009, most state assets had been privatized to the benefit of urban economic elites; land tenure rights had also been returned to landlords. In addition, most state subsidies that benefited workers and peasants were reduced or cut all together, including those on rice, sugar, cooking oil, fuel, power, and transportation. Privatization ended job security and associated social provisions.[142] Observers have noted deteriorating social conditions in Egypt since the early 1990s, and although certain social indicators such as life expectancy and infant mortality have improved, unemployment, poverty, and income gaps reportedly increased in the 1990s.[143]

Given the strains on social equity generated by the marriage between wealth and political authority in Egypt, how can we explain the government's decision to implement politically motivated economic reforms? The evidence suggests a calculation by the upper echelons of the state and government to build a social base of support from rent-seeking urban and economic elites, and enrich themselves in the process.

Effectively economic liberalization in Egypt had stalled between the late 1970s and early 1990s. However, in the 1990s significant economic reforms were implemented, signaling an end to the logjam.[144] Between February and October 1991, the government changed the foreign exchange system into a largely market-determined rate. In January 1991, banks became free to set interest rates. In the same year, parliament approved a budget to cut the government budget by 9.5 percent of the GDP. Beginning in 1990, subsidies were reduced on a large variety of goods, especially energy products. Subsidies for basic foods, cigarettes, and fertilizers were also cut.[145] Most fundamentally in terms of a deepening of economic reforms and a shifting of social relations in Egypt, privatization of state assets began seriously in the early 1990s.

What caused the logjam against economic reforms in Egypt and what ended it? The Egyptian government's resistance to most elements of an orthodox economic reform program, especially privatization, throughout the 1970s and the 1980s has been explained in various ways. Domestically, some scholars argue, the balance of class power was against reform.[146] It was asserted that states had difficulties imposing policies that noticeably discriminated against urban populations, especially labor, that could protest and demonstrate against reforms; and since governments typically give top priority to political stability they were not willing to deepen economic reforms to include privatization and higher unemployment. Similarly, structural adjustment harmed the interests of other citizens working in the public sector and they, along with labor, successfully organized against a deepening of reform. In contrast, those who stood to benefit most from the implementation of a full orthodox economic reform program included commercial agriculture, private industrialists, and export sectors that would have to anticipate future but uncertain gains; the latter groups were more weakly organized to complete the economic reform process than the defenders of the public sector who stood to lose much quickly.[147] This perspective, however, is blind to the real possibility of economic elites being aware of potential gains and organizing to pursue the uncompetitive appropriation of state-owned assets. In this light, the formation of new ruling coalitions built upon state privatization policies provides a plausible explanation for the breakdown of state resistance to full economic liberalization.

Other related factors posited that contributed to the stalemate of economic reform included the threat of destabilization from a population that was as a whole unwilling to accept a violation of the social contract implied by the regime's statist and welfare policies. Finally, it was argued that internationally Egypt was strategically important to the West and therefore able to earn rent in the form of large amounts of foreign aid that delayed economic reform.[148] In a similar vein, worker remittances and oil sales stalled reforms.

To explain the breakdown of regime resistance to a deepening of economic reform and privatization in the early 1990s, some scholars referred to a change of hearts and minds among high-level Egyptian government officials and Western donors who came to believe that the statist policies and partial economic reforms were not sustainable and that delaying full reform meant sacrificing Egypt's economic future and causing persistent economic crises that typically lead to political stability. Egypt's growing foreign debt contributed to this sentiment and weakened the government's autonomy in the economic policy process.[149]

Samir Sulayman made the case that the availability or lack of sufficient government revenue has been the decisive factor in Egypt's economic reform trajectory.[150] According to him, in 1987 the state signed an economic reform agreement with the World Bank due to a financial crisis stemming from a decline in oil prices, a decline in Suez Canal revenues, and a decline in immigrant labor remittances from Egyptians working in the Gulf. The state then signed an agreement with the IMF and rescheduled its external debt with the Paris Club. The state failed to abide by these agreements and in 1990 the Egyptian government began to appear like a hopeless case and an international beggar.[151] However, in 1990, the first Gulf War erupted and the rewards Egypt received for its military and political help contributed to the implementation of more economic reforms to satisfy its creditors. After the war, Egypt experienced an economic upturn from contributions from Western and Arab governments and their cancelation of debts that totaled around 24 billion dollars. This influx of foreign exchange reserves increased the political feasibility of implementing all measures of the structural adjustment and stabilization packages that Egypt had signed with the IMF and World Bank.

In terms of accelerating economic reforms, analysts also pointed to an improved ability to manage the implementation of economic policies: the government timed policy changes on holidays when street protests were unlikely. Reform by stealth strategies included removing subsidized goods from shelves rather than cutting the subsidies. The government made the reforms more of their own initiative rather than IMF or World Bank initiatives by presenting the policies as locally designed. Finally, the 1989 collapse of the Soviet Union made alternative ideologies less appealing.[152]

Changing views on economic reform in Egypt had to reach the very top. Mubarak had to change his position from his stance in the 1980s when he talked of public and private sectors as complementary partners and referred to the IMF as a quack doctor reflected by its belief that the private sector, which had never met investment targets, could work wonders in Egypt.[153] Due in part to the already described factors, Mubarak and his top officials changed their minds about deepening economic reforms in the early 1990s. Mubarak's speeches began to embrace the once-scorned IMF and World Bank prescriptions and he endorsed their suggested reforms.[154]

In a Labor Day speech in 2006, Mubarak extolled the virtues of economic reform and privatization.[155] In that speech, he backed economic reform in Egypt because it was a policy package that had proved successful in many developing and advanced countries alike, including the former Eastern bloc. He stated that Egypt could not ignore global trends reflected in market economics, privatization, and the World Trade Organization. He argued that the global context made privatization beyond debate, and that it was a means to encourage private investment, raise the growth rate, and create more jobs. He remarked that the privatization program was meant to save the public money by divesting the state from enterprises that the private sector could handle more efficiently. For Mubarak the question had become *how* to privatize state assets and protect workers' rights and benefits. On this point, he asserted that privatized companies, even foreign-owned ones, operated under Egyptian laws that protect worker rights and benefits.

In a sense Mubarak's change of position reflected long-term changes in the balance of class power in Egypt and the formation of a new distributional coalition of urban and rural economic elites who were poised to gain from privatization. The upper echelon of state officials, some within Mubarak's family, stood to profit from the government's privatization policies. Beginning in the late 1970s, businessmen and their organizations emerged as a strong and unified force, increasingly independent from government control, even as the trade unions remained under considerable government control. Business groups mostly favored the full orthodox reform package including privatization and began participating in its design in parliament, and in the ruling NDP in greater numbers.[156] Powerful elements of the business community and landlords realized that they could anticipate gains from market reserves made available by state withdrawal. Government elites, including the military, also had formed growing alliances with business families and stood to gain personally from privatization. In this manner, economic reform characterized by patronage contributed to a change in the balance of class power within Egypt and helped alter the economic policy preferences of powerful government officials and economic elites while creating a new set of allied interests and coalition partners that buttressed the regime's ability to govern.

Beyond providing support for the NDP, businessmen and landlords operating within the NDP contributed to the formation of economic reform policies from which they decisively benefited. A powerful group within the NDP has been characterized by Ahmad al-Sayyid al-Najjar as a new ruling coalition of capital-owning bureaucrats who have been behind the recent steps in economic liberalization and have amalgamated themselves with private capital when crafting economic reform policies.[157]

Economic elites in parliament allied with the NDP, strongly influencing government policies to conform to their interests in privatization, tax law, antitrust, trade agreements, and labor laws.[158] They head important legislative committees, such as the Planning and Budget, Economic, and Industrial Committees. In 2005, the new taxation law 91 placed an increasing burden on the shoulders of the middle and lower classes while cutting taxes for the wealthy. The law cut the highest tax rate from 40 percent to 20 percent. The top rate was also applied to a greater number of people; anyone earning over 40,000 Egyptian pounds a year owed the same amount of taxes. The difference between taxes paid by the poorest and richest Egyptians was reduced to 10 percent. This meant that businessmen making millions paid insignificant tax rates relative to their income and also benefited from industrial and commercial public services that small businesses paid out of their own pockets.[159]

Employees working for the state also were disadvantaged by the new tax policy. Taxes are deducted directly from their monthly salary, while powerful business owners continue a high rate of tax evasion.[160] In addition, new antitrust laws did not provide strong enough regulation to end the monopolies formed from privatizing state assets.[161] Businessmen in Egypt have also influenced the state in their adoption of trade agreements. For example, members of the Egyptian press charge that Egyptian textile and apparel entrepreneurs negotiated the establishment of a Qualified Industrialized Zone with Israeli counterparts without parliamentary debate.[162]

Labor policy in the form of the Egyptian Unified Labor Law 12, implemented in 2003, reflected the desires of capital much more than labor.[163] The labor law increased the power of the state-allied ETUF leadership, and weakened the power of the rank and file. The right to strike was exchanged for the right to fire, but strikes from the base, where militants operated, had to be approved by the leadership.[164] All of these laws were enacted in spite of the objections of the leftist opposition parties. There were two Nasserist deputies and six from Tagammu in parliament when these laws were implemented. They raised fierce arguments about these laws, but the voice of the NDP majority prevailed.[165]

In sum, during Mubarak's political opening, landed elites and business classes within the NDP successfully pressed for their material interests and personal freedoms in parliament, while the new system largely excluded the mass public from these same opportunities. In addition to state policies and laws favoring economic elites, the expansion of judicial powers during the era of multiparty politics has been utilized primarily to ensure new property rights to the benefit of the urban bourgeoisie and landlords, while secondarily protecting the right of the masses to assemble and protect themselves from state abuses.[166]

Finally, for the reasons described at the beginning of this section, the Egyptian government felt that they had a quiescent-enough population and a strong-enough base of support in the early 1990s to deepen privatization and market reforms in the manner that they did. This sense of state control also came from the limited opposition to Egypt's participation in Gulf War I. Regime leaders felt that they could move ahead on economic reform without the dangerous widespread demonstrations of the 1977 bread riots. They were partially correct. Protests in Egypt against economic reform in the 1990s and early twentieth century did not provoke the generalized instability of 1977, but protests have been widespread among workers, peasants, and Islamist organizations.

Legitimacy

All of the recent elections in Egypt attest to the regime's pursuit of electoral legitimation. Maintaining eudaemonic legitimacy, the promise to improve people's lives and welfare, has been difficult for a Mubarak regime implementing neo-liberal economic reforms in the manner that they have done. The rational legal legitimacy earned from the successes of economic reform ring hollow when privatization has benefited a rent-seeking urban and rural economic elite. In response to the changes in social relations and setbacks to workers and peasants that have resulted from new policies, the regime has sometimes sought to hide the unpleasant realities. The distributive effect of economic liberalization, especially privatization, led the Egyptian government to restrict the media. Law 93 of 1995 significantly widened the definition of crimes such as the propagation of false information and punished citizens convicted of these crimes more severely. The aim was to make it easier for the regime to suppress information that either explicitly or implicitly contained accusations of corruption. The law also led to the suppression of various periodicals, including state prevention of the distribution of *Al-Destour* and the *Cairo Times*.[167] Law 93 targeted the broad coverage of corruption in which politicians, higher civil servants, top managers of the public sector, or private business people were involved. The law followed on the heels of rumors that the sons of President Mubarak had received an important commission for the sale of Airbus aircraft to Egyptair.[168]

The regime also has sought to maintain a patina of continued populism. The World Bank supports Egypt's Social Fund for Development that aims to create employment and provide a social safety net.[169] Early retirement programs and selling shares of state-owned enterprises to workers exist but are flawed and limited.[170] Coerced charity forms a similar function. Mubarak cajoles Egypt's rich private-sector entrepreneurs to support state programs such as his voluntary school-building program. There is the implied threat that the rich should remember how they made their money in the first place and how they may lose it or lose future opportunities.[171]

Defining legitimacy as political stability without the need for coercion leads to pessimistic conclusions about Egypt under Mubarak. The secret police and military bureaucratic structures in Egypt can be both generally repressive and sharply coercive. Egyptians have been living under a state of emergency law since Sadat's assassination. The law allows the government to detain people without charges. Security services in Egypt have been accused of torturing detainees by domestic and international human rights organizations. The Egyptian government is moving toward replacing emergency laws with counterterrorism laws that will achieve the same ends.[172] Military trials with dubious links to justice are often used against the civilian opposition. In a 2007 case that garnered international attention, the Egyptian government refused to allow Human Rights observers to attend as requested the military trials for thirty-three leaders of the Muslim Brotherhood.[173]

Beginning in the early 1990s, Egypt experienced a substantial degree of political deliberalization and state coercion that was spurred by the violence of the Islamic Group but extended to other parts of civil society. Repressive amendments to the penal code in 1992 and to legislation governing professional syndicates and trade unions, as well as unprecedented electoral fraud, were some of the indicators of broad repression. As Eberhard Kienle notes, "Though related to the conflict between the regime and armed Islamic groups, the erosion of political participation and liberties also [reflected] other factors, including attempts to contain opposition to economic liberalization."[174] Amendments to the penal code aimed largely to combat Islamist violence also were invoked against the secular Tagammu party.[175] As previously discussed, repressive measures were also taken against opposition-party members who supported sharecroppers against the effects of law 96 of 1992 that reversed Nasser's land reforms. Unpopular economic-reform laws also provoked the regime to seek larger majorities in parliament and led them to take measures to prevent workers most harmed by privatization from participating in union elections.[176]

By the end of 1997, it appeared that the armed Islamic group(s) no longer posed a major threat, yet the general repressive measures of the mid-1990s remained. However, the government emphasized that the threat remained as well, and in 2004 attacks against tourists in the Sinai killed thirty-three. There were new deadly Sinai attacks against tourists and Peacekeepers in April 2006, raising the specter of a new period of sustained terrorist attacks.[177] Teasing out repression and coercion for genuine security reasons as opposed to coercion for other state reasons is difficult to do, especially in the face of a government that can limit public scrutiny in a variety of ways.

Finally, two high-profile cases illustrate how the government utilizes repression to remove the threat of individual opposition leaders. In 2005, the presidential candidate, Ayman Nour, was imprisoned and wrote from behind bars, "Letter from Prison: 'Did I Take Democracy Too Seriously?'" Nour antagonized the Egyptian government by using his assembly seat to push for concrete reforms to make Egyptian elections more competitive. His principled stand led to strong popular support for the presidential elections of 2005 and the regime jailed him, allegedly for forging signatures of support in his election campaign, a charge he and his supporters have denied.[178] Egypt's best-known advocate for democracy, the sixty-eight-year-old social scientist Saad Eddine Ibrahim, was jailed for three years beginning in 2000. In 2005, he left Egypt for a year of work at the Woodrow Wilson International Center for Scholars. He was warned not to return home.[179] Since 2007, Ibrahim has been in self-imposed exile in Qatar.

The New Authoritarianism in Syria

Syria's timid turn toward democratization took an initial step in the 1970s when Hafez Al-Asad took power in a military coup. Asad implemented another round of political reforms in the early 1990s, a process that was accelerated by his son, Bashar Al-Asad, after he took power in 2000. During the 1990s, privatization characterized by crony capitalism became a part of state policy. A ruling coalition of rent-seeking economic elites and state officials has gradually evolved in Syria, despite the complication of a sectarian divide between state and economic elites. Economic policies have also eroded material gains of workers and peasants achieved under the Ba'th in the 1960s. Political institutions have moved toward what one Syrian dissident has described as the modernization of authoritarianism along Egyptian lines: a dose of controlled pluralism that could still be contained by the high levels of state control and centralization afforded by single-party institutional structures.[180] By the time of the 2005 Ba'th Party congress that focused on the legalization of multiple political parties, it was apparent that the regime hoped to profit from electoral legitimacy.

Political Institutions

This section describes recent institutional changes in Syria and analyzes leadership decision making regarding the initiation of political reforms. Political reforms in Syria include the creation of a façade of multiparty politics cloaking continued single-party rule. Presidential powers were increased. Economic reform policies have alienated workers and peasants, who have responded with protests while their state corporatist union leaders side with the regime. The ruling Ba'th Party has been able to use its organizational resources to contain this disaffection during the country's tepid processes of political reforms. Economic elites, even those from traditional Sunni groups histori- cally hostile to the Alawi minority in control of the state and military apparatus, have become more supportive of the Ba'thist state as Syria implements tentative political and economic reforms that enhance their interests. The evidence suggests that Syrian regime leaders are con- scious of the fact that the ruling party and state assets can be deployed as resources to transform authoritarian rule and enrich themselves in the process.

In 1990, a new opening in Syria's political system was implemented by Hafez Al-Asad. The new parliament of that year reserved about one-third of its seats for independents, a far greater number than at any time during Ba'thist rule. Thousands of political prisoners were set free. The independents largely represented rising social forces of businessmen, the educated middle class, and traditional religious and economic elites. While the next section will discuss details about the nature of economic reforms in Syria and why the Syrian leadership pursued them, it is worthwhile to note here that analysts of the Syrian political scene contended that this creation of political space for social forces outside the Ba'th's original social base served as a substitute for the loss of allegiance on the part of losers of economic adjustment.[181] As Volker Perthes noted at the time, "Syria's 1990 elections, while hardly democratization, might indicate gradual remodeling of the politi- cal structure and the socio-political base that Asad relies on."[182] The incorporation of new elements in parliament and the rising profile of economic and traditional elites also served as a warning to popular constituencies that the regime had options: "The incorporation into parliament of both private sector businessmen . . . and traditional lead- ers might thus be a warning to some of the traditional components— the party, the unions, and the bureaucracy—that the regime is ready to dispense with the critics in its own ranks."[183]

In addition to movement toward molding a new ruling coalition, some argued that the regime also took political-reform steps favorable to economic and traditional elites because the state needed these social forces to generate foreign exchange for the regime and employment for an economy in transition and thus had to incorporate them politically as well.[184] Finally, international factors influenced leadership decisions. Pressure for political reforms emerged from the collapse of the Soviet

Union and the Eastern bloc and the tentative democratic transitions in that region. With its orientation toward the East and the Soviet Union both economically and politically, some demonstration effect was unavoidable.[185]

In 2000, Hafez Al-Asad died of natural causes. He had been grooming his son Basil as his successor but the latter had been killed in an automobile crash in 1994. After that, a second son, Bashar Al-Asad, an ophthalmologist living in England, was brought home and prepared for the job that he took over in 2000. Many internally and internationally hoped that Bashar Al-Asad would bring a more liberal and democratic vision to Syrian rule.

There was a Damascus Spring in Syria spurred by Bashar Al-Asad's assumption of presidential power in 2000. Initially, the president demonstrated his relative political openness by not shutting down new, more assertive political activists and groups calling for political reforms. Forums of debate, demands for greater freedom of speech and association, and a broad civil society movement emerged and spread across Syria in 2000 and 2001. In April 2001, the first large, multifaceted, and diverse opposition political movement under Ba'thist rule ever was created, called the Committees for Reviving Civil Society. These new associations that appeared in every Syrian city discussed all aspects of social, economic, and political life.[186]

Civil society associations, intellectuals, and political opposition movements during the Damascus Spring called for canceling the state of emergency in Syria, in place since 1963. They also demanded the restoration of political freedoms, freedom of the press, a new electoral law leading to a multiparty political system, the independence of the judiciary, economic justice, the end of the Ba'th as leading party of the country, gender equality, and the resolution of citizenship concerns held by part of Syria's Kurdish population.[187] The Damascus Spring movement also aimed to turn the page on the conflict between Islamists and the state that had led to the 1982 Hama bloodbath. The groups called for the cancelation of law 49 of 1980 that made membership in the Muslim Brotherhood a capital offense punishable by death.[188]

The civil society movement attempted to include the entire Syrian political spectrum in its discussions. Ba'thists were invited to answer their critics. However, when many of them started to voice that they shared many of the groups concerns and goals, the authorities cracked down by sending prominent activists to trial in state security courts. Asad himself publicly warned the movement not to put society at risk of instability. At the time, the regime claimed that a threat of civil strife and bloodshed from radical Islamists along the lines of the Algerian Civil War were the causes of the clampdown of political space, even though religious ideas and Islamist groups were not dominant in the movement.[189]

After the government crackdown, the Damascus Spring was scaled down but lurked below the surface. The 2005 discussion of political reforms at the Ba'th Party congress in June 2005 is considered by some to have been partly the result of the activities of the movement, along with the shock of the assassination of former Lebanese Prime Minister Rafiq Hariri reportedly by well-connected Syrian operatives.[190] The assassination led to international pressure and the abrupt withdrawal of Syrian troops from Lebanon, where they had been an occupying force since the Lebanese Civil War (1975–1990). That shock prompted more calls for political reforms. If single-party rule based partly on Arab nationalism could not prevent this humiliation, why not consider pluralism?

President Bashar Al-Asad promised that political reforms would be accelerated in the 2005 Ba'th Party congress in his speech on the withdrawal of troops from Lebanon.[191] Regional demonstration effects also added pressure for political reform, as there was movement toward democracy in Lebanon, and the Jordanian example of competitive parliamentary elections involving numerous political parties was next door.[192] Egypt opened up somewhat temporarily as well. The fall of Iraq at the hands of the United States and allied forces exerted pressure on the Syrian single-party regime to move toward increasing pluralism in the formal political system. Some argue that serious consideration of a multiparty political system emerged in Syria in 2005 because the government and Ba'thists believed, with reason, that the Ba'th Party was strong enough in terms of public support and social control mechanisms that it could gain some democratic legitimacy without risking much.[193] Political dissident Yassin Hajj Saleh, who was imprisoned for sixteen years and freed in 1996, asserted that discussion of multiparty politics in Syria is part of a project to emulate Egypt's controlled political pluralism: "We have an archaic authoritarian regime, which is now a burden on itself. They want to streamline it and make it more attractive. The old model has ended, it is outdated, its age has passed and they want to renew it." He called the regime's tentative political reform steps "the modernization of authoritarianism."[194]

Prior to rumblings in 2005 about the implementation of multi-party politics, Bashar Al-Asad and others around him appeared to favor implementing economic and social reforms while delaying political ones. His appointment of Issam Al-Zaim as minister of industry indicated support for a Chinese model of economic and political development. In a published interview, Al-Zaim has spoken favorably about the People's Republic of China: "[While no country can be exactly copied] China has a comparable political system, and they have twenty years of experience [of economic reform]. There is great change in China's southern and eastern regions, in the new economic zones, where the increases in the standard of living are remarkable. China has a national identity and solidarity that is many thousands of years old. It has a tradition of collective discipline and loyalty that is very important in its stability."[195] It is worth noting here, however, that the rent-seeking nature of Syria's economic reform process, to be described in the next section, does not augur well for economic efficiency and Chinese-style high economic growth rates.

In the end, the Chinese model of economic and social reforms under a single-party state held sway over Al-Asad's proclaimed intentions to accelerate political reforms and implement a multiparty political system. The 2005 Ba'th Party conference was a disappointment for reformers. Article 8 of the constitution that established the Ba'th Party's role as leader of state and society was not canceled. Ethnic and religious parties remained banned. The state of emergency and exceptional courts remained in force. The new political party law made it almost impossible for opposition forces to form a political party.[196] Only one new party, actually the revival of one that had been a rival of the Ba'th in Syria's earlier multiparty era, the Historic or Greater Syria Syrian Social National Party (SSNP), was allowed to compete in the elections outside the group of "socialist" Progressive National Front Parties led by the Ba'th. In the 2007 parliamentary elections, the SSNP won only two seats; the Independents lost two (see Tables 4.4 and 4.5).

There was a backlash against the failed promises of political reforms after the 2005 conference. The Damascus Declaration, held courageously inside Syria four months after the conference, called for radical change in the country, and for the rejection of all forms of cosmetic or partial reforms. Most opposition groups signed the declaration, including the Muslim Brotherhood.[197] The regime itself seemed somewhat embarrassed by the tepid reforms that were only partially realized after all the signals of evolution toward at least the controlled pluralism of Egypt. In an interview just after the 2005 conference, Ba'th Party member and reformer, Ayman Nour asserted that ultimately Syria would eliminate the one-party system: "Yes, they cannot keep on like this, especially after the fall of Iraq. Now everyone is saying that the one party dictatorships only exist in North Korea, Cuba, [China], and Syria."[198]

As in Egypt's case, Syria's state party, the Ba'th, has absorbed many businessmen and landlords. The Chambers of Commerce and Business has gained increasing access to decision makers and growing influence in intrabureaucratic politics.[199] The increasing marriage of power and money in Syria is also exemplified by the funding for Bashar Al-Asad's 2007 presidential referendum ceremonies that was provided virtually exclusively by private business.[200] In the 2007 parliamentary elections, independents lost a few seats to the Ba'th-led coalition (see Tables 4.4 and 4.5). No autonomous business party emerged, and the opposition SSNN, as noted, earned only two parliamentary seats. Unsurprisingly, given how economic liberalization policies have favored rent-seeking businessmen and landlords, there has not been any dynamic to create an autonomous business party during Syria's tepid political reform experiments.

No labor or peasant party has emerged, either, to contest the economic and political direction of the Ba'th. Some of this is due to state repression of opposition. In addition, the gains made by labor and peasants under the Ba'th have not been completely erased, and food subsidies, while reduced, still exist.[201] The regime claims that it is creating a "social market economy." According to regime figures, this includes redefining socialism to mean social justice and equality under the law and the right to have a job (a rhetorical right, since it has not been implemented in practice).[202] Still, there are signs of the discontentment felt by workers and peasants during their country's drift away from its populist past, even if these signs do not show up in Syria's highly controlled multiparty elections. They do show up in the divisions between leadership and base within the national trade union federation.

Workers have strenuously protested the Syrian state's new labor law of 2006. The law gives business owners much greater powers for dismissal without reason than they previously had, weakens workers rights to strike, and favors business demands on a minimum wage. The new law was opposed by workers and peasants within parliament and outside of it, to no avail.[203] The implementation of the policy signaled a decisive shift of the Ba'th toward the business community on labor matters.[204]

Similar to Egypt's case, the leadership of state corporatist organizations have sided with the state, represented by the ministry of labor, on labor matters. During protests over the new labor law, the head of the General Federation of Trade Unions, Muhammad Sha'ban 'Azuz, had to defend the federation against accusations of links to the government that trump workers' demands and interests. The defense was weak in that he affirmed, contrary to the rank-and-file protests, that the federation supports the state's plan to promote investment, which includes the new labor law that is the main source of recent worker protests.[205]

Overall, workers in Syria have been less willing to confront the authoritarian state, its party, and its party's affiliated corporatist organizations than has been the case in Egypt. Yet there was one notable demonstration by one hundred workers in the Syrian Company of Building and Construction in the city of Harsta. Organized around local demands, demonstrators planned to expand their local grievances to a broader protest against Syrian economic and political conditions. The protestors were headed to Damascus before they were stopped by the police.[206]

In terms of peasant reactions to reform, land privatization polices in Syria have recreated land concentration and revived many landlords. Agricultural policy in Syria during economic liberalization was transformed to encourage large-scale investment and large farms. Some peasants lost land. State policies also failed to support small peasants, beneficiaries of previous land reforms, which left them restricted in terms of production and marketing choices for the new market arrangements and new export-led growth strategy.[207]

The Peasant Union was not consulted during the privatization process, even in cases in which property rights over public lands to be privatized were contested by smallholders who had lived on and tilled the land for generations according to some aggrieved parties.[208] In addition, in 2006, despite peasant protests, the government established

Table 4.4. Syrian Legislative Elections, People's Assembly

PARTY	1971	1973	1977
Ba'th Arab Socialist Party	87 (50.3%)	122 (65.6%)	125 (64.1%)
Arab Socialist Union	11 (6.4%)	6 (3.2%)	10 (5.1%)
Communist Party	8 (4.6%)	8 (4.3%)	8 (4.1%)
Arab Socialist Movement	4 (2.3%)	3 (1.6%)	3 (1.5%)
Socialist Unionists' Party	4 (2.3%)	1 (0.5%)	3 (1.5%)
Unionist Democratic Party			
Arab Democratic Union Party			
Democratic Social Unionist Party			
Communist Party (Yusuf Faisal Faction)			
National Vow Movement			
Social Democratic Unionists			
Arabic Democratic Unionist Party			
Syrian Social Nationalist Party			
Independents	59 (34.1%)	46 (24.8%)	46 (23.7%)

Source: 1973–2000 Results from *Elections in Africa: A Data Handbook,* ed. Dieter Nohlen. The 2003 and 2007 results are from Wikipedia, accessed September 1, 2007. All of these parties except the Syrian Social Nationalist Party are part of the B'ath Party-led National Progressive Front.

1981	1986	1990	1994	1998	2003	2007
127 (65.1%)	130 (66.7%)	134 (53.6%)	135 (54%)	135 (54%)	135	134
9 (4.6%)	9 (4.6%)	8 (3.2%)	7 (2.8%)	7 (2.8%)		8
—	8 (4.1%)	8 (3.2%)	8 (3.2%)	8 (3.2%)		5
5 (2.6%)	5 (2.6%)	5 (2%)	4 (1.6%)	4 (1.6)	32	2
8 (4.1%)	8 (4.1%)	7 (2.8%)	7 (2.8%)	7 (2.8%)		6
		4 (1.6%)	4 (1.6%)	4 (1.6%)		
		—	2 (0.8%)	2 (0.8%)		
						4
						3
						3
						—
						1
						2
46 (23.6%)	35 (18%)	84 (33.6%)	83 (33.2%)	83 (33.2%)	83	81

Table 4.5. Syrian Presidential Elections

1971	TOTAL NUMBER	%
Registered Voters	2,031,306	-
Votes Cast	1,935,803	95.8
Invalid Votes	714	0.0
Valid Votes	1,935	100
Hafez Al-Asad	1,919,609	99.2
No-Votes	15, 480	0.8

1978	TOTAL NUMBER	%
Registered Voters	4,115,149	-
Votes Cast	3,991,695	97
Invalid Votes	11,168	0.3
Valid Votes	3,980,527	99.7
Hafez Al-Asad	3,975,729	99.9
No-Votes	4,798	0.1

1985	TOTAL NUMBER	%
Registered Voters	6,560,862	-
Votes Cast	6,222,262	99.4
Invalid Votes	1,456	0.3
Valid Votes	6,200,804	99.7
Hafez Al-Asad	6,200,428	99.9
No-Votes	376	0.1

1991	TOTAL NUMBER	%
Registered Voters	6,786,193	-
Votes Cast	6,727,992	99.1
Invalid Votes	753	0.0
Valid Votes	6,727,239	100.00
Hafez Al-Asad	6,727,843	100.00
No-Votes	396	0.0

1999	TOTAL NUMBER	%
Registered Voters	9,101,000	–
Votes Cast	8,961,147	98.5
Invalid Votes	917	0.0
Valid Votes	8,960,230	100.00
Hafez Al-Asad	8,960,011	100.00
No-Votes	219	0.0

2000	TOTAL NUMBER	%
Registered Voters	9,446,054	–
Votes Cast	8,931,623	94.6
Invalid Votes	219,313	2.5
Valid Votes	8,712,310	97.5
Bashar Al-Asad	8,689,310	99.7
No-Votes	22,439	0.3

2007	TOTAL NUMBER	%
Registered Voters	11,967,611	–
Votes Cast	11,472,157	95.9
Invalid Votes	253,059	2.21
Valid Votes	11,269,098	100.00
Bashar Al-Asad	11,199,445	97.62
No-Votes	19,653	0.17

a committee to compensate landowners whose lands had been confiscated in the 1958 land reforms.[209] In a similar reflection of a loss
of material and political resources, a new local elections law in 2005
abolished quotas for workers and peasants in Syria.

In sum, Syrian changes in political institutions broadly speaking
resemble those in Egypt. A controlled experiment in party pluralism has been implemented. The state party has been able to absorb
rent-seeking urban and rural economic elites. The ruling party and
affiliated corporatist organizations still control increasingly alienated
workers and peasants who are weakened and scrambling to lessen the
impact of being the losers of an economic reform process.

Finally, Syria's political reforms in 2005, while falling short on
delivering on promises of party pluralism, managed to increase Bashar
Al-Asad's executive power. He revamped the Ba'th's regional command,
ousting foes, limiting numbers, and installing allies. He also established
that, in part, the multiparty experiments in Syria are designed to separate the Ba'th from the government so that he and his inner circle can
implement policies without interference from the Ba'th in the details
of policymaking.[210]

Ruling Coalition and Policies

The political opening in Syria in the early 1990s was accompanied
by economic reforms that eroded post-revolutionary gains of workers and peasants. The policies, including some privatization, helped
to generate crony capitalism and began the process of molding a new
ruling coalition of landlords, capitalists, and high-level state officials
in Syria, including the military.

At the end of the 1980s, Syria changed its economic policies substantially in the direction of a market economy. Far-reaching reforms
strengthened the private sector, liberalized foreign trade, adjusted
the country's currency, and reduced subsidies. In 1991, Investment
Law 10 opened up all areas of the Syrian economy in order to attract
investment from Syrians living outside the country, Arab capital primarily in the Gulf, and other foreign investors. These investors were
given special privileges as well.[211] During this period, Syria's import-
substituting industrialization development strategy was ended in favor
of a development strategy based on export-oriented growth.[212] The
government also undertook specific measures to enhance the private

sector's ability to generate foreign exchange for itself and the state.[213] The switch toward a private enterprise-driven capitalist market economy was partly linked to the economic crisis of the decade and the fall of the Soviet Union, which removed a powerful patron and ideological justification for Syrian socialism. Some economic reforms, especially privatization, seem to be tied to reshaping a ruling coalition and self-enrichment by policymakers. Even with the changes toward a market economy. Syria has had trouble attracting foreign investors and Syrian ex-patriots, which has hamstrung the strategy to create needed jobs.

Syria has followed indirect strategies of privatization. One is based on self-liquidation and the substitution of the private economic sector for the workplaces and goods produced by the public sector. Investment Law 10 of 1991, which opened all economic sectors to private investment, was partly intended to gradually liquidate the public sector through competition from the private sector.[214] Under the term *cooperation,* the government has invited private-sector investment and management in a number of public enterprises, especially textiles, that has resulted in de facto privatization and loss of jobs.[215] Syria's privatization by stealth is characterized by an official government strategy of joint–private public ventures that favor leading businessmen and former landlords. The strategy culminates in de facto privatization and avoids direct opposition from trade unions, as noted by Raymond Hinnebusch:

> Joint private–public ventures are a substitute for open privatization. In these the state's contribution is likely to be land or factories while the private sector contributes capital and entrepreneurship. The state retains some control and gets a share of the economic rewards, but the firms are run by businessmen for profit. According to a leading private businessman, this approach, avoiding the opposition of the trade unions, is Syria's special road to privatization. Indeed the provision by the state of large tracts of state-owned land to agricultural companies may amount to a de facto privatization of this land. Joint ventures are an intermediary stage which encourages the alliances between state bourgeoisie on which further liberalization depends.[216]

The mixed private–state sector privatization strategy in Syria was introduced at the end of their first economic opening in 1977. Private entrepreneurs were sought to be partners with the state in tourism. These large joint stock companies were private in name only. They were also established by laws that legally protected them against competition, and therefore resulted in monopolies in parts of the tourism industry.[217] In the 1980s the mixed-sector formula was extended to transport and agriculture. Beneficiaries of the mixed agricultural joint stock companies were businessmen or crony capitalists whose economic success depended heavily on their relationship with members of the regime elite.[218] Limitations of the size of agricultural land, which had been implemented in the 1960s, were removed, resulting in the concentration of vast landholdings into few hands and the rebound of richer agriculturalists from prior eras.[219] The aim was to mobilize private capital for export activities that would earn needed foreign exchange.[220] The mixed sector as a whole also provides a legal and institutional way to transform the state bourgeoisie into a private-sector bourgeoisie. In addition, it indirectly enables the state to back away from previous commitments to labor and trade unions.[221]

Overall, economic policies characterized by joint ventures and other forms of indirect privatization are well on their way to fusing segments of the Syrian bourgeoisie, landlords, and the state bourgeoisie into a new ruling coalition while overcoming the Sunni–Alawite divide which has slowed that process. The state is doing this by selective licensing, or choosing winners, in a manner that fosters a rent-seeking urban and rural economic elite that benefits from state policy, though without gaining the ability to determine economic policies.[222]

This evolving Syrian bourgeoisie warrants further description. According to Volker Perthes, there are four segments of the Syrian bourgeoisie.[223] The old bourgeoisie, "enemies of the revolution," whose resources were largely nationalized in the 1960s, sprang from the land-owning bureaucratic class of the late Ottoman period that transformed themselves into merchants and early industrialists under the French. They were also, as noted, largely Sunni Muslims, religious, and conservative, and generally have been the most recalcitrant toward state economic liberalization policies authored by the Alawi-dominated state–military apparatus. New industrialists emerged in the 1970s economic opening. They were not from notable families but achieved success in the changing, more liberal economic environment. Top government and party officials, the top rank of the military, police, and security services, and the top managers of the public sector form the state bourgeoisie. Through personal ties and the benefits of their positions they have acquired significant political and economic power and personal wealth. A small new commercial class has flourished by utilizing connections with influential bureaucratic or political figures, with whom they share cuts from their economic activities, both legal and illegal. In varying degrees all four segments of the Syrian bourgeoisie have benefited from the states' indirect privatization policies.

By 2002, there were thirty-three mixed public sector–private sector companies in Syria in agriculture, industry, transport, and tourism.[224] Without hard data (like other MENA countries Syria either does not gather or share data on privatization), it is difficult to estimate the number of enterprises that have been privatized in this manner or to quantify crony capitalism in Syria in general.[225] In other terms, however, one can track crony capitalists linked to the regime.[226] The most important crony capitalists in Syria are the Makhlouf family, the Al-Asad family, and the Shallish family.[227] Dhu al-Himma Shallish, a cousin of Bashar Al-Asad, moved from the security apparatus to the business world exclusively. He owns a construction company, S.I.S International Corporation, that does work on roads, dams, and other infrastructure. He and his extended family have an estimated wealth of 23 billion dollars.[228]

Syria scholar Joshua Landis argues that the "sons of power" benefit most from privatization in Syria; leading businessmen from all backgrounds benefit as well, as the government widens its social alliances.[229] He gives as an example, the Al-Shams (Damascus) Holding company in which thirty powerful Syrian businessmen came together to invest in major projects in Syria, including some in the mixed sector. The businessmen raised hundreds of millions of dollars in capital. When they presented their proposal, a major player in the regime, Rami Makhlouf, first cousin of president Bashar Al-Asad, matched their price and insisted that he be included with a majority share of 51 percent. This left the group of businessmen with a hard choice. If they accepted, their company would receive preferential treatment from the government, but the endeavor risked descending into a mafia-style arrangement in which Makhlouf simply demanded revenue on a regular basis, unrelated to the profitability of the enterprise. In the end, feeling pinched, they accepted the arrangement.[230]

Mohamed Makhlouf, Bashar Assad's maternal uncle, has established himself in banking. Private banks are a new phenomena in Ba'thist Syria, and Makhlouf is the primary shareholder in all Syrian private banks, which numbered ten by the end of 2006. His wealth alone is estimated at 6 billion dollars. His company also manages all services in the Syrian oil sector.[231] Rami Makhlouf, mentioned earlier for his role in an enterprise undertaken by a number of Syrian businessmen, is Mohamed Makhlouf's son and owns Syriatel, a cell phone company that has a near monopoly in the industry. When a member of parliament criticized the mobile phone deal, he was imprisoned for five years under the trumped-up charge of tax evasian.[232] He also is a dominant force in the mixed tourism sector and is nearing a monopoly in air travel from Syria to other countries in the Middle East.[233] He is also close to gaining control of the textile industry in Damascus and throughout Syria.[234] As he is powerful as a middleman as well, observers argue that no foreign company can do business in Syria without his consent.[235]

Through other companies and consumption habits, Rami Makhlouf demonstrates how the marriage between power and wealth leads to a different world from the one in which ordinary Syrians live. He owns duty free outlet shops throughout Syria where only those with dollars can shop. There are mansions, villas, and expensive foreign cars in isolated enclaves near the new malls for the rich.[236]

Jamil Al-Asad and his descendants have attained assets said to amount to 17 billion dollars. Meher Asad has formed an alliance with Mohammed Hamsho. The Hamsho businesses are in trade, tourism, media, and import–export companies. He competes with Rami Makhlouf as the most dominant businessman in Syria.[237]

Overall, Syria's strategy of privatization through joint public private companies is an efficient mechanism for funneling rents to different parts of the Syrian bourgeoisie, and in a manner that is helping to overcome the Sunni–Alawite conflicts between Syrian elites. The assets are jointly owned and management in these companies has been turned over to private hands without state regulation and oversight, resulting in windfall gains.[238] Perhaps more crucially in a communally divided society dominated by a minority sect, "business partnerships have developed between the [Sunni] private sector and the children of the [Alawi] political elite, who increasingly felt themselves, as their fathers never had, to be part of the bourgeoisie and who were confident that economic liberalization would work for them.[239]

After stalling after the initial burst that followed the implementation of law 10 of 1991, privatization has picked up somewhat under Bashar Al-Asad. Privatization was slowed and even retrenched at the end of the 1990s and early 2000s but seemed to be picking up steam again in 2004.[240] The government declared its intention of offering some public industries for sale: the Hamah Iron company, the Shoes Factory, Tanning Factory, the Syrian Company for Batteries and Natural Gas in Aleppo, and the Al-Ghab Sugar Factory. The lack of transparency in prior sales will likely apply in these as well.[241] The Minister of Industry, Mohammad Safi Abu-Dan, announced that the support and development of the private sector in all economic activities was one of the most important goals of the 2005 five-year-plan.[242]

Despite the bias toward a rent-seeking bourgeoisie and landlords in Syria's privatization policies (why, for example, weren't the mixed enterprises privatized through shares for workers and peasants or shares to the general public?) there are some more nuanced aspects of the government strategy. The government insists that they are implementing a social-market economy that takes social justice for workers and peasants into account. In its rhetoric, the regime continues to validate the public sector, along with private and mixed sectors. At times the government turns to Syrian economists who are skeptical of elements of the Washington Consensus. An influential advisor on economic policy to Bashar Al-Asad, Nabil Sukkar, has argued that the public sector should be maintained until the private sector can replace it in terms of employment. He also has sensibly insisted that privatization should not occur before a regulatory framework to prevent rent seeking has been established and has been critical of a privatization process in Syria that has failed to do that.[243] On the other hand, he has more recently abandoned support for the public sector, asserting that it is already dying and that there is no sense wasting more resources to rescue it.[244] Previously, in his resistance to privatization Sukkar argued that loss-making public enterprises would only be bought to strip their outsets, and true to present realities he has also argued that privatizing profit-making state enterprises would mean a golden opportunity for corruption, rent seeking, and the mafia-style operations that accompany them in almost every instance.[245]

The indirect strategy of privatization undertaken in Syria belies the rhetoric of continued Syrian populism. It is designed partly to avoid labor confrontation. The agricultural sector is 90 percent private. The concentration of vast landholdings into few hands has returned.[246] The mixed private–public sector stands out most for its capacity to transform the state bourgeoisie's wealth into private wealth for the fully capitalist economy to come.

Legitimacy

Like our other cases, Syria has attempted, albeit more haltingly, to substitute electoral legitimacy for the eudaemonic legitimacy of the past. Jobs have been lost and subsidies cut, putting a severe strain on the previous social contract. Stealth privatization favoring a rent-seeking urban and rural elite erodes hopes for legitimacy from successful economic reforms. The loss of revolutionary populist legitimacy due to drawbacks from the social contract, coupled with a fundamental change in the ideological underpinnings of the regime in the direction of private-sector driven capitalism, has produced the oddly phrased and weak, in terms of the generation of legitimacy, "social-market economy" in Syria.

Nationalist legitimacy has taken twists and turns in recent years. The regime has at times opened itself to and sought cooperation with Western powers, but the assassination of the former Lebanese Prime Minister, Rafiq Hariri, and stands taken by Syria during the U.S. occupation of Iraq, have pushed them back toward pariah status in the West. Ironically, however, Syria's withdrawal from Lebanon, and the Lebanese reaction to it, revived Syrian nationalist sentiment to the benefit of the regime.[247]

Syria's stop at the brink of implementing a fully liberating political party law—while still taking a step toward controlled political pluralism—reflects what the regime thinks of its own legitimacy. The repression that followed the Damascus Spring bespeaks the same. Contrary to indications of a broad-based opposition movement led by secular groups, the regime couched this closing down of political space largely in terms of the threat of radical Islam with allusions to the pitched battle between the regime and the Muslim Brotherhood in the late 1970s and early 1980s, culminating in the battle at Hama in 1982. That battle between a largely rural, minority, and populist regime against the Muslim Brotherhood with a social base in the Sunni bourgeoisie and traditional Sunni religious leaders is a much greyer affair at this point, as these traditional elite groups have largely become regime allies who help their ability to govern rather than threaten it. In terms of the continuum between Neo-Islamic Totalitarianism and Liberal Islam, the Muslim Brotherhood in Syria publicly supports democracy and liberal rights, and seeks participation in competitive multiparty elections for government office. However, doubts about that commitment and the organization's association with acts of political violence and intimidation raise enough concerns to place them in the middle of the continuum.

The New Authoritarianism in Algeria

The transition from the old authoritarianism to the new in Algeria has been bloody and tumultuous.[248] During this transition, a civil war in the country between the regime and Islamists erupted and claimed more than 100,000 lives, most of them civilian. The initial transition away from authoritarian rule in Algeria had seemed headed for a rapid switch to a capitalist economy and substantive rather than façade democracy, before the tragic turn to violence. One prominent Algeria analyst argued that President Chadli Benjedid undertook the most decisive steps toward real democracy ever in the Arab world in order to fully implement what he termed "radical economic reforms."[249] After the horrific failure of simultaneous economic and political reforms, Algeria's political economy has settled into the familiar pattern of a landlord and crony capitalist spoils system cloaked in a multiparty façade, with a president seeking greater power, strife between base and union leadership, and attempts to forge electoral legitimacy. After losing power and support to an alternative regime party, the FLN has reemerged as a ruling party.

Serious problems in the old authoritarianism in Algeria began when a major drop in oil prices in 1986 triggered balance of payments, budget deficits, and spiraling inflation. In response, President Benjedid implemented austerity policies along the lines of Washington Consensus neo-liberal economic reforms without the benefit of World Bank and IMF backing and financial support to ease the pain of economic adjustment. The economic crisis, alienation from the regime, and perceptions of corruption sparked numerous demonstrations, strikes, and the most extensive and destructive riots in the country since independence, building to the wave of antigovernment riots known as Black October 1988. During this wave of discontent, a series of strikes and walk-outs by students and workers in Algiers degenerated into rioting by thousands of mostly young men. The riots spread to other cities and towns before the government declared a state of emergency and the Algerian national army fired on civilians, unofficially killing more than five hundred people.[250] This was the first time that the military, heroes of the revolution against France, had fired on its own citizens.

In the aftermath of Black October, Benjedid legalized multiple polit-ical parties and scheduled local and national elections among them. In addition to calming civil strife, the switch toward multiparty political competition and democracy was driven, as noted, by Benjedid's desire to deepen economic liberalization.[251] The victory of the Islamist FIS in the 1991–1992 two-round national assembly elections provoked a military coup. Islamists responded to the abortion of their victory with violence. In the late 1990s, the waves of violence between regime and Islamists that claimed more civilian lives than anything else, began to subside substantially. In the wake of this conflict, the regime has settled into an authoritarianism characterized by a façade of multi-party politics dominated by a state party and affiliated corporatist organizations deployed to contain disaffected workers and peasants. The current president, Abdelaziz Bouteflika, is attempting to increase his power vis-à-vis parliament, the ruling party, and the military in the shadows that has long been the dominant power in Algeria. Policies have eroded gains of workers and peasants and have empowered crony capitalists, landlords, and state officials (especially the military). This group of rent-seeking economic elites forms the new ruling coalition in contemporary Algerian politics. Legitimacy efforts are marked by a veneer of continued populism and electoral legitimacy.

Political Institutions

As the spearhead of the nationalist movement, the Algerian army has formed the power behind the scenes in Algeria since indepen-dence; it holds an informal power that is exercised when the FLN party state, affiliated corporatist organizations, and presidency veer in direc-tions deemed unfavorable. During Algeria's bold democratic experi-ment and multiparty competition led by Chadli Benjedid (1989–1991), the army was relegated to a backstage role. Accordingly, it withdrew its representatives from the FLN, which at the time was losing its role as Algeria's state party.[252] Benjedid apparently had decided that an acceleration of economic reforms required breaking from conservative regime forces within the FLN.[253] The military hastened the end of this democratic experiment in 1992. For most of the rest of the 1990s the military reigned supreme, without even the partial curb on the exercise of military power in the political sphere that the FLN party structure provided.[254] This phase laid bare the factionalism within the military. Various clans and factions within the military utilized certain political parties, including Islamist ones, and the press as proxies for internal struggles, thereby creating political chaos.[255]

By the end of the 1990s, representative and deliberative assemblies at national, regional, and local levels were reestablished.[256] Multiparty competition reemerged, and competitive presidential elections became part of the political landscape, indicating that the waves of bloodshed suffered by the country might have set the stage for substantive democratization and created some democrats along the way.[257] Tempering that possibility, however, has been the reemergence of the FLN as the state party and dominant force in parliament. The FIS remains banned, though other Islamist parties and Berber parties with some electoral support indicate the continued vitality of identity politics in Algeria today. One of the more moderate Islamist parties governs in coalition with the FLN.

The fall and rise of the FLN in Algeria partly tells the story of how difficult it is for political leaders in authoritarian settings to resist the advantages of a state party. It also indicates some of the fragilities of Algeria's particular state party. It is worth recalling that Algeria was remarkably stable for the thirteen-year period under Houari Boumédienne (1965–1978), but under Benjedid the FLN proved unable to contain elite factionalism in the face of economic crisis and a doctrinaire shift from Arab socialism to rigid economic liberalism. The ruling party and affiliated state corporatist organizations also struggled to contain the disaffection of workers and peasants facing sharp economic shifts against their interests and angry about years of widespread corruption. However, despite these difficulties the FLN state has been resurrected to dominate the multiparty electoral arena since "competitive" elections were reinstated in the late 1990s after the country's bloody conflict between the military and Islamists tapered off.

Political reforms in Algeria between 1988 and 1991 brought a temporary end to the one-party system. As noted, signaling the apparent end of a "state party," the military withdrew from the FLN during that period. Factions within the FLN formed their own political parties during that period as well. Having defanged the FLN and being committed to accelerating economic reform in the face of growing opposition within and outside the FLN state, Benjedid maneuvered to help the Islamist FIS become the replacement of the FLN as Algeria's populist party. In the words of one analyst, Benjedid "unleashed, legalized, and encouraged [the FIS] to take over the populist constituency in Algerian politics, by employment of the most hair-raising rhetoric if need be, in order to deny access to this constituency to [his] national-populist enemies within the FLN who were not necessarily opponents of sensible measures of [economic] reform."[258]

Apparently President Chadli Benjedid had decided to utilize democratization as an instrument to quickly implement doctrinaire economic liberalism in Algeria.[259] As the drama of multiparty elections unfolded and the Islamist FIS won the majority of local elections, the military initially seemed to believe that it could remain behind the scenes as the ultimate political power for a national unity government formed by the FLN and the FIS.[260] However, the resounding victory by the FIS in the first round of the 1991–1992 national assembly elections revealed the threat of the FIS to both the FLN and the military, and the military took over power directly, setting up the subsequent waves of violence.

Under President Liamine Zeroual (1994–1999), Algeria relaunched multiparty electoral politics, including new competitive presidential elections. This current stage of political reforms does not, however, include the FIS, which is still banned. In addition to banning the FIS, an upper house, the Council of the Nation, has been created to lessen the stakes of parliamentary elections to the executive branch and the military. The Council of the Nation is composed of 144 members who hold six-year terms. Of these, 96 are elected indirectly by members of regional assemblies. The president appoints the remaining 48. On the other hand, in order to coax political parties to participate in the new elections, the regime agreed to a proportional representation system, which should allow smaller parties to win seats in parliament and gain popular support overtime.

New rules ban parties based on identity or religion, though religious and ethnic parties under names that are not obviously identity-based are legal and participate in electoral contests. Abdallah Djaballah formed the Revival (al-Nahda), a constitutionally permitted Islamist party that has achieved some electoral success in Algeria since national assembly elections were resumed in 1997. The party has links to the Egyptian Muslim Brotherhood. Mahfoud Nahnah founded the Movement of the Society for Peace (MSP); when he died in 2003, he was replaced by Aboudjerra Soltani. Both of these Islamist parties were born out of opposition movements and have a social base beyond their leaders' small circles, but they have been compromised by their participation in elections that the still autocratic regime uses to enhance its legitimacy. They also publicly are committed to democracy and civil liberties, a factor that puts them in the camp of liberal Islam. The MSP is a government coalition partner and thus provides significant legitimacy to the regime's controlled multiparty political system.

The regional and ethnic Berber movement has some force in electoral politics and makes claims for broader goals of democracy, but may have limited appeal for non-Berbers and nonresidents of the Berber-dominated Kabilye region of Algeria. The most prominent are Said Sadi's Rally for Culture and Democracy (RCD) and Hocine A't Ahmed's Socialist Forces Front (FFS). A Trotskyist Workers' Party led by Louisa Hanoun has achieved some electoral success as well. The results of legislative and presidential elections are given at the end of this section.

On the whole, multiparty politics in Algeria has attained more substantive pluralism than has been the case in Egypt and certainly Syria. Still, as in those two cases, a dominant party linked to the state has once again become the most important force in civilian politics. In the course of establishing a multiparty system dominated by a state party, the regime at one point (when the FLN seemed weakened) formed a new party to represent itself, the Democratic National Rally (RND). However, in the end, the FLN reemerged in electoral dominance and the RND currently has formed an alliance with the FLN as a junior partner in parliament. To an extent, the more important political change at the end of the day in Algeria may not be pluralism but the transformation of a populist state party (FLN) to a state party (RND/FLN) tied most significantly to political, military, and economic elites.

The RND was created by the regime in 1997 and was based on the premise that the executive branch needed to control the National

Assembly and that the FLN was no longer viable for that role.[261] In the 1997 elections, vigorous vote rigging was necessary to produce the RND's large majority in the National Assembly.[262] The RND was very unpopular, partly due to the implementation of structural adjustment policies under its watch. This unpopularity set the stage for the dramatic revival of the FLN.[263] While the FLN has continued structural adjustment policies including privatization, it has been more cautious. The FLN also has its revolutionary legacy and nostalgia for the FLN under Boumédienne on its side, which makes it a more appropriate ruling-party vehicle.[264]

In the 2002 legislative elections, the FLN once again became both the dominant party in Algeria and the controlling force for the executive branch in the national assembly. For the regime the FLN and its affiliated state corporatist organizations proved to be a better resource than the RND to perform the functions that ruling parties perform in autocratic regimes.

It is worth noting that the revival of the FLN did not proceed smoothly from the perspective of the executive branch. In the 2004 presidential elections the general secretary of the FLN and prime minister under President Bouteflika, Ali Benflis, competed for the presidency. As a response, Boutelflika fired Benflis as prime minister and his supporters took steps to topple the FLN leadership, ban a national FLN conference, and form a new FLN party leadership. Bouteflika won that presidential election with nearly 85 percent of the vote while Benflis tallied less than 7 percent. Massive fraud was likely involved to produce such a landslide victory. A number of candidates resigned at the last moment as a protest against expected rigged elections.

Outside electoral politics, corporatist controls in Algeria have been strained for much of the post-independence era. Under Houari Boumédienne and in the early years of Chadli Benjedid's presidency, the FLN co-opted the leadership of the General Union of Algerian Workers (UGTA).[265] This co-opted leadership exercised considerable control of the base of Algeria's labor federations prior to 1988. However, on October 10, 1988, in the midst of Black October, the General Secretary of the UGTA issued an appeal for workers to end demonstrations and provide "firm support and total trust in the leadership of President Chadli Benjedid."[266] Despite that appeal there was an intensive wave of strikes and demonstrations against Benjedid's economic policies in

Algeria between 1988 and 1991.[267] Strikes and protests were part of the context of economic crisis in the late 1980s and early 1990s that provoked Benjedid's simultaneous economic and political reforms.

Benjedid's economic and political reforms contributed to turning the UGTA into a powerful political force that was more independent of the state. In introducing competitive multiparty elections, in essence separating the FLN from the state, he gave factions within the FLN, the military, and the bureaucracy that opposed his economic reforms little reason to support his policies and to utilize their resources for social control. Those factions of the power structure could offer support to the growing militancy of the autonomy movement within the UGTA and tacit agreement to limit repression of their activism. In order to neutralize the UGTA, Benjedid's 1989 constitution that ended single-party rule also ended the UGTA's role as the only legal national labor organization. Multiple national trade unions were permitted for the first time in Algeria's post-independence history.[268] Still, the regime continued to negotiate exclusively with the UGTA. Legalizing multiple trade unions led the FIS to found their own trade union federation. However, they were largely unsuccessful at attracting workers to this new organization, partly because the government continued to utilize the UGTA as the organization with which to negotiate wages and other issues.[269]

Strikes and demonstrations were constants in Algeria in the 1990s. There have also been leadership base chasms within the UGTA. In 1991, the UGTA staged a national strike to protest higher prices and diminished buying power. Participation rates were above 90 percent in urban areas and above 60 percent in rural areas.[270] In 1992, worker protests declined due to the rise of the FIS, the assassination of President Mohamed Boudiaf, a war hero brought to power to calm tensions after the cancelation of legislative elections, and the National Emergency declared after the military takeover of power.[271]

The UGTA president, Abelhak Benamouda, supported the 1992 military coup. The rift between the UGTA and the Islamist FIS has never been repaired, though a minority current within the UGTA sympathized with the FIS and favored dialogue rather than eradication as state policy to overcome the political crisis generated by the usurpation of the FIS's victory in the 1992 National Assembly elections.[272]

Between 1992 and 1994, resistance to privatization by the UGTA led Prime Ministers Abdesselam Belaid and Redha Malek to stall the program. However, comprehensive debt rescheduling according to an IMF agreement in 1994 made the formal and direct initiation of privatization inevitable.[273] The social costs were painfully borne by workers, as noted by Bradford Dillman: "The privatization process was marked by confusion and arbitrariness. . . . It was unclear how many companies were being privatized and who the buyers were. Moreover, a number of companies were liquidated and their remaining assets transferred (often illegally) into private hands. In 1997 an estimated 100 state companies were liquidated with a loss of 400,000 jobs."[274]

In 1995, Labor Minister Mohamed Liaichoubi called for a social pact with laborers and employers to manage a gentle transition and soften the blow of the movement to a market economy.[275] During the return to electoral politics orchestrated by President Liamine Zeroual in 1995, the leadership of the UGTA, including its General Secretary Abelhak Benamouda, supported the president. This firm support remained despite near rage at privatization policies that the government under Zeroual implemented. Although industrial unrest at the base was widespread, the UGTA did its best to limit the extent of stoppages.[276] In 1997 Abelhak Benhamouda was assassinated, apparently by Islamic guerrillas.[277]

Numerous workers' strikes occurred in 1998. More than 100,000 people participated in one day alone, March 9, 1998.[278] The widespread strikes and work stoppages were undertaken to force the government to listen to their protests against firings and privatization, according to Ahmed Slimani, a member of the trade union committee orchestrating the strikes.[279] Initially the government did not respond."[280]

Negotiations between the government and the UGTA at the end of 1998 led to the government meeting some of the workers' demands about purchasing power, wages, factory closures, firings, and an end to privatization. The head of government at the time, Ahmed Ouyahia, announced the agreement, but added that the government would not abandon previous commitments made due to the overwhelming economic conditions of the time.[281] Prior to the state's labor negotiations, workers in some sectors pressed the UGTA leadership to be aggressive in their demands and not backtrack as it commonly did in negotiations with the government, including promising to lead street protests of a national scope to protest privatization policies if they continued. This issue threatened to break the trust between the UGTA leadership and public sector workers.[282]

Strikes against privatization soared again in 2000 and 2001. The UGTA leadership in discussions with the government emphasized the improved financial health of the state and sought investments to create jobs and incomes.[283] Striking industrial workers protested plans to privatize more industries and called for worker participation in decisions concerning the future of state-run companies.[284]

In 2003 and 2004, labor unrest figured into the battle between Bouteflika and his former prime minister and general secretary of the FLN, Benflis, who challenged him for the presidency in 2004. After supporting Bouteflika in 1999, the UGTA dropped support for him in 2003 with indications that they would favor Benflis in the elections. The UGTA was displeased about the privatizations and economic reforms carried out by Bouteflika's staff.[285] On October 15, 2003 the UGTA led a general strike.[286] By early 2004, Bouteflika had ousted Benflis as prime minister and his supporters orchestrated a takeover of the FLN from Benflis's leadership. Before the 2004 elections, the UGTA leadership announced its public support for Bouteflika in the presidential race.[287]

In 2003 and 2004 independent trade unions organized a committee to defend rights, including the right to strike. They were said to fear for their existence against the centralizing forces of the FLN and UGTA. Through his attorney, the spokesman for this committee, a Mr. Osmane, said, "Today we are going backwards. They want to erase 15 years of fighting for the promotion of democracy and to rehabilitate the old system."[288]

While less chronicled, peasants have also mobilized against Algeria's privatization policies. In the district of al-Shalf, land was given back to landlords, which led to a sit-in strike in protest.[289] Similar protests occurred in Constantine.[290] There were also protests against development policies that increased rural unemployment.[291]

In sum, since the return to electoral politics in the mid-1990s, the executive branch, the military, and the new FLN state overall have been attempting, with uneven success, to once again secure dominion over the country's labor movement and peasants by co-opting the UGTA leadership, some wage concessions, and small unemployment and early retirement programs. These measures only partially offset the redundancies generated by privatization and the pain of austerity policies. A leadership-base divide in the UGTA has been prominent during this period.

Despite the evident discontent of workers and peasants in Algeria, exemplified by the conflicts within state corporatist institutions, no viable secular worker, peasant, or capitalist opposition party has emerged. The FLN, though less populist and with a different social base, has returned to dominate the National Assembly on behalf of the executive branch (see Tables 4.6–4.8). To dominate multiparty elections, the FLN exploits its exclusive access to public resources. Gerrymandering to the benefit of the FLN is widespread. New oil and gas revenues have supplied the current FLN state with greater resources to maintain a veneer of continued populism and attract the votes of workers and peasants. The FLN promises to distribute state resources, the benefits of the welfare system, however diminished, to the disadvantaged. By doing that, the FLN/RND can be the party, which brought the pain of privatization and austerity, and also be the only political party that offers hope for any state help for the many who find themselves in dire economic circumstances.

The state bureaucracy is utilized to the benefit of the FLN during electoral contests, including the Ministry of the Interior, the Municipal and Wilaya Councils, and the Ministry of Mudjahideen (Veterans).The FLN, especially in the last two parliamentary elections, has used financial incentives, threats, and sometimes has resorted to violence in town meetings in various towns and villages.[292] Ruling-party operatives are sometimes called Father Christmas for the employment, housing, and money promised and distributed around election time.[293]

When asked about the FLN and elections in the countryside, one Algerian journalist replied: "Concerning the FLN, it must be said that . . . they spend a lot of money to be elected, they hold meetings in rural areas and the administration gets involved in the selection of candidates. This means that it is the local authorities who decide elections. This is to say that there is no democracy at all."[294]

In the 2007 elections Said Sadi, head of the Rally for Culture, one of the political parties that supports rights for Algeria's native Berber community, said that electoral officials told him that they were instructed to make sure that the results favored the FLN or the National Democratic Rally: "The problem in Algeria is with the administration.

It's easy to have a good campaign and difficult to have good results. Electoral officials have told me they received calls telling them to make sure the results favor the FLN or another leading party allied with the FLN, the National Democratic Rally."[295]

During the 2002 local elections, patronage promises were vital for FLN support in elections. Then Benflis, the general secretary of the FLN, focused on large projects that the FLN planned to implement in order to give new hope to Algerian youth. Le Matin, an antigovernment daily, said Benflis had run a brilliant campaign leading up to the local elections by focusing on FLN projects that would generate jobs and help revive buying power in an economy in which voters had seen the average national per capita income slashed by half in ten years, dropping from $3,000 per annum to $1,500. Unemployment surpassed 30 percent.[296]

In addition to the return of the FLN state with its social control functions, current President Abdelaziz Bouteflika has increased presidentialism in Algeria. He has been attempting to wrest control of the government from the military, thereby uniting formal power with real power.[297] The battle is most visible in two areas: first, in presidential control over the designation of ministerial posts, including prime minister; and second, in presidential control over the military through holding or appointing the minister of defense, and achieving dominance over the military general staff created under previous administrations.

The war against Islamist terrorists that has led external powers to cooperate with and bolster the Algerian military and security forces provides the military with "ammunition" to reassert its fuller role in the Algerian political sphere. In contrast, the military's role in the bloodshed of the last fifteen years strengthens Bouteflika's political project to establish the presidency in place of the army high command as the supreme arbiter of policy debates.[298] President Bouteflika has undertaken measures to increase his own power vis-à-vis both the generals in the shadows and in the legislative branch. In addition, according to Algerian journalist Rezak Tarik, "President Bouteflika has in fact always ill concealed his contempt for the National Assembly, denying it the constitutional right to censure government action or even to express a judgment of its programme. He believes that the presidential majority alone legitimizes the work of the executive and has often repeated 'the head of government's programme is my programme.'"[299]

Table 4.6. Algerian Legislative Elections, People's National Assembly

PARTY	1991	1997	2002	2007
Front for National Liberation	15 (23.4%)	14.3%	199	136
Islamic Salvation Front, FIS	188 (47.3%)			
El-Islah, Movement for National Reform			43	3
Democratic National Rally		33.7%	47	61
Movement of the Society for Peace (MSI Hamas)	0 (5.4%)	14.8%	38	52
Workers' Party		1.9%	21	26
Algerian National Front			8	13
Harikat al-Nahda al-Islamiyya (Islamic Renaissance Movement)	0 (2.2%)	8.7%	1	5
Party of Algerian Renewal	0 (1%)	1.9%	1	4
Movement of National Understanding			1	4
Social-Democratic Front for Socialists	23	20		
Berber Rally for Culture and Democracy	0 (2.9%)	4.2%	Boycott	19
Independents	3 (4.5%)	4.4%	30	33
El-Infitah Movement				3
Movement for Youth and Democracy	0.1%	0.5%		5
Ahd 54				2
National Republican Alliance		2%		4
National Party for Solidarity and Development				2
National Movement for Nature and Development				7

PARTY	1991	1997	2002	2007
National Front of Independents for Understanding				3
Algerian Rally		0.8%		1
National Movement of Hope				2
Republican Patriotic Rally				2
Republican Progressive Party	0%	0.6%		0
National Democratic Front				1
Democratic and Social Movement				1
Socialist Workers' Party				0
Socialist Forces Front	25 (7.4%)	5%	Boycott	
Movement for Democracy in Algeria	0 (2%)		Boycott	
Social Democratic Party	0			
Algerian Movement for Justice and Democracy	0.4%	0.6%		
Union for Democracy and Freedom	0.1%	0.5%		
National Movement of Algerian Youth		0.9%		
Movement of the National Entente		0.8%		
National Constitutional Rally		0.5%		
"Work" Movement		0.5%		
Others	3.2%	3.1%		

Source: Daniel Brumberg, "Liberalization Versus Democracy: Understanding Arab Political Reform," Working Paper No. 37 (Washington D.C.: Carnegie Endowment for International Peace, 2003), 17–19; 2005 Election Results from Wikipedia, accessed September 1, 2007.

Table 4.7. Composition of Parliament after Final Correction by the Constitutional Council

PARTY	SEATS (OF 380)	100%
National Democratic Rally	156	41.0
Movement of the Society for Peace (MSI Hamas)	69	18.2
National Liberation Front	62	16.3
Nahda Movement	34	8.9
Socialist Forces Front	20	5.3
Berber Rally for Culture and Democracy	19	5.0
Workers' Party	4	1.0
Republican Progressive Party	3	0.8
Liberal Social Party	1	0.3
Union for Democracy and Freedom	1	0.3
Independents	11	2.9

Source: Dieter Nohlen, Florian Grotz, and Christof Hartmann, *Elections in Asia and the Pacific: A Data Handbook,* Vol. I: *Middle East, Central Asia, and South Asia* (Oxford: Oxford University Press, 2001), 47–49.

Ruling Coalitions and Policies

Given the catastrophic results of simultaneous economic and political liberalization in Algeria, what explains the regime's shift to doctrinaire and rapidly introduced liberal economic reforms, especially under Chadli Benjedid? The evidence suggests a mixture of reasons. In terms of privatization policies under Benjedid and beyond, there is clear evidence that the policies served to create a coalition of regime support from powerful rent seeking social forces rather than steps to improve economic efficiency and productivity.

Early reasons to begin economic reform in Algeria were pragmatic and linked to difficulties encountered by Houari Boumédienne's statist development strategy, as noted by John Entelis:

> By . . . 1979 many of the shortcomings associated with Boumediene's centralized development strategy had become evident. The strategy, based on [state-led] heavy industrialization, had created

Table 4.8. Algerian Presidential Elections

1963	TOTAL NUMBER	%
Registered Votes	6,581,340	-
Votes Cast	5,850,133	88.9
Invalid Votes	22,515	0.4
Valid Votes	5,827,618	99.6
Ahmed Ben Bella (FLN)	**5,805,103**	**99.6**
No Votes	22,515	0.4

1976	TOTAL NUMBER	%
Registered Votes	8,352,147	-
Votes Cast	8,107,485	97.1
Invalid Votes	87,663	1.1
Valid Votes	8,019,822	98.9
Houari Boumédienne (FLN)	**7,976,568**	**99.5**
No Votes	43,242	0.5

1979	TOTAL NUMBER	%
Registered Votes	7,888,875	-
Votes Cast	7,809,438	99.0
Invalid Votes	23,803	0.3
Valid Votes	7,785,635	99.7
Chadli Benjedi (FLN)	**7,736,697**	**99.4**
No Votes	48,938	0.6

1984	TOTAL NUMBER	%
Registered Votes	10,154,715	-
Votes Cast	9,776,952	96.28
Invalid Votes	56,322	0.58
Valid Votes	9,720,630	99.42
Chadli Benjedi (FLN)	**9,664,168**	**99.42**
No Votes	56,462	0.58

1988	TOTAL NUMBER	%
Registered Votes	13,060,720	–
Votes Cast	11,634,139	89.08
Invalid Votes	264,835	2.28
Valid Votes	11,369,304	97.72
Chadli Benjedi (FLN)	**10,603,067**	**93.26**
No Votes	766,237	6.74

1995	TOTAL NUMBER	%
Registered Votes	15,965,280	–
Votes Cast	11,965,280	74.9
Invalid Votes	345,748	2.9
Valid Votes	11,619,532	97.1
Liamine Zeroual	**7,088,618**	**61.0**
Mahfoud Nahnah (MIS-Hamas)	2,971,974	25.6
Sayid Sadi (RCD)	1,115,796	9.6
Noureddine Boukrouh (PRA)	443,144	3.8

2004	TOTAL NUMBER	%
Registered Votes	18,097,255	–
Votes Cast	10,508,777	58.1
Invalid Votes	329,075	3.1
Valid Votes	10,179,702	96.9
Abdelaziz Boutefika— National Rally for Democracy	**8,651,723**	**85.0**
Ali Benflis— National Liberation Front	652,951	6.4
Abdallah Djaballah— Movement for National Reform	511,526	5.0
Said Sadi— Rally for Culture and Democracy	197,111	1.9
Louiza Hanoune—Workers' Party	101,630	1.0
Ali Fawzi Rebaine—Ahd 54	63,761	0.6

Source: Presidential election data 1963–1995 from Dieter Nohlen, Florian Grotz, and Christof Hartmann, *Elections in Asia and the Pacific: A Data Handbook*, Vol. I: *Middle East, Central Asia, and South Asia* (Oxford: Oxford University Press, 2001). Wikipedia for 2004 Elections, accessed 1 September 2007.

dualistic economic structures, threatened Algiers and other coastal cities with hyerurbanization, caused intolerably high unemployment in both rural and urban areas, exacerbated income inequalities despite theoretical salary ceilings, and so neglected domestic food production that it increasingly failed to meet the country's needs. Also Algeria's substantial foreign debt, contracted mainly to pay for industry, was causing concern, particularly because it implied an unwelcome vulnerability to pressure from overseas.[300]

Under then new President Chadli Benjedid, Algeria's five-year development plan announced by the FLN in 1980 began the shift in development strategy toward a market economy driven by private enterprise. Led by Prime Minister Abdelhamid Brahimi, the early focus was on decentralization and deconcentration to foster more effective utilization of Algeria's human, natural, and industrial resources. "Brahimi thought that the bad management of the economic units [and their inability to generate profits outside of oil and natural gas exports] was caused by their size."[301] A number of state-owned enterprises, including the oil and gas company SONATRACH, were restructured and broken up into multiple state companies which were to receive better management and administration in their smaller form.[302] To improve upon the Boumédienne legacy, there was a mild shift from heavy to light industry and a focus on agriculture, the shortage of water, the housing crisis, and the absence of public infrastructure.[303] Of course, the steep drop in oil and gas revenues in the 1980s brought the need for economic efficiency in Algeria to the forefront. Overall, however, this phase of Algeria's economic reforms emphasized the downsizing of the large public sector firms that had come to dominate Algerian society and the encouragement of private industry without widespread privatization and austerity state budgets.[304]

The steps taken in the early 1980s were avowedly pragmatic, with an emphasis on common sense, realism, and practicality. The pragmatic and mild economic liberalization measures were intended as a contrast to supposedly doctrinaire Arab socialist policies of the 1970s and they received for that broad consensus within the Algerian power structure as a whole.[305] These gradual reforms, however, lacked broad social support outside the state.[306]

In the mid- to late 1980s, Algeria began to implement ambitious and radical economic liberalization measures. According to Hugh Roberts, "by the late 1980s the issue of liberal economic reform was no longer being presented by its supporters as a matter of pragmatism and common sense, but as an ideological crusade" for capitalistic economic reform.[307] Chadli Benjedid, an embattled president due to the searing economic crisis, had stopped being an impartial arbiter between regime factions favoring modest reforms to make adjustments to Boumédienne's legacy versus radical factions intent upon rapidly making the full transition to a free market economy driven by private enterprise, and a balanced state budget shorn of most food and other subsidies. Chadli Benjedid became identified with the most aggressive economic liberalizers. This put his presidency at odds with the general public and segments of the Algerian power structure.[308] To achieve the radical economic transition it pursued, Benjedid's government had to overcome public, military, and bureaucratic resistance.

In the face of resistance and in the midst of economic crisis, beginning in the late 1980s Algerian economic reforms released the Central Bank from control by the Ministry of Finance and placed severe limits on public borrowing for the first time. The Algerian dinar was devalued, some food subsidies removed, and imports of consumer goods were liberalized.[309] Plans were made to privatize state land and enterprises, outside of the oil and natural gas giant SONATRACH, which would be decentralized and would invite foreign partnerships. New laws on trade unionism were introduced to foster pluralism and end the monopoly on trade unions held by the Algerian General Workers' Union that opposed the reforms. While mirroring much of the Washington Consensus, these reforms were undertaken largely without the guidance and completely without the material support of the World Bank and IMF in the early years due to concerns about Western influence and interference in policy making after decades of fervent nationalist and anti-imperialist government discourses.[310]

Explanations for the shift to a radical program of economic reforms in Algeria are varied. Close observers focused on the political functions that doctrinaire liberal economic reforms served for the Benjedid regime.[311] Initially, the regime hoped to garner legitimacy from delivering higher living standards through pragmatic economic management, but when the oil price slump contributed to ending that possibility the regime sought a more ideological legitimacy from its crusade for doctrinaire, rapid economic liberalization. They aimed to appeal to a private sector middle-class constituency, technocrats, journalists, and academics favorably disposed ideologically toward capitalism and free enterprise. In addition, the crusade for reform attracted external support from Western powers that it hoped would compensate for the regime's lack of domestic support. The crusade for economic reform was also utilized to delegitimate opposition to the Benjedid regime from other elements in the power structure by labeling them as uncompromising hardliners and intransigents of a status quo that included FLN "Barons." The decisive shift by Chadli Benjedid toward free market economics and private enterprise also reflected the capture of the presidential agenda and government policy by a younger generation of technocrats that surrounded him.[312]

In terms of economic reasons for the adoption of privatization policies, analysts highlight the failure of state-led industrialization and the possible rise of the private sector to dominance over state capital. Private capital, in this view, combined with foreign capital to pursue open markets and full integration into the global capitalist economy.[313] Some analysts point to Chadli Benjedid's family roots as responsible for his inclination to support rigid doctrinaire economic liberalism. Benjedid had been the commander and chief of the fifth military region, Oran, during the War of Independence, and that region had an especially active business sector that had made a strong impression on the future president.[314] Louis Martinez has argued that the Algerian state's decision to privatize the economy was partly meant to reward certain patronage networks within the state sector that had been destroyed by Islamist guerrillas during the bloody civil conflict of the 1990s.[315]

Opposing voices in the Algerian parliament insisted that privatization was merely a process to clean illegal money accumulated through corruption by government officials and others in the previous decades.[316] The leader of the opposition party Al-'Ahd, Ali Fawzi Ruba'in, asserted that Algeria is controlled by an economic lobby that failed in running a socialist system and are now accumulating wealth through corrupt means that they conceal in Swiss Bank accounts. He declared that this exploitation of the country's resources came at the expense of the lower social classes and poorer regions.[317] Communist labor party leader Louisa Hanoun denounced corruption in announcing that state banks possessed $33 billion in revenue from the selling of state-owned enterprises, while the Algerian people suffered from unemployment and poverty.[318]

Undeniably, privatization in Algeria has benefited groups linked to the ruling class, especially to powerful military officers and clans, and has created a crony capitalist and landlord spoils system for economic elites as well.[319] Until 1998, Algeria's formal privatization program was relatively small, but similar to the clandestine privatization strategy employed in Syria, de facto privatization in the 1980s and 1990s was widespread as the government dismantled socialist farms, abandoned fruit and vegetable trading, sold off public real estate, pulled out of retailing, liberalized importing, "and in a corrupt frenzy in 1996–1997, the government sold off or liquidated most of its 1,000 local public enterprises."[320]

Thomas Hasel described a complete reorientation under Benjedid's regime toward a private-sector-driven economy.[321] However, he claimed that Benjedid's reforms became an instrument for self-enrichment of the people in power. His study indicates that it was mostly high officials who profited from privatization laws. Obtaining state assets did not depend on merit; what mattered were good connections. The majority of the Algerian population suffered during the economic reform process,[322] and their increasing impoverishment stood in sharp contrast with the accumulating wealth of the upper class.[323]

Djillali Hadjadj, an Algerian journalist who has evolved into one of the most vehement fighters of Algerian corruption, specifies that the sectors most permeated by corruption are the police, customs, justice, and the ministries of agriculture, industry and tourism.[324] While some, such as Hasel and Hichem Aboud, mention the involvement in corruption scandals by relatives of President Benjedid,[325] Hadjadj points an accusing finger not at Algeria's successive presidents but rather at the circles of the ministers. In his book *Corruption et démocratie en Algérie*, Hadjadj reports on numerous corruption scandals at the time of the privatization of state-owned enterprises. Typically, contracts would be made between a state-owned enterprise and a foreign company without the offer having been put out on the markets, that is, excluding the market competition necessary to efficiently allocate resources. In most cases, personal ties with Algerian high officials and large sums of money transferred to them were needed to conclude the transactions. Among others, Hadjadj asserts that deals of this type have occurred between Air Algérie and Boeing; between the Caisse Nationale d'Epargne et de Prévoyance (CNEP) and the American construction company Chadwick; and between the national railway company SNTF and Siemens Austria.[326] Apart from that, Hadjadj highlights the sectors of health care and agriculture as particularly infested with corruption.[327] Ahmed Rouadjia provides a detailed explanation about the workings of the corrupt customs system.[328]

One of the most infamous scandals in Algeria's business world was the Khalifa affair in 2007.[329] This case involved the fall of the Khalifa commercial and financial group, which for several years had been expanding at a surprising pace until issues were raised by media investigations. "Significant resource deficits" were reported, "disguised by false declarations."[330] The Khalifa Group had owned companies in the service sector, aviation, construction, and others, and the affair cost the Algerian state 100 billion dinars.

Newspaper articles document the corruption present in the Algerian construction sector, the most gruesome evidence of which was demonstrated by the earthquake of 2003.[331] The quake hit the northeast part of the country and caused numerous buildings to collapse, leading to more than four thousand deaths and injuries. The disaster caused outbursts of anger among the Algerian people, since the collapse of the buildings was generally attributed to bad construction practices. Construction regulations had been widely neglected, and deals of self-enrichment between contractors and suppliers systematically lead to the purchase and usage of inferior materials.

In the real estate sector, Rouadjia also documents the unequal distribution of dwellings in Algeria. The average Algerian would frequently be placed on a list for social housing. An endless wait would often ensue while a small layer of top officials, called by Rouadjia "la mafia politico-financière," were granted luxurious palaces.[332] Jean-Claude Brulé confirmed in his article on the privatization of real estate in Algeria that legal practices in this sector have been the exception, that Algeria "has remained a kind of no man's land with regard to real estate," and that this sector constitutes a source of major insecurity and anxiety for the underprivileged majority of the country's population.[333]

Numerous efforts have been made by Algerian journalists and dissidents, as well as by scholars, to bring corruption within the Algerian political economy to light. While a number of intellectuals and corruption-fighting officials have been exiled or physically eliminated, the materials written on this subject are still numerous and detailed enough to provide concrete insights into the identity of the fortune-making elites. As part of the army, which since the independence of the country has played a very dominant role in ruling Algeria, a group of generals who led the fight for independence drained the country's resources and became a source of inequality. The literature also mentions a power struggle between several clans, among whom the Oujda clan and later on the Annaba clan stand out. Aboud makes a hierarchical classification of Algeria's privileged groups in three layers. The top one would be constituted by "le club des onze," defined as "le clan mafieux qui governe l'Algérie" (The Club of Eleven defined as the mafia clan that governs Algeria). Under them would be "les sous-traitants" (entrepreneurs who operate as sub-contractors for the club of eleven), who themselves would be surrounded by "le troisième cercle" (third circle).[334] Aboud discusses the most prominent individuals in each of these layers by name. As the five core players of the top layer he identifies Khaled Nezzar, Larbi Belkheir, Benabbes Gheziel, Mohammed Mediene (called "Tewfik"), and Abdelmalek Guenaïzia.

In line with other authors, Hasel made it clear that the Algerian president was not the axis of this system. Benjedid has accused several officials of corruption. Under him, as under current president Bouteflika, anticorruption committees and regulations were established and numerous scandals made public.[335] The recommendations of the committees, however, were generally not executed. The successive presidents appear in the anticorruption struggle as seemingly well-intentioned but powerless agents. In the case of Bouteflika, his criticisms of corruption appear in part to be an effort to keep the military off balance and limit the ultimate control that they have over him.

Overall, a pro-liberalization rent-seeking coalition of government and private-sector elites has been formed in Algeria where a liberalized economy operates through circulating rent between the military, a deficient public sector, and a largely commercial private sector.[336] Privatization also appears to be fostering deindustrialization in Algeria as the private sector is not taking up the slack for the decrease in production of state enterprises in hydrocarbons, textiles, and food processing.[337] According to Dillman, instead of bolstering productivity and entrepreneurship, the private sector responded to incentives arising from state rent distribution, clientelism, ungovernability, and incompetence.[338]

With regard to privatization of land, during Algeria's gradual and accelerated economic reform periods, erstwhile egalitarian land-reform measures were reversed, frequently to the benefit of former landlords. As discussed in chapter 3, Boumédienne's agrarian reforms of 1971 nationalized state and some private large landholdings and redistributed them to farmers who lacked land.[339] The only condition behind land reform was that peasants had to join government-organized cooperatives, which would provide them with state loans, seed, fertilizers, and agricultural equipment. By 1974, this agrarian revolution had given 10 hectares of private land to each of 60,000 peasants and had organized them into 6,000 agricultural cooperatives.[340] Boumédienne then inaugurated a new program to construct 1,700 socialist villages that would house 140,000 farmers.

Between 1980 and 1984, Chadli Benjedid began a process of transferring state farms to private hands. In 1987 the government broke up 3,400 state or socialist farms (about 700 hectares each) and transferred them into privately owned farms averaging 80 hectares each.[341] Benjedid's land reform of 1990 returned land to owners who twenty years earlier had seen their land nationalized during Boumédienne's agrarian revolution. This law generated many conflicts among the "owners" who had been working on the land since receiving it in the agrarian revolution of 1971.[342] Peasants who enjoyed usufruct rights to public agricultural land sought private property rights, but generally speaking their requests were denied and in numerous cases the land was given back to pre-revolution owners. The state claimed that the 1990 reforms and similar steps taken later in the decade would enhance production, and no reasonable alternative existed.[343] The *autogestion* movement (the populist self-management movement initiated under Algeria's first post-independence war president, Ahmed Ben Balla) had fallen into the hands of agricultural engineers with no field experience and productivity had dropped.

During the course of the worst years of the civil conflict between the state and Islamists, state commitment to economic reform waxed and waned. During the worst years of the bloody waves of conflict,

1993–1996, government after government went back on reforms, but did not disavow the discourse toward a transition to capitalism and a free market. The regime gradually entered into agreements with the IMF, the World Bank, and the European Union. IMF agreements required structural adjustment, including privatization, as a condition.[344] The structural-adjustment measures have carried a high social cost and the burden has been heaviest on the weakest. In 1997, the head of the privatization council, Dr. Abd al-Rahman Mabtul, estimated that the number of unemployed in Algeria could reach three million people as a result of privatization and the unemployment rate could climb to 28 percent.[345] The 1990s saw a 50 percent increase in unemployment, nearly one-third of the labor force. This figure was double the figure for the depression era in the United States in the 1930s.[346]

The unemployment grants and early retirement compensation designed to aid workers hurt by privatization and a general economic crisis proved to be inadequate in terms of addressing the difficulties facing workers and peasants. Describing the social costs of structural adjustment, Azzedine Layachi noted as follows:

> Structural adjustment entailed a set of stringent measures, which included a devaluation of the Algerian dinar by more than 40%, the curtailment of remaining subsidies on basic consumption items such as milk, bread, and cooking oil (prices increased by 15% to 200%). . . . Close to 500,000 workers were laid off as a result of the restructuring or shutting down of public enterprises between 1994 and early 1998 alone; 815 public enterprises were dissolved; and Public Economic Enterprises laid off 60% of their workers . . . The number of people living below the poverty line [between 1991 and 2001] substantially increased, reaching a high of 12 million out of a population of 30 million people. Given the fact that most people tend to spend today 70% of their income on food, this situation has hurt people with fixed-income the most. However, the already small middle class has not been spared; it has largely collapsed, as many of its members have been pulled towards lower living standards.[347]

Legitimacy

Algeria's transition to the new authoritarianism has been tumultuous and bloody. The bloodshed hit the civilian population, ostensibly outside of the conflict between the Islamists and the government, hard. Some believe that the regime now relies on its ability to protect life from political violence as the main source of regime legitimacy.[348] The revolutionary and populist legitimacy of the FLN state has been deeply compromised by the country's economic reforms. Still, it claims to represent nationalism and poses as the guardians of the benefits of the revolution.

Until the recent upturn in oil and gas revenues, eudaemonic legitimacy from the provision of material needs was largely beyond the reach of the state. Electoral legitimacy cannot be deep without the participation of the FIS and the public sense that the electoral game is indeed a game orchestrated by *le pouvoir* (the power, especially the military behind the FLN state). The FIS has also been compromised by long years of bloodshed and waves of violence, which may provide an opening for the moderate Islamist parties constitutionally permitted to compete in Algerian elections. Potentially, this can become a route to bolster the legitimacy of both elections and the National Assembly. That scenario would be hampered, however, if the demilitarizing of the regime and progress in electoral legitimacy were not accompanied by a redress in the balance of power between the executive and legislative branches of government.

Finally, discussions of legitimacy in Algeria have to include the FIS. Rhetorically accepting democracy, the FIS adopted a strategy to gain power by accepting the rules of multiparty competition. The party won power, but never got the chance to implement its policies and program in Algeria. Is the banned FIS an organization within the tradition of Liberal Islam: true believers in democracy, advocating equal rights for women and non-Muslims in Islamic countries, supporting freedom of thought, and standing hostile to obscurantist impulses? Not fully probably, but much more so than the GIA and al-Qaeda in the Islamic Maghreb, which places the FIS in the middle of the continuum between Neo-Islamic totalitarianism and Liberal Islam.

The New Authoritarianism in Tunisia

In the 1980s Tunisia's accelerated transition to the new authoritarianism began with the rise to power of Tunisia's second post-independence president, General Zine el-Abidine Ben Ali. Citing the mental

infirmity of President Habib Bourguiba, Ben Ali—in succession director of national security, minister of the interior, and prime minister
under Bourguiba—executed a bloodless coup in 1987 in the name of
democratic reform, respect for human rights, and national reconciliation. The end of Bourguiba's rule had been marked by an escalating
conflict against Islamists that threatened public order and by a number
of rash and unpredictable changes in government ministers by the
octogenarian president.

Ben Ali's political opening seemed impressive at first. He pledged
to separate the historic Destour Party from the state and to make the
substantive transition to pluralism and competitive elections in Tunisia.
During Ben Ali's first year in power, for the first time in modern
Tunisian history an entire year passed without the banning of books,
the suppression of newspapers, or cases of capital punishment.[349] The
new ruler ended the presidency-for-life established by Bourguiba, and
mandated a three-term limit. Many jailed Islamists, whose persecution
by Bourguiba and their own coup plotting was hurtling the country
toward civil war, were released. Ben Ali began to negotiate with the
leadership of the national trade union federation (UGTT) that had spearheaded the national strike in 1978 that had shaken the regime to its
foundation. Under the guidance of Ben Ali, a national pact signed by
all of the country's social forces in 1988, just prior to the introduction of
National Assembly and presidential elections, seemed to bring together
soft- and hard-liners and inspired optimism about Tunisia's democratic
reforms.[350] The name of the historic ruling party was changed to the
Democratic Constitutional Rally (RCD).

After the promising start, Ben Ali's political reforms settled into a
façade of multiparty politics, overshadowed by RCD hegemony and a
shift in its social base to becoming largely a party of rural notables and
well-connected capitalists. A banned Islamist party, al-Nahda, became
the only opposition party with strong popular support.

The RCD co-opted the UGTT leadership in order to control workers and peasants facing a turn against them in state policy. The growing opposition political parties that represented the interests of workers and peasants faced an impossible political terrain that included
severely restricted public liberties that damaged their ability to organize, the rapid muzzling of the press, gross financial disadvantages,
and the determination of the RCD state to use all of the resources at its

disposal to maintain hegemonic control. Presidential powers were also increased and the ban on a presidency for life was compromised.

The regime began to count on coerced charity, limited electoral legitimacy, spurts of economic growth, and the radical shutdown of political space and civil liberties to maintain power and control. The civil war in neighboring Algeria also gave resonance to Ben Ali's claim of providing Tunisians with peace and prosperity. On the economic front, the privatization of state land and state-owned enterprises during the country's political opening provided the regime with resources to build a new ruling coalition of rent-seeking urban and rural economic elites, as well as resources to enrich the president's extended family and others close to the regime.

Political Institutions

In Tunisia, as in our other cases, the ruling elite has been able to manipulate regime resources to ensure its repeated electoral domination in the country's multiparty elections. The RCD state has used all of its material and organizational advantages to maintain hegemonic control of Tunisia's transformed political economy. With his implementation of multiparty elections, what President Ben Ali appeared to have in mind was a form of consensual authoritarianism in which opposition political parties supported the regime, accepted that they would never be competitive electorally against the RCD, and backed a Bourguiba-style presidency-for-life. In exchange, they received limited policy input.

Beyond creating a façade of multiparty politics and increasing executive powers, subjugating the UGTT has been critical to consolidating both the economic and political dimensions of the new authoritarianism in Tunisia. Economically, the objectives of neo-liberal economic policies meant certain losses to workers and peasants. The UGTT leadership was co-opted by the regime to contain dissent from the base provoked by new regime policies. The regime also succeeded at preventing dissenting members within the UGTT from establishing a labor-based political party, an option discussed within the union.[351]

Despite the UGTT's bureaucratic ties to the state apparatus, this mass organization did not hesitate in the 1970s and 1980s to defend the important gains made by workers and peasants during the country's populist authoritarian period.[352] The UGTT's independent streak is tied to its history: it became the first independent trade union federation in Africa when it was founded by detaching itself from French trade union organizations during the colonial era. It then quickly became a darling of the International Confederation of Free Trade Unions (ICFTU). As discussed in chapter 3, the UGTT was an important part of the nationalist movement, contributing to establishing a post-independence regime of national unity led by the single party and affiliated state corporatist organizations as an alternative to class conflict and political pluralism. The statist development strategy that was modified in 1969 also earned UGTT support for the regime.[353]

The gradual liberalization of the economy beginning in 1970 led to periodic tripartite collective negotiations and agreements among the UGTT, the National Business Association, and the state. The position taken by the state during these negotiations and the signed agreements did not always favor the interests of the UGTT base, and as a consequence, strikes that had barely existed in post-independence Tunisia until that time increased in number and intensity during the 1970s.[354] In addition, the UGTT began to question the role of a "unique" party and began to demand pluralism, democratic reforms, and human rights along with advocating for the material needs of its members. The absence of freedom of expression and freedom of assembly in Tunisia at that time also made the UGTT the haven for opposition of all kinds.[355]

The UGTT led the destabilizing national strike of 1978. However, it formed an alliance again with the government for the 1981 aborted elections, though this step splintered the organization and led to the formation of a rival trade union federation.[356] The UGTT was heavily involved in the bread riots of 1984, and by 1985 was involved in open conflict with the government. The UGTT leadership claimed that workers' standard of living fell 20 percent between 1983 and 1985.[357] At that time, fearing the growing strength of the UGTT and increasing dissatisfaction with its domestic policies, the regime took steps to neutralize the UGTT. The head of the UGTT, Habib Achour, and more than one hundred other UGTT unionists were arrested, accused of mishandling union funds and lack of patriotism, and jailed. Security forces and state party members took control over provincial offices of the UGTT and its headquarters in Tunis. The control over the UGTT was handed over to state party loyalists.[358]

In the 1970s and 1980s the UGTT envisaged creating its own

political party, the Workers' Party, but regime pressure and opposition from UGTT leaders close to the regime led to the abandonment of that idea.[359] For the legislative elections planned for 1986, the UGTT head Habib Achour and opposition political parties called for a boycott.[360] While not a part of mass mobilization against the regime led by the UGTT in the 1970s and early 1980s, by the mid-1980s the main Islamist organization in Tunisia, the Islamic Tendency Movement (MTI), also began to attract popular support, and its growing strength added to the troubling context that characterized the end of Bourguiba's rule. At the end of his rule, Bourguiba faced a labor movement that was confrontationally demanding social equity and democratization. A growing opposition Islamist movement and unofficial new parties were also beginning to sprout. Observers described the once populist authoritarian regime as "declining into atrophy, centralization, increasing authoritarianism and corruption. The exclusion of progressive, leftist, and democratic tendencies left it weakened in an increasingly heterogeneous and conflict-ridden political environment."[361]

When Ben Ali took power in 1987 (ushering in the "new era," as his regime prefers to call it), he probably had to include a commitment to pluralism and democracy in order to restore civil order and surmount the lack of legitimacy, domestic unrest, and economic deterioration that characterized the end of Bourguiba's rule. However, he apparently did so with the intent to neutralize the mobilization potential of both the UGTT and the MTI. Ben Ali's rehabilitation of the UGTT came at a high cost to UGTT independence. Any strikes at any level now had to be officially approved by the general secretary of the UGTT. No strikes were allowed at places of work. The regime had to be notified ten days in advance of the intention to strike. A closer collaboration between state party authorities and the UGTT leadership was instituted.[362] The UGTT leadership for all intents and purposes had to be chosen by the regime. Dissident unionists were harassed by the security police.[363]

The co-opted leadership of the UGTT signed on to Ben Ali's economic policies, thereby making a break from its former militancy and eschewing a strategy of opposition that had the potential of resulting in a political party capable of representing the interests of labor and peasants in Ben Ali's multiparty political experiment. By 1992, the UGTT general secretary offered full support for the regime's economic policies:

> Our union . . . has chosen in principle to adapt to international trans-
> formations by adopting new methods of work and intervention . . .
> in order to expand social justice and prosperity. Today, the union
> is trying to adapt to changes in the international economic sys-
> tem, the structural adjustment program, the new world order and
> the market economy. The task of meeting these challenges is the
> union's preoccupation.[364]

The UGTT leadership has also backed Ben Ali's political project. The UGTT leadership has, in every election, issued an appeal to workers to vote for Ben Ali as president of the republic. They supported his back-stepping on presidential term and age limits. The official position of the UGTT in legislative elections has been neutrality toward all of the legal political parties that adequately serve the function of political pluralism in the new era.[365] In reality, of course, by containing the dissent of its members, it joins with the RCD in maintaining hegemony in the political arena.

To neutralize the other possibility of popular mobilization, the Islamic Tendency Movement (MTI), Ben Ali banned political parties based on religion. In response, the MTI changed its name to Al-Nahda (the renaissance) and pledged a commitment to pluralism, democracy, and human rights, but still was not allowed to participate in elections as a political party. In the 1989 elections Al-Nahda ran as independents and won up to 20 percent of the vote, the most of any opposition organization. This steeled the resolve of the regime to keep them out of the electoral arena. In the early 1990s, the regime launched major repressive measures against Al-Nahda intended to eradicate them as a political force. By that time, Al-Nahda had begun to plan and implement violent actions of their own. The leader of the movement, Rached Ghanouchi, was chased into exile in London.

With the UGTT defanged as a political force and Al-Nahda banned, multiparty elections in Tunisia under Ben Ali have consisted of contests between the hegemonic RCD and seven legal political parties, none of which has a discernible base of support. Indeed, after the embarrassment of winning every seat in the 1989 legislative elections, the regime changed electoral rules to guarantee 20 percent of seats for opposition political parties. These parties never win more than the allotted 20 percent, and the RCD wins consistently more than 95 percent of the vote according to government tallies. Apparently perturbed about even

Table 4.9. Tunisian Legislative Elections: Number of Seats Won in Chamber of Deputies

PARTY	1989	1994	1999	2004
Democratic Constitutional Rally, RCD (formerly PSD, Parti Socialiste Destourien, renamed 1988)	154	135	148	152
Movement of Socialist Democrats, MSD		10	13	14
Unionist Democratic Union, UDU		3	7	7
Party of Popular Unity, PUP		2	7	11
Movement for Renewal, MR (communist)		4	5	3
Social-Liberal Party, PSL (liberal)			2	2
Movement for Popular Unity (MUP)				
Tunisian Communist Party				
Leftist Coalition				
Social Party Progress				
Socialist Progressivist Rally				
IRSP				
MDU				
PPS				
Independents				

Source: 1989–1999 results from Dieter Nohlen, Florian Grotz, and Christof Hartmann, *Elections in Asia and the Pacific: A Data Handbook,* Vol. I: *Middle East, Central Asia, and South Asia* (Oxford: Oxford University Press, 2001), 47–49. Results for 2004 from Mena Election Guide, accessed 1 September 2007.

this amount of opposition in the national assembly, the government created an upper house in 2002, partly appointed by the president. In presidential contests the opposition has been known to call for voters to vote for Ben Ali. He wins these contests with nearly 100 percent of the vote (see Tables 4.9–4.10).

To the degree that these vote counts have anything to do with citizen preferences, it is notable that capital has good reason to support

Table 4.10.Tunisian Presidential Elections

1989	TOTAL NUMBER	%
Registered Votes	2,762,109	-
Votes Cast	2,102,351	76.1
Invalid Votes	15,348	0.7
Valid Votes	2,087,028	99.3
Zine El-Abdine Ben Ali (RDC)	2,087,028	100

1994	TOTAL NUMBER	%
Registered Votes	3,150,612	-
Votes Cast	2,989,880	94.9
Invalid Votes	2,505	0.1
Valid Votes	2,987,375	99.9
Zine El-Abdine Ben Ali (RDC)	2,987,375	100

1999	TOTAL NUMBER	%
Registered Voters	218,400	
Votes Cast	195,906	89.70%
Valid Votes	194,680	99.37%
Invadlid Votes	1,226	0.63%
Zine El-Adidine Ben Ali, Constitutional Democratic Rally	190,814	98.01%
Aberrahmane Tlili, Unionist Democratic Union	1,942	0.99%
Mohammed Belhai Amor, Popular Unity Party	1,924	0.98%

2004	TOTAL NUMBER	%
Total (turnout %)	4,449,558	91.5
Invalid Votes	14, 779	
Total Valid Votes	4,464,337	
Zine El Adidine Ben Ali—Democratic Constitution Rally	4,202,294	94.5
Mohamed Bouchiha—Party of People's Unity	167,986	3.8
Mohamed Ali Hafouani—Renewal Movemnet Ettajdid	42,213	1.0
Mohamed Mouni Béji—Social Liberal Party	35,067	0.8

Sources: 1989, 1994 results provided by Dieter Nohlen, Florian Grotz, and Christof Hartmann, *Elections in Asia and the Pacific: A Data Handbook,* Vol. I: *Middle East, Central Asia, and South Asia* (Oxford: Oxford University Press, 2001), 911–925. 1999 results accessed from IFES Election Guide Profile on Tunisia, September 15, 2007. 2004 results from MENA Election Guide, accessed 1 September 2007.

the RCD state that anticipates and provides for its needs,[366] and worker and peasant opposition has been contained in other ways. While it exists on occasion, for the reasons discussed above and effective government repression, there have been few strikes in Tunisia to protest recent policies that have eroded the social gains of workers. In the Tunisian countryside, peasants have to an extent withdrawn from formal political participation in the farmers' union and elections, and have retreated into clientelism and neo-traditional social organization as land policies have turned against them. Islamic welfare mechanisms have encouraged the wealthy to redistribute some wealth on important days in the Islamic calendar. Favoring large landowners in policy, RCD operatives at the local level pressure rural elites to participate in these traditions.[367]

Ruling Coalition and Policies

The evidence suggests that economic stagnation and leadership preferences contributed to Ben Ali's decision to implement the full array of Washington Consensus neo-liberal economic reforms, including privatization. The manner of privatization, largely to the benefit of a rent-seeking urban and rural elite including prominent members of Ben Ali's family, suggests a desire by leaders of the regime to transform its social base and foster personal enrichment.

The decade between 1977 and 1987 was a difficult one economically for Tunisia. The state had been implementing a gradual policy of economic liberalization since 1970, but by 1977 it had started to falter. The sound economic growth of the first half of the 1970s appeared by the end of the decade to be overly dependent on Tunisia's small oil revenues. The country experienced a rise in balance of payments and state budget deficits. It began to borrow heavily abroad and showed no productive base capable of absorbing excess labor and of exporting a diversified and competitive range of goods.[368] Tunisia's Sixth Development Plan (1982–1986) was an austerity plan designed to make economic adjustments to counter the deteriorating economic situation. Severe controls were maintained on external debt and balance of payments; public investments and consumption were restricted through wage freezes and import restrictions.[369] Despite those measures, growth rates remained poor, and in 1986 Tunisia experienced its first year of negative growth since independence.[370]

The economic problems provoked social unrest led by the national trade union federation, UGTT. At the start of economic liberalization in 1970, the UGTT entered into collective agreements with the Tunisian government and the national business association in order to work together on national development goals and to fairly share the benefits of economic growth.[371] However, despite the UGTT's official support of government policy in the 1970s, dissension grew as economic conditions worsened, real wages were reduced, and the cost of living increased. Finally, in 1978, the UGTT leadership backed a national strike that shook the regime to its foundation.

After recovering from the 1978 national strike, in 1984 the Tunisian government introduced measures to reduce food subsidies. Bread prices suddenly doubled. Violent demonstrations, "bread riots," ensued across the country. The state's response was extremely violent. State security forces fired on crowds in towns across the country, including the capital Tunis. President Bourguiba declared a state of emergency.[372]

Economic stagnation and social unrest lead to the implementation of a World Bank- and IMF-backed Structural Adjustment Program beginning in 1986. Tunisia's privatization policy was launched in 1987 under new president, Ben Ali.[373] He appeared to enter the presidency convinced of the wisdom of privatization. As soon as he took office he surrounded himself with technocrats that backed the policy.[374] He also took advantage of his honeymoon period and international support to begin the full transition to an economy driven by the private sector.[375]

By 2007, Tunisia had an economy dominated by the private sector, The country was regarded as a star pupil of the World Bank and IMF, heralded as an exemplary case for achieving successful economic reforms in the Arab world.[376] However, the Tunisian "economic miracle" deserves scrutiny. On the positive side, the government's economic reform policies reduced inflation from 9 percent to 5 percent between 1986 and 1986, and the budget deficit was reduced from 5 percent to 3 percent. But the numbers are less clearly positive in terms of growth rates. Economic growth during the crisis period just before Ben Ali took power (1982–1986) was 4 percent. Between 1987–1991, it rose to 4.2 percent, then dropped to 3.5 percent between 1992 and 1996.[377]

The social costs of structural adjustment in Tunisia are partially hidden by the government. After twenty years of structural adjustment in Tunisia, it is still difficult to ascertain the social consequences of state policy. Official statistics on these consequences are nonexistent or not credible.[378] For example, official statistics claim that salaries increased 11–16 percent between 1991 and 1996, yet independent analysts have asserted that "there is no doubt that the standard of living for lower socioeconomic groups decreased during that period . . . and the numbers don't add up."[379] Virtually no official data exists for the impact of cutting social outlays on the standard of living for the poor and lower classes.[380] Furthermore, the government restricts independent research about the subject. Researchers are required to gain government permission for studies and surveys well in advance. Their projects can be outright rejected, and in addition they risk receiving a visit at home by the security police. The result is that it is very difficult and unsafe to contest official statistics in sensitive areas.[381]

The state has progressively abandoned its social contract, replacing it with a patina of continued populism under the patronage of the RCD and President Ben Ali. These include the solidarity program, 2626, a form of coerced charity. This fund, also called Ben Ali's "black cash box," constitutes a form of private tax levying in that it obliges private entrepreneurs, contractors, and public officials to pay a monthly contribution based on their income. This supplemental tax is, according to the president, invested in the fight against poverty. Refusal to pay leads to dismissal from public service or other sanctions, but information about the expenses of the 2626 fund is not made public and the actual revenues of the fund are thought to be much higher than the official estimate of 10 million euros annually. According to Beatrice Hibou, lists of recipients, details of the management of the fund, and distribution plans of the revenues are all unavailable.[382] In addition to the 2626 program, free meals are distributed to the needy in Tunisia during Ramadan. However, these are largely symbolic political measures that do not begin to replace the losses in social policy.[383]

Privatization policy in Tunisia has favored a rent-seeking urban and rural economic elite beginning with the kin of the president.[384] The family of the president's wife (Leila) is a main party in privatization deals, in addition to some other well-placed families.[385] Those who have successfully lobbied to gain access to state assets fall into three camps. First, there are the sons-in-law of the president, the best-known of whom is Slim Chiboub, who married Ben Ali's oldest daughter. He is followed by Marouane Mabrouk, husband of Cyrine Ben Ali, the president's daughter from his first marriage. Cyrine owns Tunisia's only Internet service provider (which explains why oppositional and dissident Web sites are frequently blocked in the country). Marouane Mabrouk has acquired a concession for the sale of Fiat and Mercedes cars. Chiboub, or "Si Slim" as he is called, has for nineteen years been the president of l'Espérance Sportive de Tunis, the capital's soccer team. He is also active in real estate, insurance, and publicity. In the past several years, Chiboub appears to have been marginalized by the president, in favor of the clan alliance Trabelsi-Djilani.[386]

The Trabelsi clan consists of the brothers and sisters of the president's wife. According to Bernhard Schmid, before Leila's marriage to the president, the Trabelsi's lacked assets. Today, however, they own Radio Mosaïque (the only private radio station in the country), Carthago Airlines (Tunisia's most important airline and hotel company), and important stakes in the sectors of wholesale, services, and agribusiness.[387] The family is said to enjoy free telephone services,[388] and it is believed that as soon as an enterprise runs well in Tunisia, one of the Trabelsi's will demand a share of 20–30 percent.[389] The Trabelsi clan has allied itself through intermarriage with Hedi Djilani, head of the Union Tunisienne de l'Artisanat et du Commerce (UTICA), who is referred to as "le patron des patrons tunisiens."[390] The strong rivalry between the Chiboub clan and the Trabelsi-Djilani group was demonstrated by a campaign to discredit Slim Chiboub on Radio Mosaïque. According to a contributor to the censured Web site "L'Autre Tunisie," the clans are fighting a dirty battle.[391] Several dissident Web pages report on the practices of bribery, self-enrichment, and excessive luxury of the three groups. A typical story relates, for example, how ordinary Tunisians are physically removed from their homes, which are then torn down and upon which new residences are built by cousins of Leila Trabelsi.[392]

The central bank in Tunisia has been utilized to help create the new ruling coalition of rent-seeking urban and rural economic elites. A referendum issued by the bank on November 23, 1997 allowed all other banks to give loans to businessmen willing to buy state-owned-enterprises without appropriate guarantees. This referendum encouraged dozens of businessmen affiliated with government officials to buy SOEs as a way to seek wealth without improving output. Many bought the enterprises only to lay off their workers and sell their machinery and land. This was the case with the factory of Littihad Bijmal, the Tismuk Company, and the Sutabakis Company. Most of the loans to purchase these and other state-owned enterprises were not repaid. Due to this policy, Tunisian banks return only 20 percent of its loans.[393]

Since 1985, Tunisian leaders have engaged in an agrarian counter-reform in which the state is transferring over 600,000 hectares of the country's best land to a rural elite.[394] With the support of World Bank agricultural sector loans, state land held in cooperatives is being privatized in twenty-five–forty-year leases at rates far lower than market prices, prior to a future move toward outright ownership.[395] In addition, over 2.7 million hectares of communal land is being privatized in Tunisia with negative consequences for the small peasantry that already had insecure access to land and employment.[396] To counter losses by the small peasantry, the regime has pressured rural notables, who have benefited from state policy, to participate in redistributive measures in their communities organized along the Islamic calendar. The precarious economic situation has fostered neo-traditional social relations, including increased clientelism.

Legitimacy

Ben Ali's regime appears to view itself as a type of East Asian or Chinese developmental state power, delivering improved living standards and welfare under the leadership of the party-state, though with growth rates less than half that of the Asian economies during their periods of rapid growth.[397] This regime has also taken steps to maintain a patina of continued populism through the use of coercive charity in both urban and rural areas. With lingering signs still remaining of the bloodshed in neighboring Algeria, the regime rules under a mantle of relative peace and prosperity.

With vote counts for the state party above the 90th percentile, democratic legitimacy appears to carry less weight for the regime. They rely on the support of women by maintaining Bourguiba's progressive policies in that domain, and are quick to claim national security needs to combat Islamic radicalism and prevent the rise of Islamic groups and instability that occurred in neighboring Algeria and Egypt.

The current regime in Tunisia is a police state, which says something about its own sense of legitimacy. Civil and public liberties are severely restricted. The press is perhaps the least free of any in the Arab world, which is saying a lot. The security police seems omnipresent. The opposition and their families face harassment. Even after release from imprisonment, opposition figures often face a form of social death; they are banned from participation in public functions and denied most economic opportunities. In particular there has been unnecessary repression and torture of the MTI, and emasculation of the Tunisian Human Rights movement. The paradox of these circumstances is that in terms of socioeconomic indicators and political culture, Tunisia should be in the avant-garde of Arab states moving toward democracy.

Implications of the Argument

To sum up, new authoritarian outcomes were the result of political openings in all four of the single-party Arab socialist regimes. All four currently share a number of fundamental characteristics: political institutions are characterized by a façade of multiparty politics, increasing presidentialism, and strained political dynamics within the corporatist organizations allied with state parties that were designed to control labor and the peasantry. The ruling coalitions in Egypt, Syria, Algeria, and Tunisia are now all composed of rent-seeking urban and rural economic elites, along with a state bourgeoisie composed of upper-echelon state and military officials that have moved into the private sector, taking state assets with them. The policy context has shifted towards economic liberalization characterized by patronage, and electoral politics constitute a core part of their new legitimacy formula. In the hands of autocratic regime elites, changes in domestic structural conditions caused by the privatization of state assets and the historical legacies of single party rule served as primary drivers of transformed authoritarian rule. This argument contributes to several bodies of literature.

Politics under Authoritarian and Hybrid Regimes

There is a long literature of theorizing authoritarianism in post–World War II social science, and a new emerging literature has again taken up the job of analyzing politics under authoritarian rule. The literature also studies transitions to and not away from this regime type. Recent writing, however, is weakened by a nearly singular focus on the competitiveness of elections. Due to this focus on democratization, the literature tends to describe these regimes in terms of what they are not, instead of what they are. In contrast, this book contributes to recent scholarship on authoritarian and hybrid regimes by exploring the transformation in the substance of authoritarianism in the former Arab socialist single-party republics through an examination of multiple regime dimensions, including ruling coalitions, strategies of legitimation, and policies, in addition to the political institutions that are the focus of most of this new research.

Within the dimension of political institutions, autocratic leaders in Egypt, Syria, Algeria, and Tunisia follow all the tactics described in Andreas Schedler's "menu of manipulations" to subvert the possibility of losing power through recently installed multiparty elections.[398] Algerian rulers follow the tactic of reserved positions by maintaining military power behind the scenes. Divide-and-rule tactics to marginalize inexperienced opposition groups are followed in all four countries, as are restrictions on public and civil liberties to prevent fair knowledge of available choices in elections. Informal disenfranchisement through techniques, such as barring voters from polling stages and illicitly adding or deleting names, have been observed in Egypt and Tunisia. Concerns about clientelistic control of poor voters in the countryside are warranted in all four countries and add up to the violation of the norm of insulation of the vote from undue outside pressures. Electoral fraud is too common, with Tunisia standing out with its return of votes in the high 90th percentile for the state party and incumbent president. Even reversibility of a free and fair vote occurred when the military prevented the Islamic FIS from winning the 1991–1992 national assembly elections. Schedler did not mention strategies to gain real regime support during elections, concentrating instead on tactics to subvert the opposition. The use of patronage-based economic liberalization to gain support for transformed authoritarian rule is one such strategy.

Steven Levitsky and Lucan Way's conceptualization of competitive authoritarianism identifies authoritarian regimes that create democratic institutions and hold meaningful elections—elections that they could conceivably lose, although incumbents utilize a variety of subtle measures to make that outcome unlikely.[399] Benchmarks of competitive authoritarian regimes focus on the percentage of legislative seats held by the ruling party and percentage of votes held by the ruling party's presidential candidate. For presidential candidates, Levitsky and Way suggest as a rule of thumb that regimes in which presidents are reelected with more than 70 percent of the vote cannot be considered as competitive authoritarian regimes.[400] A similar two-thirds or better electoral result for legislative seats held by the ruling party also suggests noncompetitiveness.[401] Under those criteria for elections, all four cases in this study are closed authoritarian, though Algeria and Egypt are less so than Tunisia and Syria.

Utilizing the research of Levitsky, Way, and Schedler, Larry Diamond classifies a large number of regimes in transition. He classifies Egypt, Tunisia, and Algeria as (hegemonic) electoral authoritarian and Syria as politically closed authoritarian.[402] This assessment is reasonable enough since Syrian elections are even less competitive than those in the other three countries, although ruling parties in the others also always obtain more than two-thirds of the legislative seats at stake in any election. Still, my judgment would be to place Syria in the category of hegemonic electoral authoritarianism because of the hegemony of the ruling parties in all four and because of Syria's movement over time toward the electoral schema of the other Arab republics. Diamond's scheme does not attempt to account for change over time. The present study contributes to the literature by highlighting that authoritarianism in the MENA is both persistent and dynamic.

These recent studies are obviously important. They demonstrate that modern authoritarianism is categorically different in that autocratic rulers seek to legitimate themselves through elections and the trappings of multiparty democracy.[403] This hallmark trait of contemporary authoritarianism is one also manifested by the MENA republics. The recent studies of authoritarian and hybrid regimes also sift through the democratic claims of devout autocrats and reveal many of their techniques to subvert "democratic" elections. Any student of the Middle East will readily recognize Schedler's "menu of manipulations." Daniel Brumberg's formulation of liberalized autocracy and Marina Ottaway's conceptualization of semi-authoritarian regimes with Egypt as a primary case, classify a number of MENA countries along the lines of Schedler's electoral authoritarianism.[404]

While important, most of these recent studies of authoritarianism are limited by their near singular focus on the degree of electoral competitiveness. One presumably wants to know more about politics under authoritarian regimes than whether or not their elections are becoming competitive. Overall, there are only minimal attempts in these recent studies to investigate the sociological foundations of new forms of authoritarian rule: to seek to understand the economic and political projects that these regimes are devoted to and the consequences of their projects for various social groups beyond the electoral arena. Without examining these other dimensions of new authoritarian regimes, one misses much of what contemporary politics are about in the Arab republics, and presumably elsewhere in the world.

More satisfying in terms of capturing the forms and dynamics of emerging authoritarian regimes has been Raymond Hinnebusch's conceptualization of post-populist authoritarianism (PPA), which he has applied to Egypt and Syria in a number of articles.[405] Hinnebusch primarily describes and explores changes in coalitions, policies, and political infrastructure. Similar to the new authoritarianism described here, his PPA regimes are built around a new bourgeois-state-landed elite alliance. However, he does not emphasize the rent-seeking nature of this new state coalition, nor does he argue that new rent-seeking distributive coalitions can serve as a causal factor in transforming authoritarianism while maintaining power and control.

Clement Henry and Robert Springborg usefully view a number of MENA regimes in light of their efforts to integrate into the global economy by implementing the Washington Consensus or doctrinaire economic liberalism.[406] Their interest in economic policy reforms is combined with a typology of regime types in the MENA region. Their typology includes bunker states, bully praetorian states, globalizing monarchies, and fragmented democracies. The emphasis in the typology is on the tenor of state–society relations. Syria and Algeria are classified as bunker states in which a minority social force controls the state and is in such conflict with their societies that they are forced to govern from behind bunkers. Egypt and Tunisia are classified as bully praetorian states that dominate, sometimes brutally, their societies, but representing no one social force they are not obliged to retreat behind bunkers.

Henry and Springborg's position on implementing neo-liberal economic reforms in the MENA is inconsistent. On the one hand they argue that countries in the MENA must respond to globalization and attain economic development by implementing neo-liberal economic reforms commonly called the Washington Consensus: "The working hypotheses of this book are that politics drives economic development and that the principal obstacles to development in the region have been political rather than economic or cultural in nature. Political rather than economic factors have been the primary cause of the rate and method by which countries of the region have been incorporated into the globalized economy within the framework of the Washington consensus."[407] Here there is an implied acceptance of the value of the Washington Consensus as an economic policy blueprint and the implication that merely implementing the policies of this consensus constitutes successful economic reform, rather than judging the reforms by their ability to foster economic growth and improve human welfare. There is also little discussion of the desirability or possibility of legitimating the reforms through the electoral process.

This position makes one wonder if the full and rapid implementation of all tenets of the Washington Consensus in the MENA would have produced impressive economic growth. Worldwide, the results of this economic consensus have been uneven and nowhere as successful as in the developmental state model of East Asia, a market reform model that emphasizes shared growth as the economy expands, egalitarian land reform, a focus on small and medium enterprises, successful state business cooperation, some protectionism, an industrial policy, and selective integration into the global capitalist economy.

This apparent faith in the Washington Consensus is, however, diluted by their reference to the possibility of an integration of its economic reform policies with domestically inspired economic policy preferences, including the possibility of an Islamic variant of the Washington Consensus, though they do not spell out what this variant would look like.[408] The authors also note in the empirical chapters the high degree of rent seeking involved in economic reform, especially for the Algerian case.

The analytic utility of separating bunker states, Algeria and Syria, from bully praetorian states, Egypt and Tunisia, is also questionable since they yield just about the same authoritarian results: economic liberalization characterized by elite rent seeking, façades of multiparty politics and other institutional adjustments, and legitimacy deficits that encourage brutal repression. The authors also do not examine these authoritarian regime types in a cross-regional perspective.

Notably, the older literature on authoritarianism shares more of the present study's focus on *both* the economic and political projects to which authoritarian regimes devote themselves, and on the sociological foundations of authoritarian rule. Conceptualized by Guillermo O'Donnell, bureaucratic authoritarian regimes (BA) are ruled by a coalition of the state, technocrats, the military, the domestic *haute bourgeoisie*, and multinational corporations. This coalition emerged from populist authoritarian regimes to increase investment, deepen the industrialization process, and shift economic strategy to a reliance on markets, private enterprise, exports, and integration into the international capitalist order.[409] The new pattern of capital accumulation was built on shrinking real wages. To do this, BA regimes had to exclude the popular sectors from political representation and expand private investment, both domestic and foreign. This they did brutally. A coalition of the military, technocrats, and foreign and national capital underpinned BA regimes and their project to deepen industrialization by switching to a liberal economic order.

The economic determinants of a new authoritarianism in Latin America described by O'Donnell and others do not apply to the cases of the Arab republics. These are not regimes devoted primarily to deepening their countries' industrial structure. Privatization and trade liberalization combined with rampant rent seeking associated with economic liberalization has led to deindustrialization in Egypt, Syria, Algeria, and Tunisia. Local industries suffer in the new policy context, which has a static view of comparative advantage. Replacing import-substitution by import-competition damages domestic manufacturing.[410] In addition, the rational, technocratic, bureaucratic approach to policymaking implied by the term *bureaucratic authoritarianism* cannot be applied to regimes characterized by rent-seeking urban and rural economic elites and high-level state officials.

Closer to the mark in terms of regimes in Latin America that resemble the new MENA authoritarianism described in this study is Hector Schamis's conceptualization of Neo-conservative authoritarianism.[411] These regimes—Argentina, Chile, and Uruguay in the 1970s—also combined economic liberalization with deindustrialization and created ruling coalitions similar to those of the new MENA authoritarianism. Their primary project, Schamis argues, was not economic—the deepening of industrialization—but ideological: a commitment to laissez-faire economics, a social order regulated by market relations, anti-Keynesian and monetarist policies, and a Reaganism and Thatcherism of South America. Their adherence to laissez-faire postulates led them to dismantle the apparatus of state intervention by establishing a minimal state, shorn of its regulatory and distributionist role. While deepening industrialization was not their main goal, these regimes shared with BA a commitment to transforming capital accumulation to a strategy based on holding wages low, private investment, and repressing the masses to achieve their economic aims. In the end, according to Schamis their goal was to create the conditions for the emergence of a hegemonic bourgeois class that could group other social forces in society behind their economic projects and ideological commitments. Notably, Schamis highlights rent-seeing economic elites in his analysis.

While past the point of no return, the commitment to laissez-faire economics in the Arab world in general is probably the weakest of any of the world's regions. Because of a lacking of this ideological fervor, other factors including economic stagnation and foreign pressure enter prominently in explaining the policy shifts in Egypt, Syria, Algeria, and Tunisia. Attempting to transform mechanisms of capital accumulation and establish a powerful bourgeoisie that can dominate the countries' political economies only partly rings true in regimes where economic elites typically utilize rent seeking for their own conspicuous consumption rather than for productive investment.[412]

In sum, an older literature on forms of authoritarian rule that examines authoritarian politics beyond the degree of electoral competitiveness shares more of the concerns of the present work than much of the more recent literature on authoritarianism. The present study highlights political change in a region often considered changeless and authoritarian. It examines these changes in a cross-regional perspective (see chapter 5), exploring dimensions of authoritarian regimes often unexamined in the recent literature on the forms and dynamics of authoritarian rule. The changes in policies, coalitions, political institutions, and strategies of legitimation in the MENA republics described and analyzed in this book contribute to a new and broader understanding of how politics currently operates under authoritarian rule in the MENA and possibly elsewhere in the world.

The Links between Economic
and Political Liberalization

The relationship between economic and political liberalization has been a central focus of comparative research for decades. Some analysts presume a reciprocal and mutually reinforcing dynamic between democratization and economic liberalization, others discern inherent contradictions, and some argue that these two arenas of change are not necessarily interactive, at least not in a patterned way. The thesis of this book, which views economic liberalization as a force against democratization in the Arab republics, contributes to this literature on simultaneous economic and political reform by filling gaps in our understanding of how economic reforms seemingly reinforce authoritarianism in a number of MENA cases.

Those that view economic and political liberalization as mutually reinforcing typically assume that the economic reforms implemented in developing countries will improve economic efficiency and produce economic growth, partly by eliminating rent seeking.[413] Those results would tie economic reform to the well-established historical link between capitalist economic development and democracy. In explaining this link, analysts in the modernization school argued that the benefits of economic development foster a democratic political culture. These benefits include widespread education, urbanization, a more beneficial class structure—rich people less fearful of the poor and democracy, mollified lower classes not enticed by revolutionary politics—and civil society growth. As a result, most people have a stake in how politics are conducted and therefore begin to insist that public officials be held accountable. In such an environment, authoritarian politics cannot be sustained.[414] Related arguments contend that capitalism disperses resources and power, and in general economic liberty and political liberty go together.

Explanations for why capitalism engenders democracy also focus on how capitalist development created and empowered the groups that historically have been the agents for democratization. Depending on the study, these social groups included the bourgeoisie, other elements of the middle class, and labor, or most powerfully a democratic coalition comprising all three.[415] In late developers, however, the material interests of the bourgeoisie and the organized "labor aristocracy" have frequently been tied to or dependent upon authoritarian states, yielding little incentive for these groups to fight for democracy.[416]

Economic reforms in the MENA republics alienated labor and peasant support for authoritarian rule but reinforced the bourgeoisie and landlord support for a transforming authoritarian regime. To adjust to these changes and sustain authoritarian rule, autocrats in Egypt, Syria, Algeria, and Tunisia relied on single-party institutional resources to maintain mass control, pressured their private sector allies favored in policy to participate in community welfare mechanisms, and ramped up coercion when needed to avert mobilization from below.

Authoritarian trends in the MENA were also bolstered by economic liberalization characterized by patronage and rent seeking, which did not produce the economic growth or more beneficial class structure historically associated with capitalist development and democratization. One possible way to avert this outcome would have been to design economic reforms in the region to target small and medium-sized enterprises and the small peasantry as was done in the East Asia during their phase of rapid export-led growth.[417]

More recent updates of modernization theory indicate that the strongest predictor of transitions *to* authoritarianism is poverty.[418] The MENA Republics are all lower-middle-income countries according to World Bank categories, with GNI per capita between $876 and $3,465.[419] While poverty is still common in these countries and the inequalities and inefficiencies of their economic reform programs fuel authoritarian tendencies, they are relatively better off in their extents of poverty than the low-income countries of the world. On the other hand, their economies still have far to go to reach the income level at which statistical studies pinpoint countries that are invulnerable to democratic breakdown. Adam Przeworski, Michael Alvarez, Jose Cheibub, and Fernando Limongi have researched places that earn $6,055 per capita. At $4,200 per capita, democracy has a better than average chance of surviving.[420] Of course, these studies only apply to countries that have made a democratic transition in the first place. Notably, the MENA region contains a number of high-income oil- and gas-exporting countries that are firmly autocratic and never completed a democratic transition.

More proximate studies of twin transitions that view political and economic reform as mutually reinforcing focus on how marketization produces economic growth by developing a state capable of securing property rights and well-specified, transparent, and consistent rules of economic gain. In this economic environment, competition allocates resources and produces efficient outcomes.[421] Economic reform in the Arab republics, however, has been characterized by private ownership and crony capitalism, not free market policies that combine private ownership and competition. The result has been monopolies and grossly inefficient economic outcomes. Similarly, political reforms in the Arab republics have failed to produce the rule of law required for genuine political competition.

Another instance of lost opportunities by the Arab republics to implement policies that reinforce both economic and political reforms is related to the policy process that produces economic reform programs. Adam Przeworski and a diverse group of comparativists argue that reforms in both arenas can support each other if publics are included in the economic reform process. Reforms shaped in a more democratic context would be more sensitive to public concerns, more effective as policy, and more likely to get public cooperation and enhanced legitimacy for economic reforms and fragile new democratic institutions.[422]

The global implementation of new democratic institutions and multiparty elections of relative degrees of competitiveness developed at the same time as widespread economic stagnation. This was a root cause of the rejection of ISI populism, the collapse of the Soviet Union, and the cross-regional implementation of the Washington Consensus. Since these political openings and authoritarian collapses occurred in tandem with economic crisis, it is not surprising that scholarly attention has been focused on the link between the two. Most prominently, Stephan Haggard and Robert R. Kaufman argue that authoritarian regimes are most vulnerable to collapse when poor economic performance undermines the ability to purchase social compliance and prevent elite fragmentation.[423] The Arab republics were clearly affected by the economic stagnation that engulfed many countries globally in the 1970s and 1980s. However, in Egypt, Syria, Algeria, and Tunisia economic liberalization characterized by patronage provided autocratic incumbents with resources to purchase the compliance of key groups while ruling-party organizational capacities helped maintain elite consensus and control of the popular sectors.

Rent Seeking and Economic Reform

The neo-classical political economy literature and the politics of economic adjustment literature make the claim that marketization efforts dissipate rents.[424] That claim does not withstand empirical scrutiny in the main cases of this study. Instead, privatization reforms generated new rents that authoritarian incumbents utilized to build a new core coalition of support for transformed authoritarian rule.

Sustaining Authoritarianism in the Middle East and North Africa

The present argument establishes that in an important subset of MENA countries, the former Arab socialist single-party republics, economic reform created and favored a rent-seeking urban and rural elite favoring authoritarian rule and took resources away from the workers and peasants increasingly with the most to gain from democratization. Thus, changing domestic structural conditions fostered by the privatization of state-owned enterprises and land contributed to persistent authoritarian rule. Single-party institutions and their affiliated state corporatist organizations also helped the authoritarian leadership in Egypt, Syria, Algeria, and Tunisia remain in power while reinforcing control over a new authoritarian system that includes economic liberalization and some controlled pluralism. Leading explanations for persistent authoritarianism in the Middle East and North Africa, including cultural dispositions, coercive institutions, divide-and-rule tactics, electoral manipulations, and single-party strengths at social control can be enriched by recognizing how privatization provided a new social base of support for autocracy, and fostered a domestic social structure unfavorable to democratic outcomes.

To further highlight the role of single-party institutions and patronage-based economic liberalization in sustaining authoritarian rule during a global era of democratic reforms, the next chapter examines transitions away from authoritarian regimes that culminated in democracy. These cases were not characterized by dominant parties and privatization rooted in patronage.

FIVE

Political Openings without Patronage-Based Privatization and Single-Party Institutional Legacies

This book has argued that single-party institutional legacies and new sources of patronage from the privatization of state assets provided MENA autocrats with tools to sustain authoritarian rule despite the implementation of multiparty politics. This chapter highlights these causal dynamics in contrasting cases and outcomes by examining the unfolding of democratization in countries that differed institutionally (none single-party regimes) from Egypt, Syria, Algeria, and Tunisia. These different countries also had other forms and timings of privatization than Egypt, Syria, Algeria, and Tunisia. In the cases discussed below, labor drove democratization, unhinged from state parties and affiliated state corporatist controls. The bourgeoisie's roles in democratic transformations were mixed, but overall they were less willing to support authoritarian rule than in the Arab socialist single-party republics, where they have profited handsomely from rents generated by the privatization policies of authoritarian incumbents.

Democratization in Argentina

After decades of multiparty liberal democracy interrupted by multiple coups, Argentina achieved democratic consolidation after 1983, with a democratic opening and breakdown of military rule. Privatization, while characterized by the same rent-seeking behavior of capitalists that occurred in Egypt, Syria, Algeria, and Tunisia, took place after the transition to democracy and under a democratic government. Privatization was undertaken rapidly and extensively between 1990 and 1992.[1]

In terms of democratization, it is commonly argued that the defeat of the Argentine military in the Falkland Islands/Malvinas War led to the collapse of the military authoritarian regime and a democratic transition in 1983.[2] Countering that view are analyses arguing that labor played an important role through intensive protests, which contributed to dividing the military into hard-liners and soft-liners and propelled it to invade the Malvinas/Falklands to overcome the divisions.[3] Labor protests in the view of these analysts also destabilized the military regime by demonstrating the regime's lack of social support and inability to maintain order.[4] Finally, the Argentine union movement kept pressure on the regime through mobilizations and strikes to ensure that the withdrawal of the military and transitional elections scheduled by military officers in October of 1983 would indeed occur.[5]

There is a long history of labor militancy and dense social networking that united the workplace and the working-class community in Argentina. Between the 1940s and the 1980s, two opposing challengers battled for political and economic control of the country. The working and middle classes, organized by unions and under the leadership of populist general Juan Peron, struggled against the military and the five coups d'etat orchestrated by them between 1943 and 1976. When there were elections, in 1946 and 1973, the Peronists were able to win and therefore favored democratic elections.[6]

The military regime that took power in the 1976 coup harshly repressed labor and entered into a "dirty war" against urban guerrillas that killed up to thirty thousand people.[7] They had a political goal to decapitate the combative labor leadership and pursue economic liberalization policies, though privatization was not an important element.[8] The regime was able to replace labor leadership with a more supine group; though labor unrest was quelled for a short time, a new labor leadership emerged from the shop floor and spearheaded a more combative trade union movement.[9] It is worth noting that in contrast to the political context in Egypt, Syria, Algeria, and Tunisia, where labor unions had started out as nationalist or single-party allies or creations, in Argentina the opposition Peronists had established the state corporatist system. Partly for that reason, the military was never able to fully establish state control over the trade union movement.[10]

The more independent labor movement in Argentina mounted a general strike in 1979, and by the eve of the invasion of the Malvinas/

Falklands in 1982 labor was in an openly offensive mode and demanded full democratization.[11] They were joined by the lower middle classes, a phenomenon that recreated the previously successful Peronist coalition.

In addition to taking the initiative in mobilizing opposition to the military regime in Argentina, labor groups attempted to coordinate opposition with other social sectors. Business groups were divided about this push for democratic transformation.[12] Small and medium manufacturers that were exclusively oriented toward the domestic market supported labor; by contrast, the internationalized industrial bourgeoisie that formed joint ventures with multinational corporations along with the agrarian upper class favored continued military authoritarian rule.[13] Within a context of economic deterioration and labor protests, open divisions emerged within the ruling authoritarian regime. A divided labor movement came to agreement on an openly combative stance and demand for democracy.[14] The union movement organized another general strike in 1981; massive demonstrations took place that threatened the stability of the government before the military launched the Malvinas/Falklands invasion. Extrication of the military from political control and a democratic transition followed the military loss in that venture.

In sum, the institutional context in Argentina differed from that in Egypt, Syria, Algeria, and Tunisia, in ways that hindered autocratic rulers' ability to thwart substantive democratization led by a mobilized labor movement. The military in Argentina did not have as a resource a hegemonic state party to dominate the founding 1983 elections of the transition and therefore could not maintain authoritarian rule in a context of multiparty "competitive" elections.[15] Privatization occurred past the time when it could be turned into a political resource to generate support for authoritarian rule.

In contrast to the Argentinean case, political leaders in the Arab republics possessed patronage and institutional resources that they utilized to sustain authoritarian rule during timid turns towards democracy in the 1980s and 1990s. Political leaders in Egypt, Syria, Algeria, and Tunisia all alienated labor through their neo-liberal economic policies, especially privatization, enough in some instances to cause union and peasant demands for democracy and numerous demonstrations and strikes. Autocratic incumbents in the Arab republics, however, survived the multiparty elections they established to enhance legitimacy. They were able to rely on a legacy of an alliance between state parties and coopted labor union leaders that helped tip the scale in their favor despite labor and Islamist mobilization from below against their policies. During dissent and protest in Egypt, Syria, Algeria, and Tunisia, the ruling parties also provided a better anchor throughout society, and the state parties' monopoly of public resources, which they distributed as patronage, secured electoral dominance. The new sources of patronage from the privatization of state-owned enterprises and land helped autocrats in the former Arab socialist regimes replace their labor- and peasant-core base of support by shifting to an authoritarian regime anchored by big capital and landlords.

Privatization in Argentina

Privatization in Argentina was characterized by rent seeking, but it occurred largely after the 1983 democratic transition and thus did not serve as a patronage resource to build support for the military authoritarian regime. Still, for comparative purposes it is useful to briefly describe the privatization process that took place there. Argentina's privatization program, implemented between 1990 and 1992, was one of the broadest and most rapid in the world.[16] As was the case in the Arab republics, the process was characterized by crony capitalism.[17] Privatization as a source of rents for capitalists was also a political tool to build support for a government implementing difficult structural-adjustment policies.[18]

Three other features of the privatization process in Argentina are worth noting in terms of comparisons with divestiture in Egypt, Syria, Algeria, and Tunisia. First, privatization in Argentina occurred on the heels of a series of hyperinflationary episodes in 1989–1990. The year 1989 was catastrophic. From December to the following December, inflation almost reached 5,000 percent; at the peak of March 1989–March 1990, it was higher than 20,000 percent.[19] The experience of breathtaking hyperinflation created a widespread sense of need for massive reforms and enabled public support for privatization, a situation that President Carlos Menem used to his advantage.[20] Hyperinflation, and at a much lower level, was only present in the Algerian case. Second, Menem, despite being elected, governed largely through executive decrees. Thus Argentina's delegative democracy under his rule had some authoritarian aspects.[21] Finally, the privatization program in Argentina implemented by Menem differed from the programs in the Arab republics by including a larger element of employee-share ownership, as seen in the Participatory Property Program.[22]

Democratization in Spain

Spain represents a crucial early case in the transitions literature.[23] It has been viewed as the core model of a democratic transition driven by incumbent elite choices and dispositions. However, more recent scholarship has challenged that view and has characterized the Spanish democratic transition that began in 1975 as one driven by both elite negotiations and mobilization from below.[24] Privatization and the conversion of state assets into a patronage resource to sustain authoritarian rule was not a factor in the Spanish democratic transition because the privatization of significant public enterprises in Spain had begun in 1985, after the consolidation of democracy.[25] Notably, industrial capitalists played an important role in the democratic reform movement in Spain.[26]

A military authoritarian political regime ruled Spain from the end of the Civil War in 1939 until the death of its dictator General Francisco Franco in 1975. After his death, a three-year process of democratic transformation took place. Franco's rule had been characterized by fascist rhetoric and a state corporatist form of political organization. However, over time an independent trade union movement developed in association with the Communist Party.[27] The communist leadership and Spain's corporatist representative structure, penetrable enough to be infiltrated and reoriented toward oppositional political activity, enhanced democratic prospects in Spain.[28] In contrast, the nationalist party trade union alliance in Egypt, Syria, Algeria, and Tunisia has been shaken, but not to the point that it could be used in association with a communist or socialist party to tumble the regimes and install democracy. In the Arab republics, the lack of labor-based political parties with significant organizational capacity and leadership hinders the momentum of non-Islamist opposition activity.

The Spanish labor movement opened space within the authoritarian regime and led pro-democratic protests from the beginning of the 1970s until the democratic elections of 1977.[29] In 1970 alone, there were more than 1,500 worker strikes.[30] Sustained labor protests in the first half of the 1970s led to divisions within the authoritarian regime and a search for a new formula for stability.[31] "In the early months of 1976 the workers' movement showed unprecedented strength and combativeness. In 1976, the number of working hours lost to strikes reached 150 million. The struggles and mobilizations were especially intense in the first three months of the year. In that year alone there were 17,731 strikes."[32]

In response to the demonstrations and upheaval, Franco and his successors attempted to appease the public with half measures that would soften but sustain the dictatorship. Labor, the Communist Party, and the Socialist Party, however, kept up enough pressure to prevent anything short of a democratic transition.[33] Industrialists also joined the democratic reform movement.[34] It was the combination of the mobilization of society, severe enough to threaten the political system as a whole, and the choices of the regime's elite including Aldolpho Suarez and King Juan Carlos, that drove the democratic transformation in Spain.[35]

Privatization in Spain

The timing of the main period of privatization in Spain meant that democratic transition and consolidation occurred without state-owned assets becoming a political resource as patronage. Spain had developed a public sector of the economy mainly as a consequence of the political regime established by General Franco after the Spanish Civil War. Franco's victory led to political and economic isolation, provoking a state-led development strategy and generating a substantial public sector of the economy.[36] Substantial privatization began after 1985. The methods of privatization were mainly direct sales (77 percent) and public offerings (19 percent). Some incidents during the privatization process caused public monopolies to be transferred into the hands of private monopolists.[37]

Democratization in Brazil

Democratization in Brazil began with an initiative from within the military regime that took power in 1964. Shortly after taking power, to legitimate their rule, they established a controlled two-party political system; within it, the government party was intended to hold power indefinitely.[38] For a decade, this controlled opening largely worked. In 1974, however, the opposition achieved more success than anticipated in a national election. Added to that, a grass-roots urban social movement promoted by the Catholic Church demanded substantive democracy, and a powerful union movement in opposition developed in the mid-1970s.[39] These two social movements—together with other groups demanding democratic reform, including students and industrial capitalists—destabilized the military regime to the point that its leaders finally organized competitive elections and withdrew from power in 1985.[40] As was the case in Spain and Argentina, privatization in Brazil occurred largely after the transition to and consolidation of democracy. Thus, turning state-owned assets into political patronage was not a significant factor in the outcome of Brazil's transition from military authoritarian rule.[41]

An important piece of the story of democratic transformation in Brazil was the emergence of an independent trade union movement and the socialist workers' party that it created; the party was called the Partido dos Trabalhadores (the PT) and was to be of and for the popular sectors.[42] This independent labor mobilization and labor-based political party had to emerge from within Brazil's state corporatist labor relation system, which had been established to control workers.[43] The combative labor movement developed within the official corporatist union structures. The WP was able to establish a mass base due to strong leadership and provocations by the regime that reinforced the need for independent political representation.[44] An intensive series of economic strikes in 1978–1979 was harshly repressed by the military regime, and highlighted the need for labor autonomy from state control.[45]

Industrial capitalists also supported the 1985 democratic transition in Brazil. One Brazil specialist notes that their involvement contributed to the instability in the regime and the lack of stable investment rules to protect their investments.[46] Those important and threatening conditions might have been less crucial for Brazilian industrial elites had they been simultaneously securing windfall gains from the privatization of state-owned enterprises on highly beneficial and monopolistic terms.

Privatization in Brazil

A limited amount of privatization in Brazil occurred between 1980 and 1990, but the number of enterprises was small and did not include any major state-owned enterprises that had been established in the previous three decades.[47] Brazil's serious privatization drive began in 1990.[48] The privatization policies implemented were similar to those in Egypt, Syria, Algeria, and Tunisia. Public monopolies became private. Small investors were not favored. A large numbers of jobs were lost. Few programs enabled workers to share in the privatization process.[49]

Conclusion

Unlike the outcomes in the Arab republics, the political openings in Argentina, Spain, and Brazil culminated in democracy. Labor played an important role in all three cases of substantive demoratization. The state corporatist controls in the three countries were less resilient than the single-party state corporatist systems that emerged from nationalist movements in Egypt, Syria, Algeria, and Tunisia. Nationalist movements either created or rode to power in an alliance with trade union movements in the Arab republics. The combination of ruling parties and affiliated corporatist organizations is apparently more potent than were the state corporatist systems developed under military control in Argentina, Spain, and Brazil. In those three countries, independent labor unions and associated labor-based political parties were able to develop and lead the drive for democracy.

The role of capitalists in democratic reform in Argentina, Spain, and Brazil was more mixed, but overall capitalists in all three countries favored democracy much more than the capitalists in Egypt, Syria, Algeria, and Tunisia who benefit richly from authoritarian regimes that implement elections without permitting democracy. Given that economic liberalization characterized by patronage and single-party institutional legacies add up to a political context that makes democratization difficult, the next chapter explores possibilities of overcoming these two factors.

SIX

Transitions from the New MENA Authoritarianism to Democracy?

S ingle-party institutional legacies and new sources of patronage from the privatization of state-owned enterprises and land provided autocrats in Egypt, Syria, Algeria, and Tunisia with tools to hold multiparty elections and transform authoritarian rule in other ways while maintaining power and control. In that light, the general literature that examines the unusual cases of transitions from single-party authoritarianism to substantive democracy provides insights into possible paths toward real pluralism and electoral competition in the MENA republics.

Similarly, enforced mechanisms that would introduce real competition into the market arrangements being established in the former Arab socialist single-party republics—antitrust laws, competition legislation—would undercut the foundations of patronage politics, enhance local economic opportunities for the majority, and make it more likely that incumbent autocrats will relent when pressured and consent to permitting real competition in the political system. By way of conclusion, this chapter examines the possibilities of these democratizing trends emerging in Egypt, Syria, Algeria, and Tunisia.

Privatization Characterized by Crony Capitalism and a Landlord-Spoils System

Economists and other analysts within the Arab Republics are outspoken about the rent seeking and corruption involved in their economic reform programs:

What's being applied in most Arab countries is a deformed version of the Washington consensus: unregulated markets without antitrust regulation to ensure competitiveness or distributive justice. Such markets are bound to fail to clear at decent levels of human welfare. They favor the strong over the weak, and penalize the weak and poor, inevitably creating wider disparities. In Egypt, erstwhile egalitarian land reform measures were reversed to the benefit of the former landlords, and the "freeing up" of prices, under monopolistic conditions, has resulted in huge rises in the cost of inputs for all small and micro enterprises, farming included.[1]

The Algerian experience in making reforms shows that the transition towards the market has to be a political decision that provides a legal framework for economic activities in all the competing commercial relationships. Without the public authority regulating those relationships, ensuring inter alia independence of the judiciary and trade union freedom, the market will be dominated by forces which, based on political decisions, will oppose competition. Without competition legislation there is no market. Competition destroys profiteering mechanisms and liberates an economic dynamic that cannot be opposed by privileges that have been acquired by force. This is why the market is the expression of the autonomy of the trading sphere and also the capacity of civil society (parties, unions, media, associations, etc.) to impose formal and institutional arrangements of authority that cannot easily be deviated to private ends.[2]

Competition legislation that is enforced would reduce political patronage in Egypt, Syria, Algeria, and Tunisia. Competition legislation refers to well-defined legislation governing the rules of monopoly and competition.[3] It is associated with antitrust laws that typically include anticollusion mechanisms, restrictions against monopoly power, and regulations controlling corporate acquisitions and amalgamations.[4] Competition legislation is a new presence in most Arab economies.[5] Where it exists it is supported by weak, nonindependent implementation structures. "Best practices, especially in developing countries, require that the body in charge of the implementation of competition law should be independent, an issue which takes greater prominence where governments are not elected."[6]

Typically in the Arab world, when competition legislation includes threats of prosecution for illicit gains, prosecution is threatened on political rather than economic grounds. Rent-seeking elites who oppose authoritarian regimes are threatened with prosecution. Competition legislation in the region would also be enhanced if the Arab public, who have been for decades accustomed to handling anticompetitive practices through bribery or silent forbearance, are made explicitly aware of the stipulations of competition law in order to avoid such practices or in order to be more willing to challenge them.[7] Some training of the judiciary in the Arab world on the technical aspects of competition legislation is also needed.[8]

In Egypt, as described in this book, the implementation of privatization in the absence of competition legislation led to many monopolies and the prominence of crony capitalism and political corruption. Until recently, the Egyptian government resisted supporting and implementing competition legislation. Discussion about the need for antitrust and competition legislation lasted fifteen years before its implementation in 2005.[9] By then, the private sector's contribution to the national economy had grown from 20 percent to 75 percent, leading some to proclaim that this was too late, that the damage had already been done with "the mergers, strategic alliances, buyouts, acquisitions and takeovers that took place with no regard for protection against monopolistic practices."[10] Others suggested that it was better late than never, and that the legislation if implemented would cripple the political patronage upon which the government depended.[11]

Egypt's article 27 law is considered to be the law for the protection of competition and the prevention of monopolistic practices. The law established the Anti-Trust and Competition Protection Commission (ACPC) under the supervision and authority of the cabinet. The ACPC has judicial powers to closely monitor the effect of monopolistic deals and to take abusers to court, but only with cabinet approval. The law specifically outlaws monopolistic practices, but not monopolies, a distinction that allowed prominent businessman, Ahmad Ezz, who is an influential member of the National Democratic Party and chairman of the parliament's budget committee, to acquire 70 percent of the steel market without transgressing the law.[12] Opposition MPs in parliament fear that powerful businessmen will manipulate the ACPC. They accuse the current government of being too closely tied to the business community and argue that the only way to ensure ACPC independence is to affiliate it with the Central Auditing Agency.[13]

Recently, the minister of Trade and Industry, Rasheed M. Rasheed, acknowledged that Egypt's competition legislation needed to be modified. He stated that the ministry had drafted a set of amendments to article 27 that would assess harsher penalties, increasing the fine for monopolistic practices by 500 percent, and provide companies with incentives to report monopolistic practices. The ministry would also provide companies accused of these practices with technical and logistical assistance so that they might restructure their operations in a nonmonopolistic way.[14] Of course, to be effective any changes would have to be fully implemented, something that would not occur automatically in the present context.

In terms of competition legislation in Algeria, on July 19, 2003, the Algerian government implemented Ordinance 03-03. Article 7 of this legislation prohibits any abuse of a dominant or monopolistic position over a market or segment of a market. Algeria has an organization similar to the ACPC in Egypt, responsible for monitoring and prosecuting monopolistic practices. It is called the Competition Council, and as in Egypt, it operates under the authority of the cabinet. Any citizen or organization claiming to be harmed by a restrictive practice can petition the Competition Council in Algeria. Firms, labor unions, and consumer organizations can petition it as well. The council issues injunctions in order to put an end to practices that restrict competition. If the injunctions fail, monetary sanctions may be imposed by the council. However, placing the Competition Council under the authority of the government hinders its effectiveness and opens it up to the possibilities of political manipulation. The competition legislation itself is weakly implemented.

Competition legislation in Tunisia was implemented in a series of laws: law 91-64 in July 1991, law 93-83 in July 1993, law 95-42 in April 1995, and law 99-41 in May 1999. The object of these laws in part is to combat monopolistic practices, and the minister of commerce is charged with their application. A series of accords the Tunisian government made with the European Union were aimed at the politics of economic competition. The EU accords were designed to add economic dynamism in Tunisia and other Mediterranean countries by battling cartels and monopolistic practices that did not favor the most innovative entrepreneurs that likely would produce the highest economic growth and create the most jobs. The EU Director of Competition, Jean-François Pons, asserted that Tunisia and other countries with which the EU had agreements did not do enough to enforce competition legislation.[15]

Syria has no competition legislation on the books.[16] In the other three nations, the laws on the books have been overridden by political decisions of the governments to forestall implementation or enforcement. Implementation would undercut patronage politics and result in a freer civil society. Those would be democratizing developments that would act against the continuation of the cozy relationship between wealth and power that could remain long after all state-owned assets are privatized. Trade and trade unions would be freer as well. Social forces would be more able and more likely to press for democratization. However, for such changes to occur either the incumbent elites would have to change their preferences and get serious about competition legislation, perhaps under international pressure driven by trade agreements, or individuals and organizations in civil society would have to press for it. Constituencies favoring competition legislation that are willing to struggle for it risk material interests, freedom, and even physical safety from authoritarian regimes capable of retaliation.

The lack of enforced competition legislation in the Arab Republics during the widespread privatization drive of the 1990s and early twenty-first century has fostered privatization characterized by rent seeking. However, it is useful to note that the effect of rent seeking on economic growth depends on the use to which the rent seekers put the surplus that they gain.[17] Rent seeking can be a type of primitive accumulation, as can be inherited wealth or any form of windfall profit. Privatization winners could transform rents into capital through productive investment.[18] However, the conspicuous consumption described in chapter 4 of this book provides some evidence that that is not the case in Egypt, Syria, Algeria, and Tunisia.

It is also worth noting that crony capitalism—close ties between business, government, and banks that foster rent seeking—does not hinder economic growth in some countries. East Asian economies have experienced rapid growth with moderate inequality despite widespread acknowledgement of the prevalence of crony capitalism.[19] But most developing countries lack the institutional features of developmental states that suggest such an outcome. This is the case in the Arab republics; indeed, the economic growth rates in the four countries support such a conclusion.

Evolution in the Façade of Multiparty Politics: The Democratization of Single-Party Regimes

Authoritarian regimes are diverse in their resiliency and tendency to democratize.[20] As discussed, single-party regimes are the most stable form of authoritarian rule. They last, on average, considerably longer than personalist and military authoritarian regimes. As elsewhere in the world, the single-party authoritarian regimes in the Middle East and North Africa evolved from single-party regimes in which no opposition is allowed, to dominant party regimes in which a single party rules yet opposition parties compete.[21] In a typology of authoritarian regimes that they use to investigate propensities for democratization, Alex Hadenius and Jan Teorell utilize the term-limited multiparty regimes for authoritarian regimes that hold somewhat competitive multiparty elections without any dominant party. They identify dominant-party regimes as a subtype of limited multiparty regimes in which ruling parties take more than two-thirds of the votes in parliamentary and executive elections.[22]

Hadenius and Toerell argue that when limited multiparty regimes break down, the result in most cases is the onset of democratic transformation.[23] Limited multiparty authoritarian regimes lead to democratization more than other authoritarian forms because they hold elections with a degree of openness and contestation and allow some basic political liberties. As a result, they are more amenable to the incremental progress that ends in democracy.[24]

When the subset of limited multiparty regimes (termed dominant-party regimes by Hadenius and Toerell) break down, the result is most often the start of limited multiparty regimes. This is important for democratic prospects, as dominant-party regimes that break down are likely headed toward democracy, though they will generally go through an intermediate step before full democratization.[25] Egypt, Syria, Algeria, and Tunisia are dominant-party regimes in Hadenius's and Toerell's typology.[26] The institutional step that would most signal enhanced prospects for democracy in any of these regimes would be a transition to a limited multiparty authoritarian regime without a dominant or ruling state party. An examination of a few cases should illuminate the process.

The Partido Revolucionario Institucional (PRI) in Mexico is probably the best-known case of a hegemonic party that peacefully ceded power. The PRI ceded its power to the opposition Partido Acción Nacional (PAN), thereby ending its own political dominance in multiparty elections. Mexico specialists attribute the demise of the PRI's dominance primarily to decreasing levels of public resources available to pay for the patronage that was the most fundamental reason for their ability to stay in power.[27]

The rising cost of buying public support of the masses during a series of economic crises emboldened political opposition to the regime. In that context, elite unity was lost and politicians on the Left and a business party on the Right (PAN) were able to peel away voters.[28] Transition from the statist to the free-market development model ended the PRI's access to sufficient public funds needed to dispense as patronage and to maintain dominance in the electoral arena.[29] Leading a regime committed to neo-liberal reforms, the PRI pursued unpopular economic policies and changed its legitimacy claim to one based on democracy. Its aim was to make the regime more competitive, to win by smaller margins, but still maintain power, though it was willing to share the power to a greater extent, including allowing the PAN to win some local state and congressional elections.[30] The PRI calculated that it could maintain popular support of the popular sectors because they had no viable alternative and would therefore continue to vote for the PRI.

In a shock to the PRI, a labor-based party emerged with powerful electoral support in the 1988 elections. The PRD, the party of the democratic revolution, officially won 31 percent of the vote in 1988, despite widespread voter fraud.[31] Despite backing the policies of the PRI, businessmen in Mexico developed their own political party as well, the PAN. A labor-based party (PRD) and a business party (PAN) peeled much of the PRI's base of support over successive elections. Mexico thus changed from a dominant-party regime, to a limited multiparty regime, and then to a democracy.

The prospects of similar transformations in Egypt, Syria, Algeria, and Tunisia vary. Strategic rents, oil, and gas revenue have at times refilled public coffers during the liberalizing years. The Middle East and North Africa region began privatization later and has proceeded more slowly than other regions, though at some point their ability to politicize these public resources will end. All the state assets will be privatized presumably at some point, but that does not necessarily mean that the cozy relationship between power and money that has stifled democracy in the region will end, especially without effective competition legislation.

The authoritarian regimes in the liberalizing Arab socialist single-party republics have been successful so far in preventing the development of threatening business and labor-based political parties. They have been less successful in countering identity-based parties. The emergence of moderate Islamist parties and Berber parties in Algeria with popular support suggests that they could play an important role in dislodging the FLN as the dominant party and could transform Algeria into a limited multiparty regime, if the military will allow this.

It is worth repeating that before the recent rebound of the FLN, the military and president Chadli Benjedid took steps to end the FLN's political dominance and convene more competitive multiparty elections. However, the bloody civil conflict of the 1990s may have convinced Algerian leaders of the continued necessity of a state party. Another legacy of Algeria's difficult recent past is that in order for the regime to convince opposition political parties to participate in their resumption of elections in the mid-1990s, they ceded to demands for proportional representation in parliament. This has allowed opposition parties to gradually build up support and could possibly shift the regime from dominant single-party to limited multiparty status, a step that would bode well for democratic prospects.

In Egypt, the Muslim Brotherhood obviously has a strong following. The government vacillates on allowing it to participate in formal politics, but has demonstrated a willingness to repress it forcefully. One lesson is that it will likely only be Islamist parties that the regime feels more comfortable with (and probably not the Muslim Brotherhood) that will contribute peacefully to ending NDP hegemony and move the regime into the category of a limited multiparty regime. However, alternative Islamist or secular parties would also have to have enough popular support to convince the regime to share power.

Out of the four countries, leaders in Tunisia and Syria have been the least willing to stray from dominant-party rule—ruling parties in both countries routinely "win" more than 90 percent of the votes in multiparty elections—although a coalition of splinter groups from the RCD and the Islamist Al-Nahada pressured the regime in Tunisia in that direction in the late 1980s and early 1990s.

Given the tenacity of all four regimes, it may take a coalition of labor, business, and Islamist parties to succeed at their common goal of ending single-party dominance. That could mark a crucial step toward the evolution from a façade of multiparty politics to the limited multiparty regimes that in the majority of cases have been a harbinger of democracy.

Of course, it is also possible that a collapse or opening in the new MENA authoritarianism could go against the odds for dominant-party regimes and culminate in military or theocratic Islamic regimes. Whatever the institutional outcome of transitions from the new MENA authoritarianism, the hope is that increased attention will be paid to dimensions of life under these regimes beyond the competitiveness of their elections and the potential for radical Islamist politics.

NOTES

1. Political Openings and the Transformation of Authoritarian Rule in the Middle East and North Africa

1. Samuel Huntington, *The Third Wave: Democratization in the Late Twentieth Century* (Norman: University of Oklahoma, 1991).

2. With the exception of Tunisia, which was more moderate but also went through a period of Arab socialism, these countries have been referred to as the Radical Arab republics. The general moderation of their political systems over time is part of the story of this book.

3. Michael Hudson, "After the Gulf War: Prospects for Democratization in the Arab World," *Middle East Journal* 45:3 (1991): 408.

4. Associated Press, "Syrians Vote for Assad in Uncontested Referendum," *Washington Post*, May 28, 2007, section A.

5. Roger Owen, "The Middle Eastern State: Repositioning Not Retreat," in *The State and Global Change: The Political Economy of Transition in the Middle East and North Africa*, ed. Hassan Hakimian and Ziba Moshaver (Richmond, Va.: Curzon, 2001), 238.

6. Indeed, given the reality that the entire MENA region has remained largely authoritarian in the last four decades, it is likely that a broad range of region-specific factors and international ones that are not found grouped together in other regions account for the widespread authoritarianism that prevails in the Middle East and North Africa today. For an argument along these lines, see John Waterbury, "Democracy without Democrats: The Potential for Political Liberalization in the Middle East," in *Democracy without Democrats,*" ed. Ghassan Salame (London: I.B. Taurius, 1994), 23–47.

7. See Marsha Pripstein Posusney and Michele Penner Angrist, eds., *Authoritarianism in the Middle East* (Boulder, Colo.: Lynned Rienner Publishers, 2005).

8. Larry Diamond, "Elections without Democracy: Thinking about Hybrid Regimes," *Journal of Democracy* 13:2 (April 2002): 22.

9. Tarik Yousef, *Employment, Development, and the Social Contract in the Middle East and North Africa* (Washington, D.C.: World Bank, 2004), 6–10.

10. John Williamson was the first to use the term *Washington Consensus*. See "What Washington Means by Policy Reform," in *Latin American Adjustment*, ed. John Williamson (Washington, D.C.: Institute for International Economics, 1990), 7–20.

11. John Waterbury, "The Political Management of Adjustment and Reform," in *Fragile Coalitions: The Politics of Economic Adjustment*, ed. Joan Nelson (New

Brunswick, N.J.: Overseas Development Council, 1989), 39–56. John Waterbury did not include peasants in the old coalition or upper-echelon state agents in the newer coalition.

12. Ibid.

13. Nader Fergany (lead author, Arab Human Development Report), in an interview with the author, October 2006.

14. Anthony Shadid, "Death of a Syrian Minister Leaves a Sect adrift in Time of Strife," *Washington Post,* October 31, 2005, section A.

15. Diamond, "Elections without Democracy," 33.

16. Raymond A. Hinnebusch, "Liberalization without Democratization in 'Post-Populist' Authoritarian States," in *Citizenship and the State in the Middle East,* ed. Nils A. Butenschon, Uri Davis, and Manuel Hassassian (Syracuse, N.Y.: Syracuse University Press, 2000), 143.

17. Ibid.

18. This includes the common trend in the region for candidates to run as independents and then join the state party after winning their electoral seats.

19. Hinnebusch, "Liberalization without Democratization," 143.

20. For a seminal discussion of corporatism, see Philippe Schmitter, "Still the Century of Corporatism," *Review of Politics* 36:1 (1974): 85–131.

21. Anoushiravan Ehteshami and Emma C. Murphy, "Transformation of the Corporatist State in the Middle East," *Third World Quarterly* 17:4 (1996): 753–772.

22. Stephen J. King, *Liberalization against Democracy: The Local Politics of Economic Reform in Tunisia* (Bloomington: Indiana University Press, 2003), 76–109.

23. See Marsha Pripstein Posusney, *Labor and the State in Egypt* (New York: Columbia University Press, 1997), 5. In previous state–society clashes over economic reforms in the region, the reduction or elimination of food subsidies in the late 1970s and 1980s led to public demonstrations, and sometimes violent clashes. See David Seddon, "Winter of Discontent: Economic Crisis in Tunisia and Morocco," *MERIP Reports* 127 (October 1994): 7–16. Bread riots occurred in Egypt in 1977.

24. Nathan J. Brown, Amr Hamzawy, and Marina Ottaway, "Islamist Movements and the Democratic Process in the World: Exploring the Grey Zones" (working paper 67, Carnegie Endowment For International Peace, Washington, D.C., March 2006), 5.

25. Charles Kurzman, ed., *Liberal Islam* (New York: Oxford University Press, 1998), 4.

26. For an early analysis of some Islamic groups along these lines, see Manfred Halpern, *The Politics of Social Change in the Middle East and North Africa* (Princeton, N.J.: Princeton University Press, 1962), 134–155.

27. Marina Ottaway, Foreword, "The Other Face of the Islamist Movement," in Mustapha Kamel Al-Sayyid (working paper 23, Carnegie Endowment For International Peace, Washington, D.C., January 2003). See also Kurzman, *Liberal Islam,* 4.

28. Kurzman, *Liberal Islam,* 4.

29. Alan Richards and John Waterbury, *A Political Economy of the Middle East* (Boulder, Colo.: Westview Press, 2008), 362.

30. Waterbury, "The Political Management of Economic Adjustment and Reform," 39–56.

31. Ehteshami and Murphy, "Transformation of the Corporatist State," 764.

32. See Hesham Al-Awadi, *In Pursuit of Legitimacy: The Muslim Brothers and Mubarak, 1982–2000* (London: I.B. Tauris, 2004), 3–6. Al-Awadi refers to this as a political approach to legitimacy, which emphasizes the belief in the validity of the exercise of power by both ruler and ruled. Legitimacy is a contested concept with multiple definitions that partly depend upon the ideological orientations and professional biases of the scholars defining the concept.

33. Roger Owen, "The Middle Eastern State: Repositioning or Retreat," in Hakimian and Moshaver, *The State and Global Change,* 245.

34. King, *Liberalization against Democracy,* 76–109.

35. See Eberhard Kienle, *A Grand Delusion: Democracy and Economic Reform in Egypt,* (London: I.B. Tauris, 2001), 144–160, Ehteshami and Murphy, "Transformation of the Corporatist State in the Middle East," and Daniel Brumberg, "The Trap of Liberalized Autocracy," *Journal of Democracy* 13:4 (October 2002): 56–68.

36. This literature includes Larry Diamond, "Thinking about Hybrid Regimes." See also Steven Levitsky and Lucan Way, "The Rise of Competitive Authoritarianism," *Journal of Democracy* 13:2 (April 2002): 51–65; Andreas Schedler, "The Menu of Manipulation," *Journal of Democracy* 13:2 (April 2002): 36–50; Daniel Brumberg, "The Trap of Liberalized Autocracy"; and Marina Ottaway, *Democracy Challenged: The Rise of Semi-Authoritarianism* (Washington: Carnegie Endowment of International Peace: 2003).

37. See Gretchen Bauer and Scott Taylor, *Politics in Southern Africa: State and Society in Transition* (Boulder, Colo.: Lynne Rienner Publishers, 2005), 340–350. For an argument that state-led economic liberalization led to new opportunities for rent seeking throughout the developing world, see Steven Heydemann, ed. *Networks of Privilege in the Middle East: The Politics of Economic Reform Revisited* (New York: Palgrave Macmillan, 2004), 1–34.

2. Sustaining Authoritarianism during the Third Wave of Democracy

1. Diamond, "Elections without Democracy," 33.

2. Barbara Geddes, "Authoritarian Breakdown: Empirical Test of a Game Theoretic Argument" (paper presented at the annual meeting of the American Political Science Association, Atlanta, September 1999).

3. James Mahoney and Richard Snyder, "Rethinking Agency and Structure in the Study of Regime Change," *Studies in Comparative International Development* 34:2 (Summer 1999): 3–32.

4. Jason Brownlee, "Low Tide after the Third Wave: Exploring Politics under Authoritarianism," *Comparative Politics* 34:4 (July 2002): 33.

5. Huntington, *The Third Wave.*

6. In a comprehensive global survey of political regimes, Alex Hadenius and Jan Teorell claimed that out of the changes of regimes which occurred roughly during the period of the third wave, 1970s–1990s, 77 percent were changes from one form of authoritarianism to another, and only 23 percent were regime changes from authoritarianism to democracy. See Alex Hadenius and Jan Teorell, "Authoritarian Regimes: Stability, Change, and Pathways to Democracy" (working paper 331, Kellogg Institute, Notre Dame, 2006).

7. Guillermo O'Donnell, Philippe C. Schmitter, and Laurence Whitehead, eds., *Transitions from Authoritarian Rule* (Baltimore: Johns Hopkins University Press, 1986).

8. Guillermo O'Donnell, "Debating the Transition Paradigm: In Partial Defense of an Evanescent Paradigm," *Journal of Democracy* 13:3 (July 2002): 7.

9. Thomas Carothers, "The End of the Transition Paradigm," *Journal of Democracy* 13:1 (January 2002): 5–21.

10. See Seymour Martin Lipset, "Some Social Requisites of Democracy: Economic Development and Political Legitimacy," *American Political Science Review* 53 (March 1959): 69–105. On the development of a national political culture hospitable for the emergence and consolidation of democracy, see Gabriel A. Almond and Sidney Verba, *The Civic Culture: Political Attitudes and Democracy in Five Nations* (Princeton, N.J.: Princeton University Press, 1963).

11. Michael McFaul, "The Fourth Wave of Democracy and Dictatorship: Noncooperative Transitions in the Post-Communist World," *World Politics* 54 (January 2002): 214.

12. Ruth Berins Collier, *Paths toward Democracy: The Working Class and Elites in Western Europe and South America* (Cambridge: Cambridge University Press, 1999), 6.

13. O'Donnell and Schmitter, *Transitions from Authoritarian Rule: Tentative Conclusions about Uncertain Democracies*. Laurence Whitehead, the third editor of the four-volume series, was not an author of the "tenative conclusions" section of the study.

14. Ibid., 4.

15. See, for example, Giuseppe Di Palma, *To Craft Democracies: An Essay on Democratic Transitions* (Berkeley: University of California Press, 1991); and John Higley and Michael Burton, "The Elite Variable in Democratic Transitions and Breakdowns," *The American Sociological Review* 54:1 (February 1989): 17–32.

16. For an early effort in this direction to explain democratic transitions, see Terry Lynn Karl, "Dilemmas of Democratization in Latin America," *Comparative Politics* 23:1 (October 1990): 1–23.

17. This became a major criticism of the transitions literature, spearheaded by the founding essay of O'Donnell and Schmitter. See Carothers, "The End of the Transition Paradigm," a point also made by Marina Ottaway for the transitions literature that followed O'Donnell and Schmitter's foundational work. See Ottaway, *Democracy Challenged*, 10–12.

18. Mahoney and Snyder, "Rethinking Agency and Structure in the Study of Regime Change."

19. Ibid., 10.

20. Ibid., 12–13

21. Ibid., 24.

22. For an early example see Anne Swidler, "Culture in Action: Symbols and Strategies," *American Sociological Review* 51:2 (April 1986): 273–286.

23. Ibid.

24. Some of these challenges were becoming evident in the 1980s; however, the acceleration of privatization in the 1990s also accelerated the transformation of the social base of the regimes and a fuller shift to multipartyism as a basis for regime legitimation. Many of these challenges and the responses to them are com-

mon to populist single-party regimes elsewhere. See Ruth Berins Collier, "The Transformation of Labor-based One Partyism at the End of the Twentieth Century," in *The Awkward Embrace: One-Party Domination and Democracy,* ed. Hermann Gilomee and Charles Simkins (Amsterdam: Harwood, 1999), 219–224.

25. A shared-growth marketizing approach based on targeting small and medium enterprises and the small peasantry in the new economic policies was apparently not considered. This approach was implemented in East Asia. See King, *Liberalization against Democracy,* 12–20.

26. Benjamin Smith, "Life of the Party: The Origins of Regime Breakdown and Persistence under Single-Party Rule," *World Politics* 57:3 (April 2005): 421–451.

27. Single-party rule that evolves to include multiparty, though uncompetitive, politics, may serve as a staging ground for substantive democratization. This possibility is explored in the conclusion of this book. See Hadenius and Toerell, "Authoritarian Regimes: Stability, Change, and Pathways to Democracy, 1972–2003." Along the lines of limited multiparty politics as a gateway to democracy, see also Beatriz Magaloni, *Voting for Autocracy: Hegemonic Party Survival and Its Demise in Mexico* (Cambridge: Cambridge University Press, 2006). For multiple-case studies of single-party regimes as potential democratizing agents in the long term, see Gilomee and Simkins, eds., *Awkward Embrace.*

28. Posusney and Angrist, eds., *Authoritarianism in the Middle East.*

29. Marsha Pripstein Posusney, "Multiparty Elections in the Arab World: Election Rules and Opposition Responses," in *Authoritarianism in the Middle East,* ed. Posusney and Angrist, 91–118.

30. Ellen Lust-Okar, "Opposition and Economic Crisis in Jordan and Morocco," in *Authoritarianism in the Middle East,* ed. Posusney and Angrist, 143–168. For an earlier argument about opposition support for authoritarian rule due to the goals that some opposition forces can achieve by political participation within state-designated parameters, see I. William Zartman, "Opposition As Support of the State," in *Beyond Coercion: The Durability of the Arab State,* ed. Adeed Dawisha and I. William Zartman (London: Croom Helm, 1988), 61–87.

31. Eva Bellin, "Coercive Institutions and Coercive Leaders," in *Authoritarianism in the Middle East,* ed. Posusney and Angrist, 21–42.

32. Jason Brownlee, "Political Crisis and Restabilization: Iraq, Libya, Syria, and Tunisia," in *Authoritarianism in the Middle East,* ed. Posusney and Angrist, 43–62.

33. Lisa Weeden, "Conceptualizing Culture: Possibilities for Political Science," *American Political Science Review* 96:4 (December 2002): 713–728.

34. Hisham Sharabi, *Neopatriarchy: A Theory of Distorted Change in Arab Society* (Oxford: Oxford University Press, 1988).

35. Hazem Beblawi and Giacomo Luciani, eds., *The Rentier State in the Arab World* (London: Croom Helm, 1987).

36. Eva Bellin, *Stalled Democracy: Capital, Labor, and the Paradox of State-Sponsored Development* (Ithaca, N.Y: Cornell University Press, 2002). Bellin's analysis did not include the privatization of state assets as a new way for the state to sponsor the bourgeoisie nor single-party institutions as the mechanism to control the alienated "labor aristocracy." Peasants and large landowner–landlords were not part of her compelling analysis.

37. Waterbury, "Democracy without Democrats," 23–47.

38. In the language of the funnel approach, new sources of economic patronage

can be considered a domestic structural variable and also a macro-structural variable if a pattern of patronage is considered to be a historically specific phenomenon that can replace some conceptualizations of culture.

39. Waterbury, "Democracy without Democrats."

40. Barbara Geddes, "What Do We Know about Democratization after Twenty Years?," *Annual Review of Political Science* 2 (1999): 369–404.

41. Ibid. Geddes also includes amalgams or hybrids of these three generic types.

42. Ibid.

43. Stephan Haggard and Robert Kaufman, *The Political Economy of Democratic Transitions* (Princeton, N.J.: Princeton University Press, 1995), 267–306. An early literature on authoritarianism also noted the resilience of single-party regimes during periods of rapid socioeconomic modernization and economic distress. See Samuel Huntington and Clement H. Moore, *Authoritarian Politics in Modern Societies: The Dynamics of Established One-Party Systems* (New York: Basic Books, 1970).

44. Dafna Hochman, "Divergent Democratization: The Paths of Tunisia, Morocco, and Mauritania," *Middle East Policy* 14:4 (Winter 2007): 75.

45. Geddes, "What Do We Know about Democratization."

46. Juan Linz and H. Chehabi, eds. *Sultanistic Regimes* (Baltimore: Johns Hopkins University Press, 1998).

47. Geddes, "What Do We Know about Democratization."

48. Hadenius and Teorell, "Authoritarian Regimes," 4.

49. Jason Brownlee, "Ruling Parties and Durable Authoritarianism" (working paper, Center on Democracy, Development, and the Rule of Law, Stanford University, 2004).

50. James V. Jesudan, "The Resilience of One-Party Dominance in Malaysia and Singapore," in *Awkward Embrace,* ed. Gilomee and Simkins, 127–172. See also King, *Liberalization against Democracy,* 25–42.

51. Though during some periods of their evolution, personalist regimes may have the resource of people's adoration of a chieftain, *za'im.*

52. Michael Bratton and Nicolas van de Walle view patronage politics as the modal form of African politics. See "Neopatrimonial Regimes and Political Transitions in Africa," *World Politics* 46: 4 (July 1994): 453–489. The MENA bureaucratic and administrative apparatus is less prone to personalism and the regimes also rely on state corporatist arrangements to rule heavily, which is not the case in Sub-Saharan Africa. Overall, the MENA regimes have had longer periods of institutionalized authoritarian rule.

53. Only Algeria, of the four cases analyzed here, depends primarily on oil and natural gas.

54. Eva Bellin, "The Political-Economic Conundrum: The Affinity of Economic and Political Reform in the Middle East and North Africa" (working paper 53, Carnegie Endowment for International Peace, Washington, D.C., 2004), 12.

55. James Bill and Robert Springborg, *Politics in the Middle East* (New York: Longman, 2000), 112–130.

56. David Waldner, *State Building and Late Development* (Ithaca, N.Y.: Cornell University Press, 1999), 39.

57. Gordon Tullock, "The Welfare Cost of Tariffs, Monopolies, and Theft," *Western Economic Journal* 5:3 (1967): 224–232; and Anne Krueger, "The Political

Economy of the Rent-Seeking Society," *American Economic Review* 64:3 (June 1974): 291–303.

58. See also Hector Schamis, *Reforming the State: The Politics of Privatization in Latin America and Europe* (Ann Arbor: University of Michigan Press, 2002), 4.

59. See Steven Heydemann, ed., *Networks of Privilege*.

3. The Old Authoritarianism

1. Posusney, *Labor and the State in Egypt*, 3.

2. Aristide R. Zolberg, *Creating Political Order: The Party States of West Africa* (Chicago: McNally, 1966), 37–65.

3. Schmitter, "Still the Century of Corporatism?"

4. See Arthur Goldschmidt Jr., *Modern Egypt: The Formation of a Nation State* (Boulder, Colo.: Westview Press, 2004), 53–82.

5. Ibid.

6. Ibid., 67–78.

7. Robert Vitalis, *When Capitalists Collide: Business Conflict and the End of Empire in Egypt* (Berkeley: University of California Press, 1995), 22–26.

8. Ibid., 25.

9. Ibid., 25–26.

10. Joel Beinin, *Workers and Peasants in the Modern Middle East* (Cambridge: Cambridge University Press 2001,), p. 114.

11. Ibid., 118.

12. Richard Mitchell, *The Society of the Muslim Brothers* (Oxford: Oxford University Press, 1969), 1–12.

13. Ibid., 7–8.

14. Ibid., 14.

15. Ibid., 12.

16. Goldschmidt, *Modern Egypt*, 103.

17. There were actually three attempts by Nasser to create a state party. The ASU was the most successful of these efforts.

18. Goldschmidt, *Modern Egypt*, 13.

19. Patrick Seale, *Asad: The Struggle for the Middle East* (Berkeley: University of California Press, 1988), 45.

20. Ibid., 42.

21. Philip S. Khoury, "The Syrian Independence Movement and the Growth of Economic Nationalism in Damascus," *British Society of Middle Eastern Studies Bulletin* 14:1 (1988): 25–36.

22. Ibid., 19.

23. Raymond Hinnebusch, "Revisionist Dreams, Realist Strategies: The Foreign Policy of Syria," in *The Foreign Policies of the Arab States: The Challenge of Change*, ed. Bahgat Korany and Ali E. Hillal Dessouki (Boulder, Colo.: Westview Press, 1991), 374.

24. Flynne Leverett, *Inheriting Syria* (Washington, D.C.: Brookings Institution, 2005), 2.

25. Beinin, *Workers and Peasants*, 49.

26. Fredrick Highland, "Night Falls on Damascus," http://frederickhighland .com/damascus/articles/lastking.htm (accessed July 15, 2007).

27. Khoury, *Syrian Political Culture: A Historical Perspective*, 22–23.

28. Ibid.

29. Khoury, "The Syrian Independence Movement," 26.

30. Steven Heydemann, *Authoritarianism in Syria: Institutions and Social Conflict, 1946–1970* (Ithaca, N.Y.: Cornell University Press, 1999), 47.

31. Ibid.

32. Ibid., 47–54.

33. Seale, *Asad: The Struggle for the Middle East*, 26. Zaqi-Al-Arsuzi of Antioch was heavily harassed by the French authorities. French suppression restricted his capacity to spur the new nationalist movement. Aflaq and Bitar fared better in this regard.

34. Ibid., 29.

35. Ibid., 30–31.

36. Beinin, *Workers and Peasants*, 121.

37. Ibid.

38. Ibid.

39. Seale, *Asad: The Struggle for the Middle East*, 50.

40. Ibid.

41. Ibid., 54.

42. Ibid.

43. Ibid., 65.

44. Ibid., 58.

45. Ibid., 60–64.

46. Ibid., 60.

47. In addition to French settlers, there were significant numbers of Italian and Spanish settlers seeking better opportunities. These colons later became French citizens; gradually, French became the primary language of their descendants.

48. John Ruedy, *Modern Algeria: The Origins and Development of a Nation* (Bloomington: Indiana University Press, 1992), 74.

49. For this periodization and a more detailed discussion of the Algerian nationalist movement, see Ruedy, *Modern Algeria*, 114–155.

50. Ibid., 99–100.

51. Algerian nationalists resisted colonization heroically. French conquest was not completed until resistance forces led by Sufi Brotherhood leader 'Abd al Qadir were defeated in the 1870s.

52. Ruedy, *Modern Algeria*, 115.

53. Ibid., 131.

54. Ibid., 132.

55. During World War I this party moved to a separatist position.

56. Ruedy, *Modern Algeria*, 137.

57. Ibid., 143.

58. On the Destour party, see Clement Henry Moore, *Tunisia since Independence* (Berkeley: University of California Press, 1965), 27–40; and Leon Carl Brown, "Stages in the Process of Change," in *Tunisia: The Politics of Modernization*, ed. C. A. Micaud (New York: Praeger, 1964), 41. See also Stephen J. King, "Economic Reform and Tunisia's Hegemonic Party: The End of the Administrative Elite," *Arab Studies Quarterly*, 20:2 (Spring 1998): 59–87.

59. Brown, "Stages in the Process of Change," 41.

60. Reynold Dahl, "Agricultural Development Strategies in a Small Economy: The Case of Tunisia" (staff paper, USAID, 1971), 32–33.

61. In this way the Neo-Destour leadership resembled nationalist parties' leaders in West Africa. See Zolberg, *Creating Political Order,* 12.

62. While these new elites of rural origin were important and are emphasized in the literature on Tunisian politics, 35 percent of the Neo-Destour leadership came from Tunis. See Elbaki Hermassi, *Leadership and National Development in North Africa* (Berkeley: University of California Press), 118.

63. Henry De Montety, "Old Families and New Elites in Tunisia," in *Man, State, and Society in the Contemporary Maghrib,* ed. William Zartmen (New York: Praeger, 1973), 176.

64. Hermassi, *Leadership and National Development,* 126.

65. Ibid., 125.

66. For further details of the organization of the Neo-Destour before and after independence, see Moore, *Tunisia since Independence,* 107–158.

67. Letter from Hedi Nouira to Habib Bourguiba, June 1936, from the prosecution dossier presented February 6, 1939, on French Colonial Courts of Justice, quoted in Hermassi, *Leadership and National Development,* 126–127.

68. John Waterbury, *The Egypt of Nasser and Sadat: The Political Economy of Two Regimes* (Princeton: Princeton University Press, 1983), 312.

69. Ibid., 313.

70. Ibid., 322.

71. Ibid.

72. Waterbury, *The Egypt of Nasser and Sadat,* 315.

73. Posusney, *Labor and the State in Egypt,* 43.

74. Joel Beinin, "Egyptian Textile Workers: From Craft Artisans Facing European Competition to Proletarians Contending with the State" (paper presented at the National Overview Egypt Textile Conference IISH, November 11–13, 2004).

75. Posusney, *Labor and the State in Egypt,* 63.

76. Ibid., 76.

77. Ibid., 87.

78. Ibid.

79. Ibid., 86.

80. Waterbury, *The Egypt of Nasser and Sadat,* 9.

81. Ibid. At first there were nine members of the RCC. Five were added later.

82. Ibid., 42.

83. Ibid., 9.

84. Robert Springborg, *Mubarak's Egypt: Fragmentation of the Political Order* (Boulder, Colo.: Westview Press, 1989), 33.

85. The rent-seeking context described in this section is the one that neoclassical political economy associates with statist regimes.

86. Waterbury, *The Egypt of Nasser and Sadat,* 48.

87. Ray Bush," Mubarak's Legacy for Egypt's Rural Poor: Returning Land to the Landowners" (working paper, UNDP Land, Poverty and Public Action Policy Paper No. 10, New York, August 2005).

88. El-Ghonemy, M. Riad, *The Political Economy of Rural Poverty; The Case for Land Reform* (New York: Routledge, 1990), 226–227.

89. Beinin, *Workers and Peasants,* 132. Ansari, on the other hand, challenges

this prevailing view and argues that many pre-revolutionary powerful landholders maintained their resources and power under Nasser. See Hamied Ansari, *Egypt: The Stalled Society* (Albany: State University of New York), 97–141.

90. El-Ghonemy, *The Political Economy of Rural Poverty*, 227–231.

91. Beinin, *Workers and Peasants*, 132.

92. Waterbury, *The Egypt of Nasser and Sadat*, 4–5.

93. Yahya Sadowski, *Political Vegetables? Businessman and Bureaucrat in the Development of Egyptian Agriculture* (Washington, D.C.: The Brookings Institution, 1991), 64–66.

94. Ibid., 67–71. See also Bush, "Mubarak's Legacy for Egypt's Rural Poor," 6.

95. Sadowski, *Political Vegetables*, 67–71.

96. Waterbury, *The Egypt of Nasser and Sadat*, 67.

97. Ibid., 72.

98. Ibid., 76.

99. Mark Cooper, *The Transformation of Egypt* (Baltimore: Johns Hopkins University Press, 1982), 17.

100. This group can also be described as a state bourgeoisie, an administrative elite, or managerial and technocratic elite that formed a new class under statist policies. See Robert Springborg, *Mubarak's Egypt*, 78. Egypt's rural middle class played an important role in the literature on Egypt under Nasser. Defined by Leonard Binder as a group of strategically situated traditional elites who were well-to-do peasants and rural notability, but not the largest of landowners, it included the village headman or *umda*, the *shuyukh* of districts, and other village notables that held between 10 and 50 feddans (1.0 acres = 1.038 feddans) of land. Binder claims that Nasser and many of the Free Officers and other ruling elites in the revolution came from that class; he implies that the Egyptian state under Nasser developed policies to serve its interests. See Leonard Binder, *In a Moment of Enthusiasm: Political Power and the Second Stratum in Egypt* (Chicago: Chicago University Press, 1978), 28. John Waterbury later established that the land interests of the rural middle class were cut dramatically by the regime's reforms. In its autonomy from classes, including its own, those at the helm of the state under Nasser can be described as a state bourgeoisie or an administrative elite. See Waterbury, *The Egypt of Nasser and Sadat*, 274–277.

101. Waterbury, *The Egypt of Nasser and Sadat*, 28.

102. Ibid., 59.

103. Ibid.

104. Ibid., 70.

105. Ibid.

106. Cooper, *The Transformation of Egypt*, 19.

107. Ahmed Akhtar et al., "The Egyptian Food Subsidy System" (Washington, D.C.: International Food Policy Research Institute), 5–6.

108. Waterbury, *The Egypt of Nasser and Sadat*, 338–342.

109. Beinin, *Workers and Peasants*, 15.

110. Waterbury, *The Egypt of Nasser and Sadat*, 341.

111. Ibid., 341–342.

112. Mitchell, *The Society of the Muslim Brothers*, 140.

113. Smith, "Life of the Party," 422.

114. Seale, *Asad: The Struggle for the Middle East*, 29.

115. Ibid., 87.

116. The remainder of this discussion on Syrian institutions relies on Seale, *Asad: The Struggle for the Middle East,* 74–103 and 170–175.

117. Ibid. See also Heydemann, *Authoritarianism in Syria,* 197–200.

118. Heydemann, *Authoritarianism in Syria,* 197–200. See also Elizabeth Longuenesse, "Labor in Syria: The Emergence of New Identities," in *The Social History of Labor in the Middle East,* ed. Ellis Goldberg (Boulder, Colo.: Westview Press, 1996), 103–112.

119. David Waldner, *State Building and Late Development,* 86.

120. Ibid. See also Heydemann, *Authoritarianism in Syria,* 197–200.

121. Longuenesse, "Labor in Syria," 121.

122. Ibid., 123.

123. Nadia Forni, "Land Tenure Systems: Structural Features and Policies," (FAO report, GCP/SYR/006/ITA, Demascus Syria, March 2001), 8.

124. Ibid.

125. Beinin, *Workers and Peasants,* 120.

126. Volker Perthes, "The Syrian Private Industrial and Commercial Sectors and the State," *International Journal of Middle East Studies* 24:2 (May 1992): 208.

127. Ibid., 209.

128. For details, see Waldner, *State Building and Late Development,* 119–122.

129. Ibid., 119.

130. Nikolaos Van Dam, *The Struggle for Power in Syria: Politics and Society under Asad and the Ba'th party* (London: I.B. Tauris, 1996), 61.

131. Raymond Hinnebusch, *Peasant and Bureaucracy in Ba'thist Syria: The Political Economy of Rural Development* (Boulder, Colo.: Westview Press, 1989); Volker Perthes, *The Political Economy of Syria under Asad* (London: Tairus, 1995).

132. Hanna Batatu, *Syria's Peasantry, the Descendants of Its Lesser Rural Notables, and Their Politics* (Princeton, N.J.: Princeton University Press, 1999).

133. Clement Henry and Robert Springborg, *Globalization and the Politics of Development in the Middle East* (Cambridge: Cambridge University Press, 2001), 126.

134. Gary Gambill, "The Political Obstacles to Economic Reform in Syria." *Middle East Intelligence Bulletin* 3:7 (July 2001), http://www.meib.org/articles/0107_s1.htm (accessed October 8, 2008).

135. Raymond Hinnebusch, *Authoritarian Power and State Formation in Ba'thist Syria: Army, Party, Peasant* (Boulder, Colo.: Westview Press, 1989), 197–220.

136. Waldner, *State Building and Late Development,* 6.

137. Seale, *Asad: The Struggle for the Middle East,* 31.

138. On the fierce Arab state, see Nazih H. Ayoubi, *Over-Stating the Arab State: Politics and Society in the Middle East* (New York: I.B. Tauris, 1995).

139. Seale, *Asad: The Struggle for the Middle East,* 92.

140. Ibid., 92–93.

141. Ibid., 163.

142. Others put the figure at between 300,000 and 600,000. See John Ruedy, *Modern Algeria,* 190.

143. Ibid., 60.

144. Ibid., 61.

145. Ibid., 67.

146. Ibid., 138.

147. Peter Knauss, "Algeria's Revolution: Peasants Control or Control of Peasants," *African Studies Review* 20:3 (December 1977): 65–78.

148. Ibid., 72.

149. Ibid., 173.

150. Ibid., 129.

151. Ibid., 131.

152. At independence, the upper class in the cities numbered about 50,000 entrepreneurs, landlords, upper managers, and professionals. There also remained several thousand families in the countryside with estates larger than 100 hectares. See Ruedy, *Modern Algeria,* 214.

153. David Ottaway and Marina Ottaway, *Algeria: The Politics of a Socialist Revolution* (Berkeley: University of California Press, 1970), 6.

154. Ruedy, *Modern Algeria,* 206–207.

155. John Entelis, *Algeria: The Revolution Institutionalized* (Boulder, Colo.: Westview Press, 1986), 162. Hugh Roberts, "The Politics of Algerian Socialism," in *North Africa: Contemporary Politics and Economic Development,* ed. Richard Lawless and Allan Findlay (New York: St. Martin's Press, 1984), 40.

156. Thomas Blair, *Auto-Gestion: The Land to Those Who Work It* (New York: Doubleday, 1969).

157. Ruedy, *Modern Algeria,* 216.

158. Ibid., 135.

159. Ibid., 133.

160. Ibid.

161. Ruedy, 222–223.

162. Knauss, "Algeria's Revolution: Peasants Control or Control of Peasants," 76.

163. Ibid.

164. Entelis, *Algeria: The Revolution Institutionalized,* 1.

165. Ibid., 69–90.

166. Ibid., 127.

167. Moore, *Tunisia since Independence,* 71–104. For a general discussion of steps frequently taken to establish single-party rule in newly independent developing countries, see Zolberg, *Creating Political Order,* 66–67.

168. Moore, *Tunisia since Independence,* 86.

169. Ibid., 108.

170. Alan Richards and John Waterbury, *A Political Economy of the Middle East* (Boulder, Colo.: Westview, 1996), 314.

171. Ibid., 235–236.

172. *State capitalism* would have been a more accurate term.

173. Lisa Anderson, *The State and Social Transformation in Tunisia and Libya* (Princeton, N.J.: Princeton University Press, 1986), 237.

174. Farther east *habous* is called *waqf.* This form of land tenure for individuals endows the land for the family until the line dies out, when it serves as a charitable institution. Religious *habous* has both charitable functions and serves as the patrimony of religious leaders.

175. Hermassi, *Leadership and National Development,* 186.

176. El Ghonemy M. Riad, *Land, Food and Rural Development in North Africa* (Boulder, Colo.: Westview Press, 1993), 55.

177. Ibid.

178. Iliya Harik, "Privatization and Development in Tunisia," in *Privatization and Liberalization in the Middle East*, ed. Iliya Harik and Denis J. Sullivan (Bloomington: Indiana University Press, 1992).

179. Ibid., 210–230; see also Boyan Belev, "Privatization in Egypt and Tunisia: Liberal Outcomes and/or Liberal Policies?" *Mediterranean Politics* 6:2 (Summer 2001): 68–103; and Bellin, *Stalled Democracy,* 21.

180. Bellin, *Stalled Democracy,* 21–22.

181. Harik, "Privatization and Development in Tunisia," 211.

182. Ibid.

183. Christopher Alexander, "Labor Code Reform in Tunisia," *Mediterranean Politics* 6:2 (Summer 2001): 108–109.

184. James Buchanan, "Rent Seeking and Profit Seeking," in *Toward a Theory of the Rent-Seeking Society,* ed. James Buchanan, Robert Tollison, and Gordan Tullock (College Station: Texas A&M University Press, 1980), 9; and John Waterbury, "The Heart of the Matter? Public Enterprise and the Adjustment Process," in *The Politics of Economic Adjustment,* ed. Stephan Haggard and Robert Kaufman (Princeton, N.J.: Princeton University Press, 1992), 186.

185. Al-Awadi, *In Pursuit of Legitimacy.*

186. Anderson, *The State and Social Transformation in Tunisia and Libya,* 232–233.

187. *Time Magazine,* "Defying Nasser," Monday, October 27, 1958.

188. Anderson, *The State and Social Transformation in Tunisia and Libya,* 169–177.

189. Susan E. Marshall and Randall G. Stokes, "Tradition and the Veil: Female Status in Tunisia and Algeria," *Journal of Modern African Studies* 19:4 (December 1981): 625–646.

190. Lisa Anderson, "The State in the Middle East and North Africa," *Comparative Politics* 20:1 (October 1987): 2.

191. Waterbury, *The Egypt of Nasser and Sadat,* 63.

192. Ellis Goldberg, "The Foundations of State–Labor Relations in Contemporary Egypt," *Comparative Politics* 24:2 (January 1992): 154.

193. Ibid., 157.

194. Ibid., 154.

195. Hans Lofren, "Economic Policy in Egypt: A Breakdown in Reform Resistance?" *International Journal of Middle East Studies* 25:3 (1993): 407.

196. Waterbury, *The Egypt of Nasser and Sadat,* 130.

197. Lofren, "Economic Policy in Egypt," 407.

198. Yoram Meital, "The Struggle over Political Order in Egypt: The 2005 Elections," *Middle East Journal* 60:2 (Spring 2006): 258.

199. Moheb Zaki, *Civil Society and Democratization in Egypt, 1981–1994* (Cairo: Ibn Khaldun Center, 1994), 18; and Raymond Hinnebusch, "The Foreign Policy of Egypt," in *The Foreign Policies of Middle East States,* ed. Raymond Hinnebusch and Anoushiravan Ehteshami (Boulder, Colo.: Lynne Rienner, 2002), 98.

200. See Waterbury, *The Egypt of Nasser and Sadat,* 354–388; Roger Owen, "Socio-economic Change and Political Mobilization: The Case of Egypt," in Salame, ed., *Democracy without Democrats,* 183–199; Richard Burrell and Abbas Kelidar,

"The Washington Papers: Egypt: The Dilemma of a Nation, 1970–1977" (report 48, The Center for Strategic and International Studies, Georgetown University, Washington D.C., 1977).

201. Zaki, *Civil Society and Democratization in Egypt*, 77.

202. Waterbury, *The Egypt of Nasser and Sadat*, 354.

203. Ibid., 366.

204. Ibid., 368.

205. "New Cabinet Sworn In," *World News Digest*, November 13, 1976.

206. Nabil Sukkor, "The Crisis of 1986 and Syria's Plan for Reform," in *Contemporary Syria: Liberalization between Cold War and Cold Peace*, ed. Eberhard Kienle (London: University of London, 1994), 42.

207. Volker Perthes, "Stages of Economic and Political Liberalization" in Kienle, ed. *Contemporary Syria: Liberalization Between Cold War and Cold Peace*, 44.

208. Raymond Hinnebusch, "Syria: The Politics of Economic Liberalization," *Third World Quarterly* 18:2 (1997): 254.

209. Perthes, "Stages of Economic and Political Liberalization."

210. Ibid., 45.

211. Ibid.; and Sukkor, "The Crisis of 1986 and Syria's Plan for Reform," 26–27.

212. Ibid.

213. Perthe, "Stages of Economic and Political Liberalization," 50.

214. Asad speech quoted in Perthe, "Stages of Economic and Political Liberalization," 65.

215. Patrick Seale, *Asad: The Struggle for the Middle East*, 92–93.

216. Ibid., 327.

217. Ibid., 334.

218. Perthes, "Stages of Economic and Political Liberalization," 64.

219. For a full account of the cooperative movement, see King, *Liberalization against Democracy*, 42–75.

220. See Mohamed Elhachmi Hamdi, *The Politicization of Islam: A Case Study of Tunisia* (Boulder, Colo.: Westview, 1998).

221. Anderson, *The State and Social Transformation*, 247–248.

4. The New Authoritarianism

1. Steven Heydemann, introduction to *Networks of Privilege*, 6.

2. There were brief periods when the U.S. administration under George Bush pressured Mubarak to implement democratic reforms, but overall U.S. policy has not sided with the democratic opposition in Egypt.

3. Marsha Pripstein Posusney, "Enduring Authoritarianism: Middle East Lessons for Comparative Theory," *Comparative Politics* 36:2 (2004): 128.

4. Zeinab Abul-Magd, "Law and Economy in Egypt: Socioeconomic Realities of the New Parliament," *Economic and Business Research Centre Chronicles, American University in Cairo* 1:3 (January 2006): 30–33.

5. Haytham Jabr, "Businessmen and Politics in Egypt," *Ahwal Misriyya* 21 (2003): 128–138.

6. Ibid.

7. Virginie Collombier, "The Internal Stakes of the 2005 Elections: The Struggle for Influence in Egypt's National Democratic Party," *Middle East Journal*

61:1 (2007): 97. On internal debate and the refashioning of elite consensus within the NDP, see also Jason Brownlee, "Ruling Parties and Regime Persistence: Explaining Authoritarianism in the Third Wave," Unpublished (2005).

8. Collombier, "Internal Stakes of the 2005 Elections," 98–99.

9. Amr Hamzawy, "Opposition in Egypt: Performance in the Presidential Election and Prospects for the Parliamentary Elections," Policy Outlook 22 (Washington, D.C.: Carnegie Endowment for International Peace, 2005); Issandr El Amrani, comment on "76," The Arabist blog, comment posted November 28, 2005, http://arabist.net/archives/2005/11/28/76/ (accessed October 8, 2008).

10. *Report on Presidential Elections* (Cairo: The Land Center for Human Rights, 2006).

11. Samer Soliman, "Political Participation in the 2005 Parliamentary Elections," The Egyptian Association for Community Enhancement," 68–69.

12. Ibid., 66.

13. *Report on the Parliamentary Elections* (Cairo: Land Center for Human Rights).

14. Ibid.

15. Ibid.

16. Federal Research Division, *Government and Politics of Egypt* (Washington, D.C.: U.S. Library of Congress), http://countrystudies.us/egypt/121.htm (accessed October 8, 2008).

17. Ibid.

18. Ibid.

19. *Report on the Parliamentary Elections* (Cairo: Land Center for Human Rights).

20. Ibid., 4.

21. Ahmad Thabit, "Idarat Tanzim al-Dawa'ir al-Intikhabiyya" (The Management and Organization of Electoral Constituencies), in *Nuzum Idarat al-Intikhabat fi Misr* (The Systems of Election Management in Egypt), ed. Amr Hashim Rabi' (Cairo: Markaz al Dirasat al-Siyasiyya wa-al-Istraigiyya, 2006), 123–143.

22. Ibid.

23. Amr Hamzawy, entry on "Egypt: Dynamics of Regime and Opposition," The Bitterlemons International blog, posted September 30, 2005, http://www.bitterlemons-international.org/previous.php?opt=1&id=104 (accessed October 8, 2008).

24. Ibid. and Meital, "The Struggle over Political Order in Egypt," 257–279.

25. Meital, "Political Order in Egypt," 258.

26. Ray Bush, "Market Violence in Egypt's Countryside," *Peace Review: A Journal of Social Justice* 19:1 (2007): 15–21.

27. Larry Diamond, *Developing Democracy: Toward Consolidation* (Baltimore: Johns Hopkins University Press, 1999), 236–237.

28. Beinin, "Egyptian Textile Workers," 17.

29. According to Marsha Pripstein Posusney, labor protests against privatization have been much stronger than against other economic reforms, partly because of nationalist sentiments. See "Egyptian Labor Struggle in the Era of Privatization: The Moral Economy Thesis Revisited," in *Privatization and Labor: Responses and Consequences in Global Perspective,* ed. Marsha Pripstein Posusney and Linda J. Cook (Cheltenham: Edward Elgar, 2002), 43.

30. Ibid., 17–18.

31. Joel Beinin and Hossam el-Hamalawy, "Strikes in Egypt Spread from Center

of Gravity," *Middle East Report Online* (May 2007), http://www.merip.org/mero/mero050907.html.

32. Paul Schemm, "Labor Movement Possible Future for Egypt Opposition" (includes an interview with Joel Beinin, Head of the Middle East Studies Department at the American University in Cairo), in *Middle East Times,* April 26, 2007.

33. Ibid.

34. Ibid.

35. Ibid., and Dina Khalifa Hussein, "Egyptian Workers Object! Resurgent Workers' Protests Make Deadline News," *Economic and Business Research Centre Chronicles, American University in Cairo* 1:2 (2005): 19–21.

36. Ibid.

37. Human Rights Watch, "Group Protests Harassment of Labor Union," April 26, 2007.

38. Ibid.

39. Beinin and el-Hamalawy, "Strikes in Egypt Spread."

40. Ibid.

41. Marsha Pripstein Posusney, "Egyptian Privatization: New Challenges for the Left," *Middle East Report* 210 (1999): 38–40.

42. Ibid.

43. "Misr tahtafil bi-id al-umaal" (includes text of President's Speech on Labor Day), *Al-Ahram,* 28 April 2006.

44. Bush, "Mubarak's Legacy for Egypt's Rural Poor."

45. *Report on Peasants* (Cairo: The Land Center for Human Rights, 2006).

46. Caroline Tingay, "Law 1996 of 1992: The Government's 'Serious Commitment to Implementation,'" 2.

47. Bush, "Mubarak's Legacy for Egypt's Rural Poor," 13.

48. Ibid., 32.

49. Ibid.

50. Ibid.

51. Ibid.

52. Ibid.

53. Ibid.

54. Tingay, "Law 1996 of 1992."

55. Ibid.

56. Ibid.

57. Ibid.

58. *Report on Peasants* (Cairo: Land Center for Human Rights).

59. Bush, "Mubarak's Legacy for Egypt's Rural Poor."

60. Tingay, "Law 1996 of 1992."

61. Bush, "Mubarak's Legacy for Egypt's Rural Poor," 20.

62. Ibid.

63. Joel Beinin, "Political Islam and the New Global Economy," *New Centennial Review* 5:1 (2005): 119.

64. Ibid., 125.

65. Ibid., 119.

66. Carrie Rosefsky Wickham, "The Path to Moderation: Strategy and Learning in the Formation of Egypt's Wasat Party," *Comparative Politics* 36:2 (2004): 208.

67. Ibid.

68. Beinin, "Political Islam and the New Global Economy," 125.

69. Ibid.

70. Ibid.

71. Ibid.

72. Derek Hopwood, *Egypt: Politics and Society, 1945–1990* (London: Harper Collins Academic, 1991), 187.

73. Owen, "Socio-economic Change and Political Mobilization," 189.

74. Ibid., 191–197.

75. Ibid.

76. Marsha Priptstein Posusney, "Behind the Ballot Box: Electoral Engineering in the Arab World," *Middle East Report* 209 (1998): 12–16.

77. Beinin, "Political Islam and the New Global Economy," 125.

78. Hosni Mubarak, "They Will Never Come to Power" (interview by Lally Weymouth), *Newsweek,* June 19, 1995.

79. Kienle, *A Grand Delusion,* 155.

80. Schedler, "Menu of Manipulation," 46–50.

81. "Egypt's Elections: A Triumph for Democracy or Thuggery?," *Mideast Mirror,* November 30, 1995.

82. Beinin, "Political Islam and the New Global Economy," 125.

83. Vickie Langohr, "Cracks in Egypt's Electoral Engineering: The 2000 Vote," *Middle East Report Online* (November 7, 2000), http://www.merip.org/mero/mero110700.html (accessed April 4, 2007).

84. Ibid.

85. *Democratic Governance/Elections: Egypt* (New York: United Nations Development Programme), 2007.

86. Osama El-Ghazali Harb, "Democracy and Its Discontents," *Al-Ahram Weekly,* December 28, 2000.

87. Hosni Mubarak, "Egypt's Parliament, Representing All Categories and Parties" (includes text of speech by President Hosni Mubarak), in *Arabic News,* September 21, 2000.

88. "Democracy in Iran Prompts Arab Introspection; Neighbors Will Scrutinize Their Ways Next, Analysts Say," *Washington Post,* March 10, 2000, section A.

89. Langohr, "Cracks In Egypt's Electoral Engineering."

90. "Doubts over NDP Reform Motives," *Oxford Analytica,* November 17, 2003.

91. Mona El-Ghobashy, "Egypt Looks Ahead to Portentous Year," *Middle East Report Online* (February 2, 2005), http://www.merip.org/mero/mero020205.html (accessed April 4, 2007).

92. Ibid.

93. Mustafa al-Sa'id, "Al-siyasat-al-iqtisadiyya lil-hukuma: Al-furas wa-altahdi-iyyat" (The Economic Policy of the Government), in *Taqrir al-Ittijahat al-Iqtisadiyya al-Istratijiyya,* ed. Ahmadd al Syyid al-Najjar (Cairo: Markaz al-Dirasat al-Siyasiyya wa-al-Istratijiyya, 2005), 19–29.

94. Ibid.

95. Gary Gambill, "Jumpstarting Arab Reform: The Bush Administration's Greater Middle East Initiative," *Middle East Intelligence Bulletin* 6:6–7 (2004): 1–4.

96. Mohammed Shakeel, "Election 2005: Egypt's Ruling Party Rattled by Impressive Opposition Gains," *World Markets Analysis,* December 9, 2005.

97. Gambill, "Jumpstarting Arab Reform."

98. Ibid.

99. El-Ghobashy, "Egypt Looks Ahead."

100. Ibid.

101. Larry Diamond, "Democracy Remains the People's Choice," *Straits Times* (Singapore), September 11, 2006.

102. Amy Hawthorne, "At the Bottom of the Bush–Mubarak Agenda? The Slow Pace of Political Reform in Egypt," *Policy Watch* 258 (Washington, D.C.: Washington Institute for Near East Policy, 2001), 1–3.

103. Ellen Knickmeyer, "Egyptian Voters Impeded in Opposition Strongholds," *Washington Post*, June 12, 2007.

104. Eric Lee, "Confronting Cairo: Changing an Illusory Democracy," *Harvard International Review* 28:2 (2006): 42.

105. Ibid.

106. "Egyptian Opposition Reels under State Crackdown," *Turkish Daily News*, November 30, 2006.

107. Waterbury, "The Political Management of Economic Adjustment and Reform," 27–56.

108. Ehteshami and Murphy, "Transformation of the Corporatist State," 764.

109. Jason Brownlee, "The Decline of Pluralism in Mubarak's Egypt," *Journal of Democracy* 13:4 (2002): 6.

110. Jeffrey Herbst, *The Politics of Reform in Ghana* (Cambridge: Cambridge University Press, 1993), 2.

111. Heydemann, *Networks of Privilege*, 6.

112. Posusney, "Egyptian Privatization," 38.

113. Ibid.

114. Brad Dillman, "Facing the Market in North Africa," *Middle East Journal* 55 (2001): 208.

115. Simon Brindle, "Privatization Programme Lumbers Slowly On," *Middle East* (April 2003), http://findarticles.com/p/articles/mi_m2742/is_/ai_n25065806 (accessed May 12, 2007).

116. Ibid.

117. Hasanayin Tawfiq Ibrahim, *Al-Iqtisad al-siyasi lil-ilsah al-iqtisadi* (Cairo: Markaz al-Dirasat al Siyasiyya wa-al-Istratijiyya, 1999): 93–94.

118. *Al-Wafd,* August 1, 2001. See also *Al-Ahali,* October1, 2001.

119. Ibid.

120. Ahmad al-Sayyid al-Najjar, *al-iqtisad al-Misri: min tajrubat yulyu ila namudhaj al-mustaqbal* (Cairo: Markaz al-Dirasat al-Siyasiyya wa-al-Istratijiyya, 2002): 147–162.

121. Layla al-Khawaja, ed., *Taqrir al-tanmiya al-bashariyya fi Misr* (Cairo: Markaz Dirasat wa-Buhuth al-Duwal al-Namiya, 2004).

122. Mahmud 'Abd Al-Fadli, quoted in "Qa'imat al-ihtikarat fi Misr: bay' al-sharikat li-mustathmir wahid yu'addi ila al-ihtikar," *Al-Ahali,* February 28, 2001.

123. "Qa'imat al-ihtikarat fi Misr: bay' al-sharikat li-mustathmir wahid yu'addi ila al-ihtikar," *Al-Ahali,* February 28, 2001; "Hikayat Ahmad 'Izz ma'a sharikat al-Dikhila lil-Hadid wa-al-Sulb: fada'ih al-fasad wa-al-ihtikar fi sina'at al-sulb," *Al-Ahali,* August 2, 2000.

124. "Ummal sharikat Tilimisr yasrukhun: man yunqidhuna min ghul al-khaskhasa?" *Al-Ahali,* May 16, 2001.

125. "Al-Nasr lil-Mawasir al-Sulb shahid 'ayan 'ala fasad al-khaskhasa," *Al-Ahali,* July 18, 2001.

126. "Fi al-Misriyya li-Tijarat al-Kimawiyyat wa-al-Ma'adin: al-Sharika al-Qabida lil-Tijara tarfud sarf mustahaqqat 2000 'amil kharaju lil-mas'ash al-mubbakir," *Al-Ahali,* November 6, 2002.

127. The Free Egyptians Blog, http://Free.Egyptians.46.com (accessed July 2004; site now discontinued).

128. Data on changes in ownership concentration over time in different industries, for example, do not exist. It is also often difficult to determine the number of companies privatized, the true value of privatized assets, and the identity of the purchasers and beneficiaries. See Dillman, "Facing the Market in North Africa."

129. The final chapter of this book will unpack cronyism and build on the recent literature largely based on East Asia, aimed at distinguishing between more and less productive cronyism in terms of economic performance. Egypt's cronyism is the less productive kind.

130. As reported by Sara Gauch, *Christian Science Monitor,* April 11, 1996.

131. Gamil Amin, "Memories of a Revolution," *Al-Ahram Weekly Online,* August 10–16, 2006.

132. Karima Korayem, "Structural Adjustment, Stabilization Policies, and the Poor in Egypt" (Cairo Papers in Social Science 18/4 Winter 1995/6).

133. Neil Macfarquhar, "Alexandria Journal; Poor Egypt's Golden Coast: The Lure (and Leer)," *New York Times,* July 30, 1996.

134. John Lancaster, "Desert Turns to Green as Egypt's Affluent Revive Colonial Links," *Washington Post Foreign Service,* February 22, 1997.

135. For a review of this literature, see King, *Liberalization against Democracy,* 118–120.

136. Bush, "Mubarak's Legacy for Egypt's Rural Poor."

137. Ibid., 12.

138. M. Riad El-Ghonemy, "The Political Economy of Market-Based Land Reform," Popular Coalition/UNRISD monograph (1999).

139. King, *Liberalization against Democracy,* 126.

140. Bush, "Mubarak's Legacy for Egypt," 12.

141. Ibid., 16.

142. Asef Bayat, "Activism and Social Development in the Middle East," *International Journal of Middle East Studies* 34:1 (2002): 2.

143. Ibid.

144. Raymond Hinnebusch, "The Politics of Economic Reform in Egypt," *Third World Quarterly* 14:1 (1993): 159.

145. Lofren, "Economic Policy in Egypt," 409.

146. Ibid.

147. Herbst, *The Politics of Reform in Ghana,* 58–75; and Waterbury, "Political Management of Economic Adjustment and Reform."

148. Lofren, "Economic Policy in Egypt," 410.

149. Ibid. See also Gamil Amin, *Egypt's Economic Predicament: A Study in the Interaction of External Pressure, Political Folly and Social Tension in Egypt 1960–1990* (Leiden: E.J. Brill, 1995).

150. Samir Sulayman, *al-Nizam al-qawi wa-al-dawla al-da'ifa: idarat al-azma al-maliya wa-al-taghyir al siyasi fi 'ahd Mubarak* (The Strong Regime and the Weak

State: Managing the Financial Crisis and Political Change under Mubarak) (Cairo: al Dar, 2006).

151. Ibid.

152. Ibid., 410–416.

153. Hinnebusch, "The Politics of Economic Reform in Egypt," 163.

154. Ibid., 164.

155. "Misr tahtafil bi-'id al-'ummal,'" *Al-Ahram.*

156. Ibid., 414. Especially a powerful group of Egyptian businessmen associated with USAID; see Sadowski, *Political Vegetables;* and Hinnebusch, "The Politics of Economic Reform in Egypt," 166.

157. Ahmad al-Sayyid al-Najjar, "Ra's al-mal wa-al-hukm fi al-intikhabat al-barmaniyya" (Capital and State in the Parliamentary Elections), *Al-Ahram,* 28 November, 2005.

158. Ibid.

159. Abul-Magd, "Law and Economy in Egypt."

160. Salah al-'Amrusi, "al-Thawra al-Daribiyya al-Jadida (The New Tax Revolution) *Ahwal Misriyya* 40 (Fall 2005), 80–88.

161. Abul-Magd, "Law and Economy in Egypt."

162. Al-Najjar, "Capital and State in Parliamentary Elections."

163. Ibid.

164. Posusney, "Egyptian Labor Struggle in the Era of Privatization."

165. Abul-Magd, "Law and Economy in Egypt."

166. Hinnebusch, "Liberalization without Democratization," 143.

167. Kienle, *Democracy and Economic Reform in Egypt,* 155.

168. Ibid.

169. Jeannie Yamine, "Egypt's Social Fund for Development," World Bank Press Release 96/25/MENA, 1996.

170. "Mafhru' jaded li-nizam al-ma'ash al-mubakkir a-idtirarai," *Al-Ahram,* April 23, 2006.

171. Roger Owen, "The Middle Eastern State: Repositioning Not Retreat," in Hakimian and Moshaver, eds., *The State and Global Change,* 245–246.

172. Bogdan Obretin, "Egypt Extends State of Emergency, *Softpedia,* http://news.softpedia.com/news/Egypt-Extends-State-of-Emergency-22518.shtml (accessed September 23, 2007).

173. Human Rights Watch, "Egypt: Flawed Military Trials for Brotherhood Leaders: Human Rights Groups, Media Barred from Observing Trial," Human Rights Watch Web site (June 5, 2005), http://hrw.org/english/docs/2007/06/05/egypt16072.htm (accessed May 15, 2007).

174. Eberhard Kienle, "More Than a Response to Islamism: The Political Deliberalization of Egypt in the 1990s," *Middle East Journal* 52:2 (1998): 219.

175. Ibid., 158.

176. Ibid., 159.

177. Michael Slackman, "Peacekeepers Targets of New Sinai Attacks," *New York Times,* April 27, 2006.

178. Suzanne Gershowitz, "Dissident Watch: Ayman Nour" *Middle East Quarterly* 12:3 (2005), http://www.meforum.org/article/753 (accessed October 8, 2008).

179. Saad Eddine Ibrahim, "The New Middle East Bush Is Resisting," *Washington Post,* August 23, 2006.

180. Quoted in: Anthony Shadid, "Syria Heralds Reforms, But Many Have Doubts: Party Weighs Gradual Moves Toward Democracy," *Washington Post,* May 18, 2005.

181. Ibid., 65–68.

182. Volker Perthes, "Syria's Parliamentary Elections: Remodeling Asad's Political Base," *Middle East Report* 174 (January–February, 1992), 16.

183. Ibid., 18.

184. Ibid. Also, see Sukkar, "The Crisis of 1986 and Syria's Plan for Reform."

185. Ibid.

186. Samir Aita, "Syria: What Reforms While a Storm Is Building," *Arab Reform Brief* 6, Arab Reform Initiative, April 2006.

187. Ibid.

188. Ibid., 7.

189. Ibid.

190. Ibid.

191. Ibid.

192. Of course, monarchical power leaves the Jordanian political system still far below any democratic threshold.

193. Sami Moubayed, "Syria's Ba'athists Loosen the Reins," *Asia Times,* April 26, 2005, Middle East Section.

194. Quoted in Shadid, "Syria Heralds Reforms, But Many Have Doubts."

195. Quoted in Gareth Smyth, "Does Syria Mean Business?," *Middle East Company News Wire,* February 16, 2002. This point was also made by Flynt Leverett in *Inheriting Syria:* 79.

196. Ellen Lust-Okar, "The Syrian Challenge," Presentation at Carnegie Endowment for International Peace, Washington, D.C., March 30, 2006.

197. Aita, "Syria: What Reforms While a Storm Is Building," 8.

198. Ayman Abdel-Nour, "Discussion on the Reform Process in Syria" (interview with Abdel-Nour—Baath Party Member), *Federal News Service,* August 1, 2005.

199. Hinnebusch, "Liberalization without Democratization," 259.

200. Joshua Landis, comment on "The Presidential Plebiscite and Pageantry: What Does it Mean?" The Joshua Landis blog, comment posted June 4, 2007, http://joshualandis.com/blog/?p=274 (accessed October 10, 2008).

201. Glenn Robinson, "Elite Cohesion, Regime Succession and Political Instability in Syria," *Middle East Policy* 5:4 (1998): 161; Hinnebusch, "Liberalization without Democratization."

202. Abdel-Nour, "Discussion on the Reform Process in Syria."

203. Ibrahim al-Lawza, "Mulahazat ala qanum al-amal" (Notes on the Labor Law), *Kassioun,* June 12, 2006; "La qima li-qarar lil-qarar ra'is al jumhuriya hawla al-madda 137 min qanun al-amilin al-muwahhad" (There Is No Value in the Presidential Decision Regarding Article no.137 of the Unified Workers' Law), Al-Majlis al-Watani lil-Adala wa-al Musalaha fi Suriya; Kastru Nisi, "Wizarat al-amal wa-tudir zahraha lil-'ummal" (The Ministry of Labor Satisfies Business Owners and Turns Back on Workers), *Kassioun,* June 10, 2006.

204. Abdel-Nour, "Discussion on the Reform Process in Syria."

205. "Azzuz: al-hukuma tatajaweb ma'a matalibina," *Kassioun,* May 29, 2005, and June 29, 2006.

206. Badar al Din Shanan, comment on "Al-tabaqa al-'amila tadduq abwab

Dimishq" (The Working Class Knocks the Doors of Damascus), the Al-Badil blog, comment posted May 30, 2006, www.albadil.net (accessed May 30, 2006).

207. Ibid.

208. "Mu'raba bayna sindan al-istimalak wa-matraqat al-mukhattat," *Kassioun* June 3, 2006.

209. Ibid.

210. Abdel-Nour, "Discussion on the Reform Process in Syria."

211. Hans Hopfinger and Marc Boeckler, "Step by Step to an Open Economic System: Syria Sets Course for Liberalization," *British Journal of Middle Eastern Studies* 23:2 (1996): 183–202.

212. Perthes, "Syria's Parliamentary Elections," 57.

213. Ibid.

214. Hopfinger and Boeckler, 191.

215. "That ghita' al-tasharukiya: al-khaskhasa taqtahim salat Sundus," *Kassioun,* June 19, 2006.

216. Hinnebusch, "Syria: The Politics of Economic Liberalization," 259.

217. Perthes, "Stages of Economic and Political Liberalization," in *Contemporary Syria: Liberalization between Cold War and Cold Peace,* ed. Eberhard Kienle, 48.

218. Ibid., 57.

219. Fred Lawson, "Domestic Transformation and Foreign Steadfastness in Contemporary Syria," *Middle East Journal* 48:1 (1994): 47–64.

220. Perthes, "Economic and Political Liberalization," 52.

221. Volker Perthes, "A Look at Syria's Upper Class: The Bourgeoisie and the Ba'th," *Middle East Report* 170 (May–June 1991): 37.

222. Ibid.

223. Ibid.

224. Fouad Laham, "Al-Qita'a Al-Mushtarak for Cooperation between the Public and Private Sectors," Paper presented at the Fifteenth Tuesday Forum on Economic and Social Development in Syria (Damascus, February 12, 2002).

225. One measure would be ownership concentration by selected industries, with follow-up analysis of the degree of competition or monopoly in those industries. This data is impossible to gather, if it is kept, for the cases in this study and probably for the Middle East in general.

226. This data is often linked to exiled opposition groups, so it should be considered with caution.

227. "The Triangle of National Theft," *Free Syria,* August 26, 2006.

228. Ibid.

229. Landis, "The Presidential Plebiscite and Pageantry."

230. Ibid.

231. Ammar Abdulhamid (director, Thawra foundation), interview by research assistant, October 25, 2007.

232. Nkem Ifejika, "Who's Who: Syria's Top Ten Political Brokers" *The New Statesmen,* June 5, 2006; Subhi Hadidi, "Assad's Corruption Cover-up," *Middle East Research Institute,* January 7, 2004.

233. "The Triangle of National Theft."

234. Najib Ghadbian (associate professor of political science and Middle Eastern studies, University of Arkansas, and founding member of the Syrian Salvation Front), interview by research assistant, October 26, 2007.

235. BBC News, "Who's Who in Syria's Leadership," March 3, 2005.

236. Ammar Abdulhamid, Interview by research assistant, October 25, 2007.

237. "Mohamed Hamsho," *Free Syria*, June 21, 2006.

238. Ibid., 134.

239. Ibid., 133.

240. *Kassioun Weekly*, issue 229, October 2004; Shadid, "Syria Heralds Reforms."

241. *Kassioun Weekly*, issue 228, August 2004.

242. *Tishreen Daily*, October 27, 2004.

243. Nabil Sukkar, "Thulathiat Hitham al-Soq Wa al-Adala al-Ejitmia'aih wa Al-Ertiqaa Al Technology fi Mwajahat al-'Awalama Wa Mutatalibat Al-Iqtisad Al-Souri," Paper presented at the Sixteenth Tuesday Forum on Economic and Social Development in Syria (Damascus, September 2, 2002); Nabil Sukkar, "Syria Faces Huge Obstacles to Market Economy" (interview by Roueida Mabardi), *Agence France Presse*, August 1, 2005.

244. Qadri Jamil, "al-islah al-iqtisadi bayna al-abyad wa-al-aswad" *Kassioun*, June 19, 2006.

245. Leverett, *Inheriting Syria*, 72–73.

246. Perthes, "Stages of Economic and Political Liberalization," 57.

247. Ayman Abdel-Nour, "Discussion on the Reform Process in Syria."

248. Hugh Roberts, *The Battlefield Algeria 1988–2002: Studies in a Broken Polity* (London: Verso, 2003).

249. Ibid., 82–104.

250. Armed Conflict Events Data, "Black October Riots in Algeria 1988," in the Armed Conflicts Events Data Web site, http://www.onwar.com/aced/nation/all/algeria/falgeria1988.htm, (accessed December 20, 2007).

251. Rafael Bustos, "Economic Liberalization and Political Change in Algeria: Theory and Practice (1988–1992 and 1994–1999)," *Mediterranean Politics* 8:1 (2003): 1–26.

252. Roberts, *Battlefield Algeria 1988–2002*.

253. Ibid.

254. Ibid.

255. Ibid., 25.

256. Ibid., 28.

257. William Quandt, *Between Ballots and Bullets: Algeria's Transition from Authoritarianism* (Washington, D.C.: Brookings), 1998.

258. Roberts, *Battlefield Algeria 1988–2002*, 94.

259. Bustos, "Economic Liberalization and Political Change in Algeria," 1–26.

260. Roberts, *Battlefield Algeria 1988–2002*, 82–104.

261. Hugh Roberts, "Musical Chairs in Algeria," *Middle East Report Online* (June 4, 2002), http://www.merip.org/mero/mero060402.html (accessed August 5, 2007).

262. Ibid.

263. Ibid.

264. Ibid.

265. On the relationship between the FLN state and the UGTA, see Christopher Alexander, "The Architecture of Militancy: Workers and the State in Algeria, 1970–1990," *Comparative Politics* 34:3 (2002); and "Opportunities, Organizations, and Ideas: Islamists and Workers in Tunisia and Algeria," *International Journal of*

Middle East Studies 32:4 (2000): 465–490; also, see Amar Benamrouche, "État, conflits sociaux et mouvement syndical en Algérie (1962–1995)," *Monde Arabe Maghreb Machrek* 148 (April–June 1995): 45–54; and Bradford Dillman, "The Political Economy of Structural Adjustment in Tunisia and Algeria," *The Journal of North African Studies* 3:3 (1998): 1–24.

266. BBC Summary of World Broadcasts, "Algeria Trade Union Issues Appeal for Workers to Support Political Leadership."

267. Benamrouche, "État, conflits sociaux et mouvement syndical," 51–53.

268. Alexander, "Islamists and Workers in Tunisia and Algeria," 481.

269. Ibid., 484.

270. United Press International, "Workers Strike Against Algerian Government," March 12, 1991.

271. Ibid.

272. Ibid.

273. Dillman, "Structural Adjustment in Tunisia and Algeria," 19.

274. Ibid.

275. *AFP-Extel News,* May 3, 1995.

276. Ali Habib, "Algeria Faces Threat of Labour Unrest," *Guardian Publication,* March 17, 1996.

277. Ibid.

278. BBC Monitoring Middle East, March 9, 1998.

279. Ibid.

280. Salima Tlemcani, *El Watan,* Novemer 22, 1998.

281. BBC Monitoring Middle East, "Government Main Trade Unions Reach Agreement," September 28, 1998.

282. "Workers Vow to Protest in September," *Info-Prod Research,* August 26, 1998.

283. BBC Monitoring Middle East, "Algerian Trade Leader Renews Opposition to Privatization, Amnesty, Liquidation of the UGTA," April 25, 2001.

284. Associated Press, "Algerian Industrial Workers Strike," May 21, 2000.

285. BBC Monitoring Middle East, "Main Trade Union Drops Support for Bouteflika," January 30, 2003.

286. Pan African News Agency Daily Newswire, "Algerian Workers Go on a General Strike," October 15, 2003.

287. "General Union of Algerian Workers Supports Bouteflika in Presidential Race," *Al-Bawaba,* March 4, 2004, http://www.albawaba.com (accessed October 10, 2006).

288. BBC Monitoring Middle East, "Algeria: Independent Trade Unions Organize to Defend Rights."

289. *Al-Fadjr,* June 21, 2004, http://www.al-fadjr.com (accessed November 10, 2004).

290. *Al-Fadjr,* October 6, 2003, http://www.al-fadjr.com (accessed November 10, 2004).

291. *Al-Fadjr,* January 10, 2004, http://www.al-fadjr.com; *Al-Fadjr,* January 19, 2004, http://www.al-fadjr.com (accessed November 10, 2004).

292. Azzedine Layachi (Algerian Scholar), interview by the author.

293. Comment on "Père NoëlPolitique," Bordj Bou Arreridj info blog, comment posted May 10, 2007, http://www.bba34.com/ (accessed May 10. 2007).

294. El Moudjahid and A.P.S., "Une campagne électorale particulière dans les Bibans," Borj Bou Arreridj info Blog, comment posted on 22 November, 2007, www .bba34.com/spip.php?article189&var_recherche=tribalisme%20 (accessed October 11, 2008).

295. Jill Carroll, "In Algeria, a Status Quo Vote," *Christian Science Monitor,* May 17, 2007.

296. Jill Carroll, "Algerian PM's Party Scores Convincing Win in Local Vote," *Christian Science Monitor,* October 11, 2002.

297. Roberts, *Battlefield Algeria 1988–2002,* 89.

298. Hugh Roberts, "Demilitarizing Algeria," Working paper 86 (Washington, D.C.: Carnegie Endowment for International Peace, 2007). The military has also influenced positions in the state bureaucracy. Bouteflika would also have to assert control over the security forces as well to limit military influence in politics.

299. Rezak Tarik, *Algeria Interface,* 2001, http://www.algeria-interface.com.

300. Entelis, *Algeria: The Revolution Institutionalized,* 124.

301. Lahouari Addi, "The Political Contradictions of Algerian Economic Reforms," *Review of African Political Economy* 33:108 (2006): 209.

302. Ibid., 125.

303. Addi, "Algerian Economic Reforms."

304. Pradeep K. Chhibber, "State Policy, Rent Seeking and the Electoral Success of a Religious Party in Algeria," *Journal of Politics* 58:1 (1996): 136.

305. Roberts, *Battlefield Algeria 1988–2002,* 88.

306. Bustos, "Economic Liberalization and Political Change in Algeria," 3.

307. Roberts, *Battlefield Algeria 1988–2002,* 88.

308. Ibid., 87.

309. Bustos, "Economic Liberalization and Political Change in Algeria," 6.

310. Ibid., 16.

311. Roberts, *Battlefield Algeria 1988–2002,* 89.

312. Ibid., 89–90.

313. Hamid Hamidi, "Khaskhasat Al-Moasasaat Al-Aomomia fi Al-Qanoun Al-Jazeeri" in "Al-Islahat Al-Iqtisadiah wa Siyasat Al-Khaskhasah fi al-Buldan Al-Arabia," Report from the Center for Arab Unity Studies (Beirut), 1999.

314. Bustos, "Economic Liberalization and Political Change in Algeria," 1–26.

315. Luis Martinez, *The Algerian Civil War 1990–1998* (New York: Columbia University Press, 2000).

316. Al-Ahram, July 12, 1997, http://weekly.ahram.org.eg.

317. Al-Fadjr, March 25, 2004, www.al-fadjr.com.

318. Al-Fadjr, March 31, 2004, www.al-fadjr.com.

319. Ibid.

320. Bradford L. Dillman, *State and Private Sector in Algeria: The Politics of Rent Seeking and Failed Development* (Boulder, Colo.: Westview Press, 2000), 82–83.

321. Thomas Hasel, *Machtkonflikt in Algerien* (Berlin: Verlag Hans Schiler, 2002), 25.

322. Hasel, *Machtkonflikt in Algerien,* 30–35.

323. Ibid., 39 and 71.

324. Hadjadj, trained as a medical doctor, had been writing on corruption for the Algerian newspaper *El Watan* until he was forced to resign. He is chairman of the Algerian branch of Transparency International, an NGO devoted to the battle

against corruption, and currently writes for *Le Soir d'Algérie,* in its weekly column on corruption. Press Release: "Algerian anti-corruption journalist forced to resign," Berlin, December 16, 1999, http://transparency.org/pressreleases_archive. http://www.lesoirdalgerie.com.

325. Aboud explicitly accuses the H'lima clan, of president Chadli's wife, of involvement in the mafioso struggle for power. Hichem Aboud, *La Mafia des généraux* (Paris: Editions J.-C. Lattes, 2002), 49.

326. Djillali Hadjdaj, *Corruption et démocratie en Algérie* (Paris: La Dispute, 1999), 105–118.

327. Hadjadj, *Corruption et démocratie en Algérie,* 121–191.

328. Ahmed Rouadjia, *Grandeur et décadence de l'État Algérien* (Paris: Editions Karthala, 1994), 345.

329. "al-Jazā'ir: istijwāb 3000 shakhs fī iflās 'majmū'at Khalīfa,'" http://www.almustaqbal.com/stories.aspx?StoryID=120829; Transparency International, *Global Corruption Report 2004,* http://www.globalcorruptionreport.org/download/gcr2004/10_Country_reports_A_K.pdf, 144 (accessed June 10, 2005).

330. *Global Corruption Report 2004,* 144.

331. "Zilzāl al-arbi'ā' 21 May 2003: Hazzat arÃiyya jadīda wa-akthar min 4000 qatīl fī l-zilzāl al-awwal," http://www.algeria-voice.org/Eco-So/Eco-So10/hauptteil_eco-so10.html; Transparency International, *Global Corruption Report 2004,* 143–146.

332. Rouadjia, *Grandeur et décadence de l'État Algérien,* 287, 289, 296–299.

333. Jean-Claude Brulé, "The Agricultural Sector in Algeria: How Far Has the Privatization of Real Estate Proceeded?," in *Economic Liberalization and Privatization in Socialist Arab Countries,* ed. Hans Hopfinger (Gotha: Justus Perthes Verlag, 1996), 207–211.

334. Aboud, *La Mafia des généraux,* 52–101.

335. Hasel, *Machtkonflikt in Algerien,* 71–72; B. Takheroubt, "Lutte contre la corruption: L'État passe à l'attaque," February 3, 2005, http://algeria-watch.org/fr/article/eco/corruption_attaque.htm; "al-Jazā'ir: al-taÎqīq fð tuham fasād tashmal 40 qāÃiyyan," April 5, 2005, http://www.albawaba.com/ar/countries/226434 (accessed June 10, 2005).

336. Dillman, *State and Private Sector in Algeria,* 21–26.

337. Henry and Springborg, *Globalization and the Politics of Development in the Middle East,* 119.

338. Dillman, *State and Private Sector in Algeria,* 28.

339. Terranti Salima, "La Privatization du Foncier Agricole en Algérie; Plus de Dix ans de Débats Silencieux," Communication at the Fourth Pan African Programme on Land and Resources Rights, Worship, Cape Town, May 2003.

340. Library of Congress, "Algeria: Land Tenure and Reform," http://www.country-studies.com/algeria/land-tenure-and-reform.html (accessed June 10, 2006).

341. Ibid.

342. Terranti Salima, "La Privatization du Foncier Agrigole en Algérie," 1–8.

343. Ibid.

344. Addi, "The Political Contradictions of Algerian Economic Reforms," 210.

345. Al-Ahram, 3/26/1997, weekly.ahram.org.eg/.

346. William, I. Zartman, "Algeria at Forty: A Midlife Crisis," *Journal of North African Studies* 9:2 (Summer 2004): 4.

347. Azzedine Layachi, "The Private Sector in the Algerian Economy: Obstacles

and Potentials for a Productive Role," *Mediterranean Politics,* December 2001 6:2 (December 2001): 35–36.

348. Henry and Springborg, *Globalization and the Politics of Development in the Middle East.*

349. Austrabal comment on, "Le multipartisme d'état en Tunisie: La débâcle," Austrabal Blog, comment posted March 22, 2005, www.nawaat.org/portail/2005/ 03/22/le-multipartisme-d'etat-en-tunisie-la-debacle/ (accessed June 7, 2006).

350. Lisa Anderson, "The Tunisian National Pact of 1988," *Government and Opposition* 26: 2. (Spring 1991): 244–60; Hochman, "Divergent Democratization," 71.

351. Mediouni Lassaad, "Government Labor Power Struggle Set to Continue," IPS-Inter Press Service, December 23, 1985.

352. Sadri Khiari and Olfa Lamloum, "Le zaim et l'artisan ou de Bourguibaa Ben Ali," *Annuaire de l'Afrique du Nord* 37 (1988): 377–395.

353. Mohamed Ennaceur, "Les Syndicats et la mondialisation: Le Cas de la Tunisie," Working Paper DP/120, L'Institute internationale d'études sociales, 2000, p. 14

354. Ibid., 6.

355. Ibid.

356. Ibid.

357. Mediouni Lassaad, "Government Labor Power Struggle Set to Continue."

358. Ibid.

359. Ibid., 23.

360. Ibid.

361. Mark Tessler, Gregory White, and John Entelis, "The Republic of Tunisia," in *The Government and Politics of the Middle East and North Africa,* ed. David E. Long and Bernard Reich (Boulder, Colo.: Westview Press, 1995), 429.

362. Sadri Khiari et Olfa Lamloum, "Tunisie: des élections en trompe-l'oeil," *Politique Africaine* 76 (December 1999): 112.

363. Ibid.

364. Secretary General of the UGTT Ismail Sahbani speaking to the UGTT national assembly in 1992. Quoted in Christopher Alexander, "State Labor and the New Global Economy in Tunisia," in *North Africa: Development and Reform in a Changing Global Economy,* ed. Dirk Vandewalle (New York: St. Martin's Press, 1996), 177.

365. Ennaceur, "Les syndicats et la mondialisation."

366. For the detailed history of state-sponsored development that benefits capitalists in Tunisia, without including the privatization policies discussed herein, see Bellin, *Stalled Democracy.*

367. For a comparison of the political participation of peasants under Tunisian socialism and the current neo-liberal era, see Mira Zussman, *Development and Disenchantment in Rural Tunisia: The Bourguiba Years* (Boulder, Colo.: Westview Press, 1992) and the piggyback study of Tebourba, in King, *Liberalization against Democracy,* 76–112.

368. Marco, R. Di Tommasso, Elena Lanzoni, and Lauretta Rubini, "Support to SMEs in the Arab Region: The Case of Tunisia," UNIDO, 2001, 9.

369. Ibid.

370. Ibid.

371. Ennaceur, "Les syndicats et la mondialisation," 6.

372. Seddon, "Winter of Discontent," 7.

373. Marco et al., "Support to SMEs," 11.

374. Rhys Payne, "Economic Crisis and Policy Reform in the 1980s," in *Polity and Society in Contemporary North Africa,* ed. William Mark Habeeb and I. William Zartman (Boulder, Colo.: Westview, 1993), 139–167.

375. Khiari and Lamloum, "Tunisie: des élections en trompe-l'oeil," 108.

376. Speech, Tunisian Ambassador in the Maghreb Center's Speaker's Series at Georgetown University, December 2007.

377. Ibid.

378. Khiari and Lamloum, "Tunisie: des élections en trompe-l'oeil," 111.

379. Ibid.

380. Ibid.

381. Ibid.

382. Bensendrin and Mestri, "Tunesien: Auch Europa hält sich seine Despoten: das Tunesische Modell," http://www.unikassel.de/fb5/frieden/regionen/Tunesien/despoten.html (accessed January 18, 2007).

383. Khiari and Lamloum, "Tunisie: des élections en trompe-l'oeil," 110.

384. Nicolas Beau and Jean-Pierre Tuquoi, *Notre ami Ben Ali: l'envers du "miracle tunisien"* (Paris: La Decouverte, 1999), 152–158.

385. Personal communication with a Tunisian opposition journalist, July 2004. Tunisia's police state, which is more repressive than Egypt's, does not allow for the relatively freer flow of information on these matters through the press and social studies' institutes. On the condition of anonymity, officials in the Tunisian U.S. embassy verify that elite corruption and the lack of transparency are the biggest criticisms related to the country's structural adjustment program.

386. El Haj Khlouf, "Ben Ali arbitre la lutte Chiboub/Trabelsi," *L'autre Tunisie,* June 12, 2003, http://tounes.naros.info/article.php3?id_article=57 (accessed January 18, 2007).

387. Bernhard Schmid, "Tunesien zwischen Präsidentschaftswahl, politischen Prozessen und 'wilden' Streiks: Wahlfarce und Soziale Kämpfe im Polizeistaats-'Musterlände,'" Trend Online Setzung, December 4, 2004, http://www.trend.infopartisan.net/trd1204/t121204.html (accessed January 18, 2007).

388. http://www.tunisnews.net/20mars05.htm (accessed January 18, 2007).

389. Dominique Lagarde, "La fronde des jeunes," L'Express.fr, May 18 2000, http://www.lexpress.fr/info/monde/dossier/tunisie/dossier.asp?ida=408871 (accessed January 18, 2007) .

390. http://tounes.naros.info/article.php3?id_article=57 (accessed January 18, 2007).

391. Ibid.

392. Sihem Bensendrin and Omar Mestri, "Tunesien: Auch Europa hält sich seine Despoten: Das Tunesische Modell," published in INAMO, May 5, 2005, http://www.unikassel.de/fb5/frieden/regionen/Tunesien/despoten.html (accessed January 18, 2007).

393. *Al-Mawqif,* October 17, 2003.

394. Stephen King, *Liberalization against Democracy.*

395. World Bank, *Republic of Tunisia: Growth Policies and Poverty Alleviation* (Washington, D.C.: World Bank, 1995), 26.

396. Ibid., 6–7.

397. I. William Zartman, "Opposition as Support of the State," in *Beyond Coercion: The Durability of the Arab State,* ed. Adeed Dawisha and I. William Zartman (London: Croom Helm, 1988), 81–84.

398. Schedler, "Menu of Manipulations," 36–50.

399. Levitsky and Way, "The Rise of Competitive Authoritarianism," 51–64.

400. Ibid., 55.

401. Diamond, "Elections without Democracy."

402. In his classification scheme, a group of countries reside in ambiguous territory between competitive authoritarianism and electoral democracy; a separate group of countries are deemed to be even more politically closed than electoral authoritarian regimes.

403. This strategy has been utilized on occasion by autocrats in the past, but the phenomenon has become generalized.

404. Brumberg, "The Trap of Liberalized Autocracy," 56–68; and Ottaway, *Democracy Challenged*. Ottaway utilizes Egypt as a paradigmatic case. Her other cases of semi-authoritarian regimes are from other regions of the world.

405. Raymond Hinnebusch, "Authoritarian Persistence, Democratization Theory and the Middle East: An Overview and Critique," *Democratization* 13:3 (June 2006): 373–395; "Liberalization without Democratization," 123–145; "The Politics of Economic Liberalization: Comparing Egypt and Syria," 111–134; *Egyptian Politics under Sadat: The Post-Populist Development of an Authoritarian-Modernizing State* (Cambridge: Cambridge University Press, 1985).

406. Henry and Springborg, *Globalization and the Politics of Development in the Middle East*.

407. Ibid., 15.

408. Ibid.

409. Guillermo A. O'Donnell, *Modernization and Bureaucratic Authoritarianism: Studies in South American Politics* (Berkeley: University of California Press, 1973).

410. Hector E. Schamis, "Reconceptualizing Latin American Authoritarianism in the 1970s: From Bureaucratic Authoritarianism to Neoconservatism," *Comparative Politics* 23:2 (January 1991): 201–220. This article builds on the arguments made in *Generals in Retreat: The Crisis of Military Rule in Latin America,* ed. Philip O'Brien and Paul Cammack (Dover, N.H.: Manchester University Press, 1985).

411. Ibid.

412. See chapter 3.

413. See Larry Diamond, "Economic Development and Democracy Reconsidered," *American Behavioral Scientists* 35:4–5 (March–June 1992):450–99; Carlos Waisman, "Capitalism, The Market, and Democracy," *American Behavioral Scientist* 35: 4–5 (March–June 2002): 500–516; and Huntington, *The Third Wave*. As advocates of neo-liberal reform policies, agencies such as the IMF, the World Bank, and USAID press for the implementation of the Washington Consensus partly on the grounds that it will foster democracy. See Bellin, "The Political Economic Conundrum." In a political atmosphere in which international actors seek ways to foster democratization around the world, the economist Robert Barro bluntly suggested that the only useful steps policy makers could and should take would be to push for the implementation of standard Washington Consensus economic reforms that are theoretically underpinned by neoclassical economic theory, which produces the economic prosperity that is the only powerful link between economic and

political development. See Robert Barrow, *Determinants of Economic Growth: A Cross Country Empirical Study* (Cambridge: Cambridge University Press, 1998).

414. Most prominently, see Lipset, "Some Social Requisites of Democracy," 69–105.

415. On the bourgeoisie as class agent of democracy, see Barrington Moore, *Social Origins of Dictatorship and Democracy: Lord and Peasant in the Making of the Modern World,* (Boston: Beacon Press, 1966); Rueschemeyer, Stephens, and Stephens emphasize labor organized in labor-based political parties and unions as the class agent of democracy. See Dietrich Rueschemeyer, Evelyne Huber Stephens, and John D. Stephens, *Capitalist Development and Democracy* (Chicago: University of Chicago Press, 1992). In a more recent study focused on the Middle East and North Africa (2006), Raymond Hinnebusch emphasizes democratic coalitions; see his "Authoritarian Persistence, Democratization Theory, and the Middle East."

416. Bellin, *Stalled Democracy.*

417. For a description of that economic model and its implication for democratization see King, *Liberalization against Democracy,* 1–25.

418. John Londegran and Keith Poole, "Poverty, the Coup Trap, and the Seizure of Executive Power," *World Politics* 42:151–83.

419. World Bank External Data/Statistics 2006.

420. Adam Prezeworski et al., *Democracy and Development: Political Institutions and Well-Being in the World, 1950–1990* (Cambridge: Cambridge University Press, 2000).

421. Schamis, *Reforming the State.*

422. Adam Przeworski, ed., *Sustainable Democracy* (Cambridge: Cambridge University Press, 1995).

423. Haggard and Kaufman, *The Political Economy of Democratic Transitions.*

424. David Collander, *Neoclassical Political Economy: The Analysis of Rent Seeking and DUP Activities* (Cambridge, Mass.: Ballinger, 1984); Nelson, ed., *Fragile Coalitions;* Haggard and Kaufman, eds., *The Politics of Economic Adjustment;* John Williamson, ed., *The Political Economy of Policy Reform* (Washington D.C.: IIE, 1994); Robert Bates and Anne Krueger, eds., *Political and Economic Interactions in Economic Policy Reform* (Oxford and Cambridge, Mass.: Blackwell, 1993).

5. Political Openings without Patronage-Based Privatization and Single-Party Institutional Legacies

1. World Bank, *Argentina's Privatization Program: Experience, Issues, and Lessons* (Washington, D.C., World Bank, 1993).

2. Collier, *Paths toward Democracy,* 119; and Marcelo Cavarozzi, "Patterns of Elite Negotiation and Confrontation in Argentina and Chile," *in Elites and Democratic Consolidation in Latin America and Southern Europe,* ed. John Higley and Richard Gunther (Cambridge: Cambridge University Press, 1992), 208–236.

3. For a review of the literature and an argument highlighting labor's role in Argentina's democratic transition in 1983, see Collier, *Paths toward Democracy,* 119–126.

4. Ibid., 124.

5. Ibid., 125.

6. Adolfo Canitrot, "Crisis and Transformation of the Argentine State (1978–1992)," in *Democracy, Markets, and Structural Reform in Contemporary Latin America: Argentina, Bolivia, Brazil, Chile, and Mexico.*, ed. William C. Smith, Carlos Acuña, and Eduardo Gamarra (New Brunswick, N.J.: Transaction Publishers, 1994), 75.

7. Laura Tedesco, *Democracy in Argentina* (London: Frank Cass, 1999), 173.

8. Collier, *Paths toward Democracy,* 121.

9. Ibid., 122.

10. George Philip, "The Military Institution Revisted: Some Notes on Corporatism and Military Rule in Latin America," *Journal of Latin American Studies* 12:2 (1980): 421–436.

11. Geraldo L. Munck, *Authoritarianism and Democratization: Soldiers and Workers in Argentina, 1976–1983* (University Park: Pennsylvania State University Press, 1998), 89.

12. Ibid., 112–124.

13. Larry Diamond et al., *Democracy in Developing Countries: Latin America* (Boulder, Colo.: Lynne Rienner Press, 1999), 110–111.

14. Collier, *Paths toward Democracy,* 123–124.

15. If indeed they wanted to maintain political power. As discussed in chapter 2, Barbara Geddes has argued that when military regimes break down they have the option to return to the barracks and still, depending on the context, be able to insure their corporate interests. See Geddes, "Authoritarian Breakdown."

16. World Bank, *Argentina's Privatization Program.*

17. Schamis, *Reforming the State,* 21.

18. Armando Pinheiro and Ben Ross Schneider, "The Fiscal Impact of Privatization in Latin America," *The Journal of Development Studies* 31:5 (June 1995): 751–776.

19. Paul Beckerman, "Central-Bank 'Distress' and Hyperinflation in Argentina, 1989–90," *Journal of Latin American Studies* 27:3 (October 1995): 663–682.

20. Schamis, *Reforming the State,* 127.

21. Guillermo O'Donnell, "Delegative Democracy," *Journal of Democracy* 5:1 (January 1994): 55–69.

22. Schamis, *Reforming the State,* 135–136.

23. Ibid., 22–23.

24. For a summary see Collier, *Paths toward Democracy,* 126–132.

25. Joaquim Verges, "Privatizations in Spain: Process, Policies, and Goals," *European Journal of Law and Economics* 9:3 (2000): 255.

26. Collier, *Paths toward Democracy,* 132.

27. Ibid., 127.

28. Ibid., 127–128.

29. Ibid., 127–129.

30. Ibid., 129.

31. Ibid.

32. Jose Mario Maravall and Julian Santamaria, "Political Change in Spain and the Prospects for Democracy," in *Transitions from Authoritarian Rule,* ed. O'Donnell, Schmitter, and Whitehead, 82.

33. Collier, *Paths toward Democracy,* 129.

34. Ibid., 132.

35. Ibid.

36. Laura Cabeza Garcia and Silvia Gomez Anson, "The Spanish Privatization Process: Implications on the Performance of Divested Firms," *International Review of Financial Analysis* 16 (2007): 392.

37. Joaquim Verges, "Privatizations in Spain," 255.

38. Collier, *Paths toward Democracy,* 134–138.

39. Ibid.

40. Ibid.

41. Rex A. Hudson, ed., *Brazil: A Country Study* (Washington, D.C.: GPO for the Library of Congress, 1997).

42. Margaret Keck, *The Workers Party and Democratization in Brazil* (New Haven: Yale University Press, 1992).

43. Ibid.

44. Ibid.

45. Ibid.

46. Leigh A. Payne, *Brazilian Industrialists and Democratic Change* (Baltimore: Johns Hopkins University Press, 1994).

47. Hudson, *Brazil: A Country Study.*

48. Ibid.

49. Werner Baer and James T. Bang, "Privatization and Equity in Brazil and Russia" (working paper, Ciber Papers, 2002).

6. Transitions from the New MENA Authoritarianism to Democracy?

1. Nader Fergany (lead author, *Arab Human Development Report, 2002–2005*) in interview with the author, October 2007.

2. Addi, "The Political Contradictions of Algerian Economic Reforms," 212–213.

3. Yusuf Mansur, "The Consequences of Distorted Competition in the Arab World," *The Daily Star,* December 15, 2007.

4. Ibid.

5. Ibid.

6. Ibid.

7. Ibid.

8. Ibid.

9. Gamal Essam El-Din, "Not Everyone Is Happy about the New Anti-Trust Bill," *Al-Ahram Weekly,* January 27–February 2, 2005.

10. Ibid.

11. Ibid.

12. Mohamed Ibrahim Fahmy Menza, (American University in Cairo), in interview with the author, October 2007.

13. Ibid.

14. Gaber Al Karmouty, *Al-Hayet,* December 29, 2007, 12.

15. Jean-François Pons, "Le rôle accru de la politique de la concurrence dans la relance du partenariat euro-méditerranéen et dans la coopération multilatérale" (Séminaire régional sur la politique de concurrence et les négociations multilatérales, Tunis, March 28–29, 2002). The Association agreements with the EU actually were

the main factors that led to getting competition legislation in these countries on the books. See Mansur, "The Consequences of Distorted Competition in the Arab World."

16. Neither does Kuwait, the Palestinian Authority, Qatar, the United Arab Emirates, Yemen, or Libya. See Mansur, "The Consequences of Distorted Competition in the Arab World."

17. Catherine Boone, "States and Ruling Classes in Post-Colonial Africa: The Enduring Contradictions of Power," *State Power and Social Forces: Domination and Transformation in the Third World,* ed. Joel Migdal, Atul Kohli, and Vivienne Shue (Cambridge: Cambridge University Press, 1994), 108–142.

18. Ibid.

19. For an incisive analysis, see David C. Kang, *Crony Capitalism: Corruption and Development in South Korea and the Philippines* (Cambridge: Cambridge University Press, 2002).

20. Axel Hadenius and Jan Teorell, "Pathways from Authoritarianism," *Journal of Democracy* 18:1 (January 2007): 154.

21. Ibid., 145.

22. Ibid., 148.

23. Ibid., 152.

24. Ibid., 153.

25. Ibid.

26. Though the power of the military in Algeria and Syria, and to a lesser extent Egypt, makes them somewhat amalgams of military and dominant-party authoritarian regimes.

27. Magaloni, *Voting for Autocracy;* and Kenneth F. Greene, *Why Dominant Parties Lose: Mexico's Democratization in Comparative Perspective* (Cambridge: Cambridge University Press, 2007).

28. Magaloni, *Voting for Autocracy.*

29. Kenneth F. Greene, *Why Dominant Parties Lose.*

30. Collier, "The Transformation of Labor-Based One-Partyism," 225–226.

31. Ibid., 229.

BIBLIOGRAPHY

Aboud, Hichem. *La Mafia des généraux*. Paris: Editions J.-C. Lattes, 2002.

Abul-Magd, Zeinab. "Law and Economy in Egypt: Socioeconomic Realities of the New Parliament." *Economic and Business Research Centre Chronicles, American University in Cairo* 1:3 (January 2006): 30–33.

Addi, Lahouari. "The Political Contradictions of Algerian Economic Reforms." *Review of African Political Economy* 33:108 (June 2006): 207–217.

Aita, Samir. "Syria: What Reforms While a Storm Is Building." Arab Reform Brief No. 6, Arab Reform Initiative, April 2006.

Akhtar, Ahmed, Bouis Howarth, Gutner Tamar, and Hans Lofgren. *"The Egyptian Food Subsidy System."* Research Report 119, International Food Policy Research Institute, Washington, D.C., 2001.

Al-Amrusi, Salah. "Al-Thawra al-Daribiyya al-Jadida." *Ahwal Misriyya* 40 (Fall 2005): 80–88.

Al-Awadi, Hesham. *In Pursuit of Legitimacy: The Muslim Brothers and Mubarak, 1982–2000*. London: I.B. Tauris, 2004.

Alexander, Christopher. "State Labor and the New Global Economy in Tunisia." In *North Africa: Development and Reform in a Changing Global Economy,* edited by Dirk Vandewalle, 177–202. Includes a speech to the UGTT national assembly in 1992 by Ismail Sahbani, Secretary General of the UGTT. New York: St. Martin's Press, 1996.

———. "Opportunities, Organizations, and Ideas: Islamists and Workers in Tunisia and Algeria." *International Journal of Middle East Studies* 32:4 (November 2000): 465–490.

———. "Labor Code Reform in Tunisia." *Mediterranean Politics* 6:2 (Summer 2001): 104–125.

———. "The Architecture of Militancy: Workers and the State in Algeria, 1970–1990." *Comparative Politics* 34:3 (2002): 315–336.

"Algeria: Independent Trade Unions Organize to Defend Rights." *BBC Monitoring Middle East*, October 7, 2003.

"Algerian Anti-corruption Journalist Forced to Resign," Press Release, Berlin: Transparency International, December 16, 1999. http://transparency.org/pressreleases_archive.

"Algerian Industrial Workers Strike." Associated Press, May 21, 2000.

"Algerian Trade Leader Renews Opposition to Privatization, Amnesty, Liquidation of the UGTA." *BBC Monitoring Middle East,* April 25, 2001.

"Algeria Trade Union Issues Appeal for Workers to Support Political Leadership." BBC Summary of World Broadcasts, March 15, 1998.

"Algerian Workers Go on a General Strike." Pan African News Agency Daily Newswire, October 15, 2003.

"Al-Islah al-iytisal bayna-alabyad wa-al-aswad." Kassioun, August 2004.

"Al-Jazā'ir: al-taÎqīq fð tuham fasād tashmal 40 qāÃiyyan." Al-Bawaba, April 5, 2005. http://www.albawaba.com/ar/countries/226434.

"Al-Jazā'ir: istijwāb 3000 shakhs fī iflās 'majmū'at Khalīfa." Al-Mustaqbal, May 12, 2005. http://www.almustaqbal.com/stories.aspx?StoryID=120829.

"Al-Jaza'ituraji' syasatha al-istithmariyya: al-fasad al-maliwa-al-rashwa." Al-Fadjr, January 31, 2004.

Al Karmouty, Gaber. "Misr: Taqrir rasmi 'an nata' ijzs saba nub al-takhtit yuzhir numuwwan malhuzan." Al-Hayet, December 29, 2007, 12. http://www.daralhayat.com/business/12-2007/Item-20071228-21fb0467-c0a8-10ed-0025-b6bf64b8a3c9/story.html.

al-Khawaja, Layla, ed. Taqrir al-tanmiya al-bashariyya fi Misr. Cairo: Markaz Dirasat wa-Buhuth al-Duwal al-Namiya, 2004.

"Al-Khawsasawa-al-fasadfi al-iqtisad al-Jaza'ir." Al-Fadjr, January 10, 2004. http://www.al-fadjr.com.

"Al-lajna al-wizariyyalil-khaskhasatabhath al-yawm: tahdidas'arashum 11 sharikali-tarhahafi al-bursa lil-afrad." Al-Ahram, August 12, 1997.

al-Lawza, Ibrahim. "Mulahazat 'ala qanum al-amal." Kassioun, June 12, 2006.

"Al-Majlis al-Watani lil-Adala wa-al Musalaha fi Suriya," Kassioun, June 2007.

Almond, Gabriel A., and Sidney Verba. The Civic Culture: Political Attitudes and Democracy in Five Nations. Princeton, N.J.: Princeton University Press, 1963.

"Al-Multaqa al-jihawi lil-ghuraf al-fi lahiyyali wilayat-gharb sa'ida." Al-Fadjr, March 25, 2004. http://www.al-fadjr.com.

al-Najjar, Ahmad al-Sayyid. Al-iqtisad al-Misri: Min tajrubat yulyu ila namudhaj al-mustaqbal. Cairo: Markaz al-Dirasat al-Siyasiyya wa-al-Istratijiyya, 2002.

———. "Ra's al-mal wa-al-hukm fi al-intikhabat al-barmaniyya." Al-Ahram, November 28, 2005.

"Al-Nasr lil-Mawasir al-Sulb shahid 'ayan 'ala fasad al-khaskhasa." Al-Ahali, July 18, 2001.

al-Sa'id, Mustafa. "Al-siyasat-al-iqtisadiyya lil-hukuma: Al-furas wa-altahdiiyyat ." In Taqrir al-Ittijahat al-Iqtisadiyya al-Istratijiyya, edited by Ahmadd al Syyid al-Najjar, Cairo: Markaz al-Dirasat al-Siyasiyya wa-al-Istratijiyya, 2005.

Amin, Gamil. Egypt's Economic Predicament: A Study in the Interaction of External Pressure, Political Folly and Social Tension in Egypt 1960–1990. Leiden: E.J. Brill, 1995.

Anderson, Lisa. The State and Social Transformation in Tunisia and Libya. Princeton, N.J.: Princeton University Press, 1986.

———. "The State in the Middle East and North Africa." *Comparative Politics* 20:1 (October 1987): 1–18.

———. "Political Pacts, Liberalism, and Democracy: The Tunisian National Pact of 988." *Government and Opposition* 26:2: (Spring 1991): 244–260.

Ansari, Hamied. *Egypt: The Stalled Society*. Albany: State University of New York, 1986.

Arabist Blog. http://arabist.net/. Comment posted November 28, 2005.

Argentina's Privatization Program: Experience, Issues, and Lessons. Adapted from Myrna Alexander and Carlos Corti, World Bank Staff. Washington, D.C.: World Bank, 1993.

"Asatizat al-qanunwa-mashru' qanun al-tijara al-jadid." *Al-Ahram,* March 12, 1997.

"Audacious Corruption." *Tunis News,* March 20, 2005. http://www.tunisnews .net/20mars05.htm.

"Ayman Abdel-Nour, Baath Party Member, Discussing the Reform Process in Syria." Interview, *The Federal News Service, Inc.,* August 1, 2005.

Ayoubi, Nazih H. *Over-Stating the Arab State: Politics and Society in the Middle East.* New York: I.B. Tauris, 1995.

"Azzuz: Al-hukuma tatajaweb ma'a matalibina." *Kassioun,* May 29, 2005.

Baer, Werner, and James T. Bang. "Privatization and Equity in Brazil and Russia." Working paper, Ciber Papers (Center for International Business Research, University of Illinois at Urgana-Champaign), 2002.

Barro, Robert. *Determinants of Economic Growth: A Cross-Country Empirical Study.* Cambridge: Cambridge University Press, 1998.

Batatu, Hanna. *Syria's Peasantry, the Descendants of Its Lesser Rural Notables, and Their Politics*. Princeton, N.J.: Princeton University Press, 1999.

Bates, Robert, and Anne Krueger, eds. *Political and Economic Interactions in Economic Policy Reform*. Cambridge, Mass.: Blackwell, 1993.

Bauer, Gretchen, and Scott Taylor. *Politics in Southern Africa: State and Society in Transition*. Boulder, Colo.: Lynne Rienner, 2005.

Bayat, Asef. "Activism and Social Development in the Middle East." *International Journal of Middle East Studies* 34:1 (February 2002): 1–28.

Beau, Nicolas, and Jean-Pierre Tuquoi. *Notre ami Ben Ali: L'envers du "miracle tunisien."* Paris: La Decouverte, 1999.

Beblawi, Hazem, and Giacomo Luciani, eds. *The Rentier State in the Arab World.* London: Croom Helm, 1987.

Beckerman, Paul. "Central-Bank 'Distress' and Hyperinflation in Argentina, 1989–90." *Journal of Latin American Studies* 27:3 (October 1995): 663–682.

Beinin, Joel. *Workers and Peasants in the Modern Middle East.* Cambridge: Cambridge University Press, 2001.

———. "Egyptian Textile Workers: From Craft Artisans Facing European Competition to Proletarians Contending with the State." Paper presented at the

National Overview Egypt, Textile Conference, International Institute of Social History, Amsterdam, The Netherlands, November 11–13, 2004.

———. "Political Islam and the New Global Economy: The Political Economy of an Egyptian Social Movement." *New Centennial Review* 5:1 (Spring 2005): 111–139.

———, and Hossam el-Hamalawy. "Strikes in Egypt Spread from Center of Gravity." *Middle East Report Online*.http://www.merip.org/mero/mero050907.html. May 9, 2007.

Belev, Boyan. "Privatization in Egypt and Tunisia: Liberal Outcomes And/Or Liberal Policies?" *Mediterranean Politics* 6:2 (Summer 2001): 68–103.

Bellin, Eva. *Stalled Democracy: Capital, Labor, and the Paradox of State-Sponsored Development*. Ithaca, N.Y.: Cornell University Press, 2002.

———. "The Political-Economic Conundrum: The Affinity of Economic and Political Reform in the Middle East and North Africa." Working paper no. 53, Washington, D.C.: Carnegie Endowment for International Peace, 2004.

———. "Coercive Institutions and Coercive Leaders." In *Authoritarianism in the Middle East,* edited by Marsha Pripstein Posusney and Michele Penner Angrist, 21–42. Boulder, Colo.: Lynne Rienner, 2005.

Benamrouche, Amar. "État, conflits sociaux et mouvement syndical en Algérie (1962–1995)." *Monde Arabe Maghreb Machrek* 148 (April–June 1995): 43–54.

Bensedrin, Sihem, and Omar Mestiri. "Tunesien: Auch Europa hält sich seine Despoten: das Tunesische Modell." *Informationsprojekt Naher und Mittlerer Osten e.V.* 41:11 (Spring 2005), http://www.unikassel.de/fb5/frieden/regionen/Tunesien/despoten.html.

Bill, James, and Robert Springborg. *Politics in the Middle East*. New York: Longman, 2000.

Binder, Leonard. *In a Moment of Enthusiasm: Political Power and the Second Stratum in Egypt*. Chicago: Chicago University Press, 1978.

"Black October Riots in Algeria 1988." Armed Conflicts Events Data. http://www.onwar.com/aced/nation/all/algeria/falgeria1988.htm.

Blair, Thomas. *Auto-Gestion: The Land to Those Who Work It*. New York: Doubleday, 1969.

Boone, Catherine. "States and Ruling Classes in Post-Colonial Africa: The Enduring Contradictions of Power." In *State Power and Social Forces: Domination and Transformation in the Third World,* edited by Joel Migdal, Atul Kohli, and Vivienne Shue, 108–142. Cambridge: Cambridge University Press, 1994.

Bratton, Michael, and Nicolas van de Walle. "Neopatrimonial Regimes and Political Transitions in Africa." *World Politics* 46: 4 (July 1994): 453–489.

Brindle, Simon. "Privatization Programme Lumbers Slowly On." *The Middle East,* April 2003, 1–4.

Brown, Leon Carl. "Stages in the Process of Change." In *Tunisia: The Politics of Modernization,* edited by C. A. Micaud, 3–66. New York: Praeger, 1964.

Brown, Nathan J., Amr Hamzawy, and Marina Ottaway. "Islamist Movements and the Democratic Process in the World: Exploring the Grey Zones." Working paper no. 67, Washington, D.C.: Carnegie Endowment for International Peace, March 2006.

Brownlee, Jason. "Low Tide after the Third Wave: Exploring Politics under Authoritarianism." *Comparative Politics* 34:4 (July 2002): 477–498.

———. "The Decline of Pluralism in Mubarak's Egypt." *Journal of Democracy* 13:4 (October 2002): 6–14.

———. "Ruling Parties and Durable Authoritarianism." Working paper, Center on Democracy, Development, and the Rule of Law, Stanford University, 2004.

———. "Political Crisis and Restabilization: Iraq, Libya, Syria, and Tunisia." In *Authoritarianism in the Middle East,* edited by Marsha Pripstein Posusney and Michele Penner Angrist, 43–62. Boulder, Colo.: Lynne Rienner Publishers, 2005.

Brulé, Jean-Claude. "The Agricultural Sector in Algeria: How Far has the Privatization of Real Estate Proceeded?" In *Economic Liberalization and Privatization in Socialist Arab Countries: Algeria, Egypt, Syrian and Yemen As Examples,* edited by Hans Hopfinger, 207–225. Gotha: Justus Perthes Verlag, 1996.

Brumberg, Daniel. "The Trap of Liberalized Autocracy." *Journal of Democracy* 13:4 (October 2002): 56–68.

Buchanan, James. "Rent Seeking and Profit Seeking." In *Toward a Theory of the Rent-Seeking Society,* edited by James Buchanan, Robert Tollison, and Gordan Tullock, 3–15. College Station: Texas A&M University Press, 1980.

Burrell, Richard, and Abbas Kelidar. "The Washington Papers: Egypt: The Dilemma of a Nation, 1970–1977." Report 48, The Center for Strategic and International Studies, Georgetown University, Washington, D.C., 1977.

Bush, Ray. "Mubarak's Legacy for Egypt's Rural Poor: Returning Land to the Landowners." UNDP Land, Poverty and Public Action Policy Paper No. 10, New York: UNDP, August 2005.

———. "Market Violence in Egypt's Countryside." *Peace Review: A Journal of Social Justice* 19:1 (Spring 2007): 15–21.

Bustos, Rafael. "Economic Liberalization and Political Change in Algeria: Theory and Practice (1988–92 and 1994–99)." *Mediterranean Politics* 8:1 (Spring 2003): 1–26.

Canitrot, Adolfo. "Crisis and Transformation of the Argentine State (1978–1992)." In *Democracy, Markets, and Structural Reform in Contemporary Latin America: Argentina, Bolivia, Brazil, Chile, and Mexico,* edited by William C. Smith, Carlos Acuña and Eduardo Gamarra, 75–102. New Brunswick, N.J.: Transaction Publishers, 1994.

Carothers, Thomas. "The End of the Transition Paradigm." *Journal of Democracy* 13:1 (January 2002): 5–21.

Carroll, Jill. "Algerian PM's Party Scores Convincing Win in Local Vote." *Christian Science Monitor,* October 11, 2002.

———. "In Algeria, a Status Quo Vote." *Christian Science Monitor,* May 17, 2007.

Cavarozzi, Marcelo. "Patterns of Elite Negotiation and Confrontation in Argentina and Chile." In *Elites and Democratic Consolidation in Latin America and Southern Europe,* edited by John Higley and Richard Gunther, 208–236. Cambridge: Cambridge University Press, 1992.

Chhibber, Pradeep K. "State Policy, Rent Seeking and the Electoral Success of a Religious Party in Algeria." *Journal of Politics* 58:1 (February 1996): 126–148.

Collander, David. *Neoclassical Political Economy: The Analysis of Rent Seeking and DUP Activities.* Cambridge, Mass.: Ballinger, 1984.

Collier, Ruth Berins. *Paths toward Democracy: The Working Class and Elites in Western Europe and South America.* Cambridge: Cambridge University Press, 1999.

———. "The Transformation of Labor-based One Partyism at the End of the Twentieth Century." In *The Awkward Embrace: One-Party Domination and Democracy,* edited by Hermann Giliomee and Charles Simkins, 219–226. Amsterdam: Harwood, 1999.

Collombier, Virginia. "The Internal Stakes of the 2005 Elections: The Struggle for Influence in Egypt's National Democratic Party." *Middle East Journal* 61:1 (Winter 2007): 95–111.

Cooper, Mark. *The Transformation of Egypt.* Baltimore: Johns Hopkins University Press, 1982.

Dahl, Reynold. "Agricultural Development Strategies in a Small Economy: The Case of Tunisia." Staff paper, USAID, 1971.

"Defying Nasser." *Time,* October 27, 1958.

Democratic Governance/Elections: Egypt. New York: United Nations Development Programme, 2007.

"Democracy in Iran Prompts Arab Introspection; Neighbors Will Scrutinize Their Ways Next, Analysts Say." *Washington Post,* March 10, 2000, Section A.

De Montety, Henry. "Old Families and New Elites in Tunisia." In *Man, State, and Society in the Contemporary Maghrib,* edited by William Zartmen, 171–180. New York: Praeger, 1973.

Di Palma, Giuseppe. *To Craft Democracies: An Essay on Democratic Transitions.* Berkeley: University of California Press, 1991.

Di Tommasso, Marco R., Elena Lanzoni, and Lauretta Rubini. "Support to SMEs in the Arab Region: The Case of Tunisia." Working Paper, Rome: UNIDO, 2001.

Diamond, Larry. "Economic Development and Democracy Reconsidered." *American Behavioral Scientist* 35:4–5 (March–June 1992): 450–499.

———. "Elections without Democracy: Thinking about Hybrid Regimes." *Journal of Democracy* 13:2 (April 2002): 21–35.

———. "Democracy Remains the People's Choice." *Straits Times* (Singapore), September 11, 2006.

———, Jonathan Hartlyn, Juan J. Linz, and Seymour Martin Lipset. *Democracy in Developing Countries: Latin America.* Boulder, Colo.: Lynne Rienner Press, 1999.

Dillman, Bradford L. *State and Private Sector in Algeria: The Politics of Rent Seeking and Failed Development.* Boulder, Colo.: Westview Press, 2000.

———."Facing the Market in North Africa." *Middle East Journal* 55 (Spring 2001): 198–215.

Dillman, Bradford. "The Political Economy of Structural Adjustment in Tunisia and Algeria." *Journal of North African Studies* 3:3 (1998): 1–24.

"Egypt: Detention of 25 Muslim Brothers Renewed." *Al-Wafd,* August 1, 2001.

"Egypt: Doubts over NDP Reform Motives." *Oxford Analytica,* November 17, 2003.

"Egypt: Flawed Military Trials for Brotherhood Leaders: Human Rights Groups, Media Barred from Observing Trial." June 5, 2005. Human Rights Watch. http://hrw.org/english/docs/2007/06/05/egypt16072.htm.

"Egyptian Opposition Reels under State Crackdown." *Turkish Daily News,* November 30, 2006.

"Egypt's Elections: A Triumph for Democracy or Thuggery?" *Mideast Mirror,* November 30, 1995.

"Egypt's Parliament, Representing All Categories and Parties." *Arabic News,* September 21, 2000. http://www.arabicnews.com/ansub/Daily/ Day/000921/2000092147.html.

Ehteshami, Anoushiravan, and Emma C. Murphy. "Transformation of the Corporatist State in the Middle East." *Third World Quarterly* 17:4 (1996): 753–772.

El-Din, Gamal Essam. "Anti-Monopoly Bill Critiqued from Left and Right: Not Everyone Is Happy about the New Anti-Trust Bill." *Al-Ahram Weekly,* January 27–February 2, 2005. Issue no. 727 in weekly.ahram.org.eg/2005/727/ ecz.htm.

"Election 2005: Egypt's Ruling Party Rattled by Impressive Opposition Gains." *World Markets Analysis,* December 9, 2005.

El-Ghobashy, Mona. "Egypt Looks ahead to Portentous Year." *Middle East Report Online,* February 2, 2005. http://www.merip.org/mero/mero020205.html.

El-Ghonemy, M. Riad. *The Political Economy of Rural Poverty: The Case for Land Reform.* New York: Routledge, 1990.

———. *Land, Food and Rural Development in North Africa.* London: IT Publications, 1993.

———."The Political Economy of Market-Based Land Reform." New York: Popular Coalition/UNRISD monograph, June 4, 1999.

Ennaceur, Mohamed. "Les Syndicats et la mondialisation: Le Cas de la Tunisie." Working Paper No. DP/120, Geneva: L'Institute internationale d'études sociales, 2000.

Entelis, John. *Algeria: The Revolution Institutionalized.* Boulder, Colo.: Westview Press, 1986.

"Fallahu al-shalf yutalibyn bi-milkiyyat al -'aradi allati yasashillunaha." *Al-Fadjr,* June 21, 2004. http://www.al-fadjr.com.

Farati, Muhammad. "Al-Khawsasa wa-in 'ikasatiha al-iztima'iyya." *Al-Mawqif,* October 17, 2003.

"Fi al-Misriyya li-Tijarat al-Kimawiyyat wa-al-Ma'adin: al-Sharika al-Qabida lil-Tijara tarfud sarf mustahaqqat 2000 'amil kharaju lil-mas'ash al-mubbakir." *Al-Ahali,* November 6, 2002.

"Five Die in Clash in Egypt." *BBC Monitoring Middle East,* March 9, 1998.

Forni, Nadia. "Land Tenure Systems: Structural Features and Policies." FAO report GCP/SYR/006/ITA, Damascus, Syria: FAO, March 2001.

Free Egyptians, The. http://Free.Egyptians.4t.com/.

Gambill, Gary. "The Political Obstacles to Economic Reform in Syria." *Middle East Intelligence Bulletin* 3:7 (July 2001), http://www.meib.org/articles/0107_s1.htm.

———. "Jumpstarting Arab Reform: The Bush Administration's Greater Middle East Initiative." *Middle East Intelligence Bulletin* 6:6–7 (June–July 2004): 1–4.

Garcia, Laura Cabeza, and Silvia Gomez Anson. "The Spanish Privatization Process: Implications on the Performance of Divested Firms." *International Review of Financial Analysis* 16:4 (2007): 390–409.

Gauch, Sara. "More Mercedes Cars Cruise Cairo's Streets as Rich Prosper." *Christian Science Monitor,* April 11, 1996.

Geddes, Barbara. "Authoritarian Breakdown: Empirical Test of a Game Theoretic Argument." Paper presented at the annual meeting of the American Political Science Association, Atlanta, Georgia, September 1999.

———. "What Do We Know about Democratization after Twenty Years?" *Annual Review of Political Science* 2 (1999): 369–404.

Gelvin, James L. "The Social Origins of Popular Nationalism in Syria: Evidence for a New Framework." *International Journal of Middle East Studies* 26:4 (November 1994): 645–661.

"General Union of Algerian Workers Supports Bouteflika in Presidential Race." *Al-Bawaba,* March 4, 2004.

Gershowitz, Suzanne. "Dissident Watch: Ayman Nour." *Middle East Quarterly* 12:3 (Summer 2005), http://www.meforum.org/article/753.

Gilomee, Hermann, and Charles Simkins, eds. *Awkward Embrace: One-Party Domination and Democracy in Industrializing Countries.* Johannesburg: Tafelberg, 2000.

Global Corruption Report 2004. Berlin: Transparency International, 2004. http://www.globalcorruptionreport.org/download/gcr2004/10_Country_reports_A_K.pdf.

Goldberg, Ellis. "The Foundations of State–Labor Relations in Contemporary Egypt." *Comparative Politics* 24:2 (January 1992): 147–162.

Goldschmidt, Arthur, Jr. *Modern Egypt: The Formation of a Nation State.* Boulder, Colo.: Westview Press, 2004.

"Government and Politics of Egypt." In *Egypt: A Country Study,* edited by Helen Chapin Metz. Washington, D.C.: Government Printing Office, 1990. http://countrystudies.us/egypt/121.htm.

"Government Main Trade Union Reach Agreement." *BBC Monitoring Middle East,* September 28, 1998.

Greene, Kenneth F. *Why Dominant Parties Lose: Mexico's Democratization in Comparative Perspective.* Cambridge: Cambridge University Press, 2007.

"Group Protests Harassment of Labor Union." Human Rights Watch, April 26, 2007.

Habib, Ali. "Algeria Faces Threat of Labour Unrest." *Guardian Publication*, March 17, 1996.

Hachana, Nejib. "210 years of Tunisian-American Relations." Lecture, Maghreb Center's Speaker's Series, Georgetown University, Washington, D.C., September 19, 2007.

Hadenius, Axel, and Jan Teorell. "Authoritarian Regimes: Stability, Change, and Pathways to Democracy." Working paper 331, Kellogg Institute, Notre Dame, South Bend, Ind., 2006.

———. "Pathways from Authoritarianism." *Journal of Democracy* 18:1 (January 2007): 143–156.

Hadidi, Subhi. "Assad's Corruption Cover-up." *Middle East Research Institute*, January 7, 2004.

Hadjdaj, Djillali. *Corruption et démocratie en Algérie.* Paris: La Dispute, 1999.

Haggard, Stephan, and Robert Kaufman. *The Political Economy of Democratic Transitions.* Princeton, N.J.: Princeton University Press, 1995.

Halpern, Manfred. *The Politics of Social Change in the Middle East and North Africa.* Princeton, N.J: Princeton University Press, 1962.

"Hal tujad 'ilaqabayna al-khawsasawa-al-istithmar al-ajnabiwa-alfasad?" *Al-Fadjr,* January 19, 2004. http://www.al-fadjr.com.

Hamdi, Mohamed Elhachmi. *The Politicization of Islam: A Case Study of Tunisia.* Boulder, Colo.: Westview, 1998.

Hamidi, Hamid. "Khaskhasat Al-Moasasaat Al-Aomomia fi Al-Qanoun Al-Jazeeri." In *Al-Islahat Al-Iqtisadiah wa Siyasat Al-Khaskhasah fi al-Buldan Al-Arabia.* Beirut: Center for Arab Unity Studies, 1999.

Hamzawy, Amr. "Egypt: Dynamics of Regime and Opposition." *Bitter Lemons,* September 30, 2005. http://*bitterlemons-international.org.*

———. "Opposition in Egypt: Performance in the Presidential Election and Prospects for the Parliamentary Elections." *Policy Outlook* 22. Washington, D.C.: Carnegie Endowment for International Peace, October 2005.

Harb, Osama El-Ghazali. "Democracy and Its Discontents." *Al-Ahram Weekly,* December 28, 2000.

Harik, Iliya. "Privatization and Development in Tunisia." In *Privatization and Liberalization in the Middle East,* edited by Iliya Harik and Denis J. Sullivan, 210–232. Bloomington: Indiana University Press, 1992.

Hasel, Thomas. *Machtkonflikt in Algerien.* Berlin: Verlag Hans Schiler, 2002.

Hawthorne, Amy. "At the Bottom of the Bush–Mubarak Agenda? The Slow Pace of Political Reform in Egypt." *Policy Watch* 258. Washington, D.C.: The Washington Institute for Near East Policy, April 2001.

Henry, Clement, and Robert Springborg. *Globalization and the Politics of Development in the Middle East.* Cambridge: Cambridge University Press, 2001.

Herbst, Jeffrey. *The Political Economy of Reform in Ghana, 1982–1991.* Cambridge: Cambridge University Press, 1993.

———. *The Politics of Reform in Ghana*. Cambridge: Cambridge University Press, 1993.

Hermassi, Elbaki. *Leadership and National Development in North Africa*. Berkeley: University of California Press, 1972.

Heydemann, Steven. *Authoritarianism in Syria: Institutions and Social Conflict, 1946–1970*. Ithaca, N.Y.: Cornell University Press, 1999.

———, ed. *Networks of Privilege in the Middle East: The Politics of Economic Reform Revisited*. New York: Palgrave Macmillan, 2004.

Highland, Fredrick. "Night Falls on Damascus." http://frederickhighland.com/damascus/articles/lastking.htm.

Higley, John, and Michael Burton. "The Elite Variable in Democratic Transitions and Breakdowns." *American Sociological Review* 54:1 (February 1989): 17–32.

"Hikayat Ahmad 'Izz ma'a sharikat al-Dikhila lil-Hadid wa-al-Sulb: Fada'ih al-fasad wa-al-ihtikar fi sina'at al-sulb." *Al-Ahali,* August 2, 2000.

Hinnebusch, Raymond. *Egyptian Politics under Sadat: The Post-Populist Development of an Authoritarian-Modernizing State*. Cambridge: Cambridge University Press, 1985.

———. *Authoritarian Power and State Formation in Ba'thist Syria: Army, Party, Peasant*. Boulder, Colo.: Westview Press, 1989.

———. *Peasant and Bureaucracy in Ba'thist Syria: The Political Economy of Rural Development*. Boulder, Colo.: Westview Press, 1989.

———. "Revisionist Dreams, Realist Strategies: The Foreign Policy of Syria." In *The Foreign Policies of the Arab States: The Challenge of Change,* edited by Bahgat Korany and Ali E. Hillal Dessouki, 374–419. Boulder, Colo.: Westview Press, 1991.

———. "The Politics of Economic Reform in Egypt." *Third World Quarterly* 14:1 (1993): 159–171.

———. "Syria: The Politics of Economic Liberalization." *Third World Quarterly* 18:2 (1997): 249–265.

———. "Liberalization without Democratization in 'Post-Populist' Authoritarian States." In *Citizenship and the State in the Middle East,* edited by Nils A. Butenschon, Uri Davis, and Manuel Hassassian, 123–145. Syracuse, N.Y.: Syracuse University Press, 2000.

———. "The Foreign Policy of Egypt." In *The Foreign Policies of Middle East States,* edited by Raymond Hinnebusch and Anoushiravan Ehteshami, 91–114. Boulder, Colo.: Lynne Rienner, 2002.

———. "Authoritarian Persistence, Democratization Theory and the Middle East: An Overview and Critique." *Democratization* 13:3 (June 2006): 373–395.

Hochman, Dafna. "Divergent Democratization: The Paths of Tunisia, Morocco, and Mauritania." *Middle East Policy* 14:4 (Winter 2007): 75.

Hopfinger, Hans, and Marc Boeckler. "Step by Step to an Open Economic System: Syria Sets Course for Liberalization." *British Journal of Middle Eastern Studies* 23:2 (1996): 183–202.

Hopwood, Derek. *Egypt: Politics and Society, 1945–1990*. Harper Collins Academic: London, 1991.

Hudson, Michael. "After the Gulf War: Prospects for Democratization in the Arab World." *Middle East Journal* 45:3 (1991): 407–427.

Hudson, Rex A., ed. *Brazil: A Country Study*. Washington, D.C.: GPO for the Library of Congress, 1997.

Huntington, Samuel. *The Third Wave: Democratization in the Late Twentieth Century*. Norman: University of Oklahoma, 1991.

————, and Clement H. Moore. *Authoritarian Politics in Modern Societies: The Dynamics of Established One-Party Systems*. New York: Basic Books, 1970.

Hussein, Dina Khalifa. "Egyptian Workers Object! Resurgent Workers' Protests Make Deadline News." *Economic and Business Research Centre Chronicles, American University in Cairo* 1:2 (October 2005): 19–21.

Ibrahim, Hasanayin Tawfiq. *Al-Iqtisad al-siyasi lil-ilsah al-iqtisadi*. Cairo: Markaz al-Dirasat al Siyasiyya wa-al-Istratijiyya, 1999.

Ibrahim, Saad Eddine. "The New Middle East Bush Is Resisting." *Washington Post*, August 23, 2006.

Ifejika, Nkem. "Who's Who: Syria's Top Ten Political Brokers." *The New Statesmen*, June 5, 2006.

Jabr, Haytham. "Rijal al-a'mal wa-al-siyasa fi misr." *Ahwal Misriyya* 21 (Summer 2003): 128–138.

Jackson, Henry. *The FLN in Algeria: Party Development in a Revolutionary Society*. Westport. Conn.: Greenwood Press, 1977.

Jamil, Qadri. "Al-islah al-iqtisadi bayna al-abyad wa-al-aswad." *Kassioun*, June 19, 2006.

Jesudan, James V. "The Resilience of One-Party Dominance in Malaysia and Singapore." In *Awkward Embrace: One-Party Domination and Democracy in Industrializing Countries*, edited by Hermann Gilomee and Charles Simkins, 127–172. Johannesburg: Tafelberg, 2000.

Kang, David C. *Crony Capitalism: Corruption and Development in South Korea and the Philippines*. Cambridge: Cambridge University Press, 2002.

Karl, Terry Lynn. "Dilemmas of Democratization in Latin America." *Comparative Politics* 23:1(October 1990): 1–23.

Keck, Margaret. *The Workers Party and Democratization in Brazil*. New Haven: Yale University Press, 1992.

Khiari, Sadri, and Olfa Lamloum. "Tunisie: des élections en trompe-l'œil." *Politique Africaine* 76 (December 1999): 106–115.

"Le zaim et l'artisan ou de Bourguibaa Ben Ali." *Annuaire de l'Afrique du Nord* 37 (1988): 377–395.

Khoury, Philip S. *Syria and the French Mandate: The Politics of Arab Nationalism*. London: I.B. Tauris and Co. Ltd., 1987.

————. "The Syrian Independence Movement and the Growth of Economic

Nationalism in Damascus." *British Society of Middle Eastern Studies Bulletin* 14:1 (1987): 25–36.

———. "Syrian Political Culture: A Historical Perspective." In *Syria: Society Culture and Polity,* edited by Richard T. Antoun and Donald Quataert, 13–28. Albany: State University of New York, 1991.

Kienle, Eberhard. "More Than a Response to Islamism: The Political Deliberalization of Egypt in the 1990s." *Middle East Journal* 52:2 (Spring 1998): 219–235.

———. *A Grand Delusion: Democracy and Economic Reform in Egypt.* London: I.B. Tauris, 2001.

King, Stephen J. "Economic Reform and Tunisia's Hegemonic Party: The End of the Administrative Elite." *Arab Studies Quarterly* 20:2 (Spring 1998), 59–87.

———. *Liberalization against Democracy: The Local Politics of Economic Reform in Tunisia.* Bloomington: Indiana University Press, 2003.

Klouf, El Haj. "Ben Ali Arbitre la Lutte Chiboub/Trabelsi." *L'autre Tunisie,* June 12, 2003, http://tounes.naros.info/article.php3?id_article=57.

Knauss, Peter. "Algeria's Revolution: Peasants Control or Control of Peasants?" *African Studies Review* 20:3 (December 1977): 65–78.

Knickmeyer, Ellen. "Egyptian Voters Impeded In Opposition Strongholds." *Washington Post,* June 12, 2007.

Krueger, Anne. "The Political Economy of the Rent-Seeking Society." *The American Economic Review* 64:3 (June 1974): 291–303.

Kurzman, Charles, ed. *Liberal Islam.* Oxford: Oxford University Press, 1998.

Lagarde, Dominique. "La Fronde des Jeunes." *L'Express.fr,* May 18, 2000, http://www.lexpress.fr/info/monde/dossier/tunisie/dossier.asp?ida=408871.

Laham, Fouad. "Al-Qita'a Al-Mushtarak for Cooperation between the Public and Private Sectors." Paper presented at the Fifteenth Tuesday Forum on Economic and Social Development in Syria, Damascus, February 12, 2002.

Lancaster, John. "Desert Turns to Greens as Egypt's Affluent Revive Colonial Links." *Washington Post Foreign Service,* February 22, 1997.

"Land Tenure and Reform." In *Algeria: A Country Study,* edited by Helen Chapin Metz. Washington, D.C.: Government Printing Office, 1993.

Landis, Joshua. "The Presidential Plebiscite and Pageantry: What Does It Mean?" Syria Comment. http://joshualandis.com.

———. "Syria Comment Blog." Syria Comment. http://joshualandis.com.

Langohr, Vickie. "Cracks in Egypt's Electoral Engineering: The 2000 Vote." *Middle East Report Online,* November 7, 2000. http://www.merip.org/mero/mero110700.html.

"La qima li-qarar lil-qarar ra'is al jumhuriya hawla al-madda 137 min qanun al-amilin al-muwahhad." *Kassioun,* June 2007.

Lassaad, Mediouni. "Government Labor Power Struggle Set to Continue." *IPS-Inter Press Service,* December 23, 1985.

Lawson, Fred. "Domestic Transformation and Foreign Steadfastness in Contemporary Syria." *Middle East Journal* 48:1 (Winter 1994): 47–64.

Layachi, Azzedine. "The Private Sector in the Algerian Economy: Obstacles and Potentials for a Productive Role." *Mediterranean Politics* 6:2 (Summer 2001): 29–50.

Lee, Eric. "Confronting Cairo: Changing an Illusory Democracy." *Harvard International Review* 28:2 (Summer 2006): 42.

"Le multipartisme d'État en Tunisie: La débâcle." Austrabal's Blog. http://astrubal .nawaat.org/2002/12/12/le-multipartisme-detat-en-tunisie-la-debacle/.

Leverett, Flynt. *Inheriting Syria: Bashar's Trial by Fire.* Washington, D.C.: Brookings Institution, 2005.

Levitsky, Steven, and Lucan Way. "The Rise of Competitive Authoritarianism." *Journal of Democracy* 13:2 (April 2002): 51–65.

Linz, Juan, and H. Chehabi, ed. *Sultanistic Regimes.* Baltimore: Johns Hopkins University Press, 1998.

Lipset, Seymour Martin. "Some Social Requisites of Democracy: Economic Development and Political Legitimacy." *American Political Science Review* 53 (March 1959): 69–105.

Lofren, Hans. "Economic Policy in Egypt: A Breakdown in Reform Resistance?" *International Journal of Middle East Studies* 25:3 (1993): 407–421.

Londegran, John, and Keith Poole. "Poverty, the Coup Trap, and the Seizure of Executive Power." *World Politics* 42 (January 1990): 151–183.

Longuenesse, Elizabeth. "Labor in Syria: The Emergence of New Identities." In *The Social History of Labor in the Middle East,* edited by Ellis Goldberg, 99–130. Boulder, Colo.: Westview Press, 1996.

Lust-Okar, Ellen. "Opposition and Economic Crisis in Jordan and Morocco." In *Authoritarianism in the Middle East,* edited by Marsha Pripstein Posusney and Michele Penner Angrist, 143–168. Boulder, Colo.: Lynne Rienner, 2005.

———. "The Syrian Challenge." Presentation at Carnegie Endowment for International Peace, Washington, D.C., March 30, 2006.

Mabardi, Roueida. "Syria Faces Huge Obstacles to Market Economy." Includes an Interview with Nabil Sukkar. *Agence France Press,* August 1, 2005.

Macfarquhar, Neil. "Alexandria Journal; Poor Egypt's Golden Coast: The Lure (and Leer)," *New York Times,* July 30, 1996.

"Mafhru' jaded li-nizam al-ma'ash al -mubakkir a-idtirarai." *Al-Ahram,* April 23, 2006.

Magaloni, Beatriz. *Voting for Autocracy: Hegemonic Party Survival and Its Demise in Mexico.* Cambridge: Cambridge University Press, 2006.

Mahoney, James, and Richard Snyder. "Rethinking Agency and Structure in the Study of Regime Change." *Studies in Comparative International Development* 34:2 (Summer 1999): 3–32.

"Main Trade Union Drops Support for Bouteflika." *BBC Monitoring Middle East,* January 30, 2003.

Mansur, Yusuf. "The Consequences of Distorted Competition in the Arab World." *Daily Star* (Lebanon), December 15, 2007.

Maravall, Jose Mario, and Julian Santamaria. "Political Change in Spain and the Prospects for Democracy." In *Transitions from Authoritarian Rule: Southern Europe,* edited by Guillermo O'Donnell, Philippe C. Schmitter, and Laurence Whitehead, 71–108. Baltimore: Johns Hopkins University Press, 1986.

Marshall, Susan E., and Randall G. Stokes. "Tradition and the Veil: Female Status in Tunisia and Algeria." *The Journal of Modern African Studies* 19:4 (December 1981): 625–646.

Martinez, Luis. *The Algerian Civil War 1990–1998.* New York: Columbia University Press, 2000

McFaul, Michael. "The Fourth Wave of Democracy and Dictatorship: Noncooperative Transitions in the Post-Communist World." *World Politics* 54 (January 2002): 212–244.

Meital, Yoram. "The Struggle over Political Order in Egypt: The 2005 Elections." *Middle East Journal* 60:2 (Spring 2006): 257–279.

"Misr tahtafil bi-id al-umaal." In *Al-Ahram,* April 28, 2006.

Mitchell, Richard. *The Society of the Muslim Brothers.* Oxford: Oxford University Press, 1969.

"Mohamed Hamsho." *Free Syria,* June 21, 2006.

Moore, Barrington. *Social Origins of Dictatorship and Democracy: Lord and Peasant in the Making of the Modern World.* Boston: Beacon Press, 1966.

Moore, Clement Henry. *Tunisia since Independence.* Berkeley: University of California Press, 1965.

Moubayed, Sami. "Syria's Ba'athists Loosen the Reins." *Asia Times,* April 26, 2005, Middle East section.

Mubarak, Hosni. "They Will Never Come to Power." Interview by Lally Weymouth. *Newsweek* June 19, 1995.

Munck, Geraldo L. *Authoritarianism and Democratization: Soldiers and Workers in Argentina, 1976–1983.* University Park: Pennsylvania State University Press, 1998.

"Mu'raba bayna sindan al-istimalak wa-matraqat al-mukhattat." *Kassioun,* June 3, 2006.

Nelson, Joan, ed. *Fragile Coalitions: The Politics of Economic Adjustment.* New Brunswick, N.J: Transaction Books, 1989.

"New Cabinet Sworn In." *World News Digest,* November 13, 1976.

Nisi, Kastru. "Wizarat al-amal wa-tudir zahraha lil-'ummal." *Kassioun,* June 10, 2006.

O'Donnell, Guillermo. *Modernization and Bureaucratic Authoritarianism: Studies in South American Politics.* Berkeley: University of California Press, 1973.

———. "Delegative Democracy." *Journal of Democracy* 5:1 (January 1994): 55–69.

———. "Debating the Transition Paradigm: In Partial Defense of an Evanescent Paradigm." *Journal of Democracy* 13:3 (July 2002): 39–45.

———, Philippe C. Schmitter, and Laurence Whitehead, eds. *Transitions from Authoritarian Rule: Tentative Conclusions about Uncertain Democracies.* Baltimore: Johns Hopkins University Press, 1986.

Obretin, Bogdan. "Egypt Extends State of Emergency." Softpedia. http://news .softpedia.com/news/Egypt-Extends-State-of-Emergency-22518.shtml.

O'Brien, Philip, and Paul Cammack, eds. *Generals in Retreat: The Crisis of Military Rule in Latin America.* Dover, N.H.: Manchester University Press, 1985.

Ottaway, David, and Marina Ottaway. *Algeria: The Politics of a Socialist Revolution.* Berkeley: University of California Press, 1970.

Ottaway, Marina. *Democracy Challenged: The Rise of Semi-Authoritarianism.* Washington, D.C.: Carnegie Endowment for International Peace, 2003.

———. Foreword to *The Other Face of the Islamist Movement,* by Mustapha Kamel Al-Sayyid. Working paper no. 23, Washington, D.C.: Carnegie Endowment for International Peace, January 2003.

Owen, Roger. "Socio-economic Change and Political Mobilization: The Case of Egypt." In *Democracy without Democrats: The Renewal of Politics in the Muslim World,* edited by Ghassan Salame, 183–199. London: I.B. Taurius, 1994.

———. "The Middle Eastern State: Repositioning Not Retreat." In *The State and Global Change: The Political Economy of Transition in the Middle East and North Africa,* edited by Hassan Hakimian and Ziba Moshaver, 232–247. Richmond, Va.: Curzon, 2001.

Payne, Leigh A. *Brazilian Industrialists and Democratic Change.* Baltimore: Johns Hopkins University Press, 1994.

Payne, Rhys. "Economic Crisis and Policy Reform in the 1980s." In *Polity and Society in Contemporary North Africa,* edited by William Mark Habeeb and William Zartman, 139–167. Boulder, Colo.: Westview Press, 1993.

"Père Noël politique." Bordj Bou Arreridj info. http://www.bba34.com/.

Perthes, Volker. "A Look at Syria's Upper Class: The Bourgeoisie and the Ba'th." *Middle East Report* 170 (May–June 1991): 31–37.

———. "Syria's Parliamentary Elections: Remodeling Asad's Political Base." *Middle East Report* 174 (January–February 1992): 15–18, 35.

———. "The Syrian Private Industrial and Commercial Sectors and the State." *International Journal of Middle East Studies* 24:2 (May 1992): 207–230.

———. "Stages of Economic and Political Liberalization." In *Contemporary Syria: Liberalization between Cold War and Cold Peace,* edited by Eberhard Kienle, 44–71. London: University of London, 1994.

———. *The Political Economy of Syria under Asad.* London: Tairus, 1995.

Philip, George. "The Military Institution Revisted: Some Notes on Corporatism and Military Rule in Latin America." *Journal of Latin American Studies* 12:2 (1980): 421–436.

Pinheiro, Armando, and Ben Ross Schneider. "The Fiscal Impact of Privatization in Latin America." *The Journal of Development Studies* 31:5 (June 1995): 751–776.

Pons, Jean-François. "Le rôle accru de la politique de la concurrence dans la relance

du partenariat euro-méditerranéenet dans la coopération multilatérale."
Paper presented at the Regional Seminar on the Politics of Competition and
Multilateral Negotiations in Tunis, 28–29 March, 2002.

Posusney, Marsha Pripstein. *Labor and the State in Egypt: Workers, Unions, and
Economic Restructuring.* New York: Columbia University Press, 1997.

———. "Behind the Ballot Box: Electoral Engineering in the Arab World." *Middle
East Report* 209 (Winter 1998): 12–16.

———. "Egyptian Privatization: New Challenges for the Left." *Middle East Report*
210 (Spring 1999): 38–40.

———. "Egyptian Labor Struggle in the Era of Privatization: The Moral Economy
Thesis Revisited." In *Privatization and Labor: Responses and Consequences in
Global Perspective,* edited by Marsha Pripstein Posusney and Linda J. Cook,
43–64. Cheltenham: Edward Elgar, 2002.

———. "Enduring Authoritarianism: Middle East Lessons for Comparative Theory."
Comparative Politics 36:2 (January 2004): 127–138.

———. "Multiparty Elections in the Arab World: Election Rules and Opposition
Responses." In *Authoritarianism in the Middle East,* edited by Marsha Pripstein
Posusney and Michele Penner Angrist, 91–118. Boulder, Colo.: Lynne Rienner
Publishers, 2005.

———, and Michele Penner Angrist, eds. *Authoritarianism in the Middle East:
Regimes and Resistance.* Boulder, Colo.: Lynne Rienner, 2005.

Przeworski, Adam, ed. *Sustainable Democracy.* Cambridge: Cambridge University
Press, 1995.

Przeworski, Adam, Michael Alvarez, Jose Cheibub, and Fernando Limongi.
*Democracy and Development: Political Institutions and Well-Being in the World,
1950–1990.* Cambridge: Cambridge University Press, 2000.

"Qa'imat al-ihtikarat fi Misr: Bay' al-sharikat li-mustathmir wahid yu'addi ila
al-ihtikar." Includes a quotation by Mahmud 'Abd Al-Fadli. *Al-Ahali,*
February 28, 2001.

Quandt, William. *Between Ballots and Bullets: Algeria's Transition from
Authoritarianism.* Washington, D.C.: Brookings, 1998.

"Rasa'il 'ajila min al-dukturYusufWaliwazir al-zira'a." *Al-Ahram,* March 26, 1997.

"Report on Peasants." Land Center for Human Rights. Cairo, February 2006.

Republic of Tunisia: Growth Policies and Poverty Alleviation. Washington, D.C.:
World Bank, 1995.

"Reports on Presidential Elections." Land Center for Human Rights. Cairo,
September 2005.

Roberts, Hugh. "The Politics of Algerian Socialism." In *North Africa: Contemporary
Politics and Economic Development,* edited by Richard Lawless and Allan
Findlay, 5–49. New York: St. Martin's Press, 1984.

———. "Musical Chairs in Algeria." *Middle East Report Online,* June 4, 2002. http://
www.merip.org/mero/mero060402.html.

———. *The Battlefield Algeria 1988–2002: Studies in a Broken Polity.* London: Verso,
2003.

———. "Demilitarizing Algeria." Working paper no. 86, Washington, D.C.: Carnegie Endowment for International Peace, May 2007.

Robinson, Glenn. "Elite Cohesion, Regime Succession and Political Instability in Syria." *Middle East Policy* 5:4 (January 1998): 159–179.

Rouadjia, Ahmed. *Grandeur et décadence de l'État Algérien.* Paris: Editions Karthala, 1994.

Ruedy, John. *Modern Algeria: The Origins and Development of a Nation.* Bloomington: Indiana University Press, 1992.

Rueschemeyer, Dietrich, Evelyne Huber Stephens, and John D. Stephens. *Capitalist Development and Democracy.* Chicago: University of Chicago Press, 1992.

Sadowski, Yahya. *Political Vegetables? Businessmen and Bureaucrat in the Development of Egyptian Agriculture.* Washington, D.C.: The Brookings Institution, 1991.

Schamis, Hector. "Reconceptualizing Latin American Authoritarianism in the 1970s: From Bureaucratic Authoritarianism to Neoconservatism." *Comparative Politics* 23:2 (January 1991): 201–220.

———. *Reforming the State: The Politics of Privatization in Latin America and Europe.* Ann Arbor: University of Michigan, 2002.

Schedler, Andreas. "Elections without Democracy: The Menu of Manipulation." *Journal of Democracy* 13:2 (April 2002): 36–50.

Schemm, Paul. "Labor Movement Possible Future for Egypt Opposition." Includes an interview with Joel Beinin, head of the Middle East Studies Department, American University in Cairo. *Middle East Times,* April 26, 2007.

Schmid, Bernhard. "Tunesien zwischen Präsidentschaftswahl, politischen Prozessen und 'wilden' Streiks: Wahlfarce und Soziale Kämpfe im Polizeistaats-'Musterlände.'" Trend Online Setzung, http://www.trend.infopartisan.net/trd1204/t121204.html.

Schmitter, Philippe. "Still the Century of Corporatism." *Review of Politics* 36:1 (1974): 85–131.

Seale, Patrick. *Asad: The Struggle for the Middle East.* Berkeley: University of California Press, 1988.

Seddon, David. "Winter of Discontent: Economic Crisis in Tunisia and Morocco." *MERIP Reports* 127 (October 1994): 7–16.

Shadid, Anthony. "Syria Heralds Reforms, But Many Have Doubts: Party Weighs Gradual Moves toward Democracy." *Washington Post,* May 18, 2005.

———. "Death of a Syrian Minister Leaves a Sect Adrift in Time of Strife." *Washington Post,* October 31, 2005, Section A.

Sharabi, Hisham. *Neopatriarchy: A Theory of Distorted Change in Arab Society.* Oxford: Oxford University Press, 1988.

Slackman, Michael. "Peacekeepers Targets of New Sinai Attacks." *New York Times,* April 27, 2006.

Smith, Benjamin. "Life of the Party: The Origins of Regime Breakdown and Persistence Under Single-Party Rule." *World Politics* 57:3 (April 2005): 421–451.

Smyth, Gareth. "Does Syria Mean Business?" *Middle East Company News Wire,* February 16, 2002.

Soliman, Samer. "Political Participation in the 2005 Parliamentary Elections." The Egyptian Association for Enhancing Societal Participation and the European Union. Cairo: 2006. Springborg, Robert. *Mubarak's Egypt: Fragmentation of the Political Order.* Boulder, Colo.: Westview Press, 1989.

Sukkar, Nabil. "The Crisis of 1986 and Syria's Plan for Reform." In *Contemporary Syria: Liberalization between Cold War and Cold Peace,* edited by Eberhard Kienle, 26–43. London: University of London, 1994.

———. "Thulathiat Hitham al-Soq Wa al-Adala al-Ejitmia'aih wa Al-Ertiqaa Al Technology fi Mwajahat al-'Awalama Wa Mutatalibat Al-Iqtisad Al-Souri." Paper presented at the Sixteenth Tuesday Forum on Economic and Social Development in Syria, Damascus, September 2, 2002.

Sulayman, Samir. *Al-Nizam al-qawi wa-al-dawla al-da'ifa: idarat al-azma al-maliya wa-al-taghyir al siyasi fi 'ahd Mubarak.* Cairo: Al-Dar, 2006.

Swidler, Anne. "Culture in Action: Symbols and Strategies." *American Sociological Review* 51:2 (April 1986): 273–286.

"Syrians Vote for Assad in Uncontested Referendum." *Washington Post,* May 28, 2007, Section A.

Takheroubt, B."Lutte contre la corruption: L'État passe à l'attaque." Algeria-Watch. http://algeria-watch.org/fr/article/eco/corruption_attaque.htm.

Tarik, Rezak. *Algeria Interface.* 2001, http://www.algeria-interface.com.

Tedesco, Laura. *Democracy in Argentina.* London: Frank Cass, 1999.

Terranti, Salima. "La privatisation du foncier agricole en Algérie; plus de dix ans de débats silencieux." Communication at the Fourth Pan African Programme on Land and Resources Rights. Cape Town, May 2003.

Tessler, Mark, Gregory White, and John Entelis. "The Republic of Tunisia." In *The Government and Politics of the Middle East and North Africa,* edited by David E. Long and Bernard Reich, 423–446. Boulder, Colo.: Westview Press, 1995.

Thabit, Ahmad. "Idarat tanzim al-dawa'ir al-intikhabiyya." In *Nuzum idarat al-intikhabat fi Misr,* edited by Amr Hashim Rabi,' Cairo: Markaz al Dirasat al-Siyasiyya wa-al-Istratigiyya, 2006.

"That ghita' al-tasharukiya: al-khaskhasa taqtahim salat Sundus." *Kassioun,* June 19, 2006.

Tingay, Caroline. "Law 1996 of 1992: The Government's 'Serious Commitment to Implementation.'" *Tishreen Daily,* October 27, 2004.

Tlemcani, Salima. "Algeria: Union Officials Accuse Government of Ignoring Workers." *El Watan,* November 22, 1998.

"The Triangle of National Theft." *Free Syria,* August 26, 2006.

Tullock, Gordon. "The Welfare Cost of Tariffs, Monopolies, and Theft." *Western Economic Journal* 5:3 (1967): 224–232.

"Ummal sharikat Tilimisr yasrukhun: Man yunqidhuna min ghul al-khaskhasa?" *Al-Ahali,* May 16, 2001.

"Une campagne électorale particulière dans les Bibans." Bordj Bou Arreridj info. http://www.bba34.com/spip.php?article189&var_recherche=tribal isme%20.

"Uyahya yurid tajmid al-birnamij al-watari lil-tanmiya al-filahiyya." *Al-Fadjr,* October 6, 2003. http://www.al-fadjr.com.

Van Dam, Nikolaos. *The Struggle for Power in Syria: Politics and Society under Asad and the Ba'th party.* London: I.B. Tauris, 1996.

Verges, Joaquim. "Privatizations in Spain: Process, Policies, and Goals." *European Journal of Law and Economics* 9:3 (2000): 255–280.

Vitalis, Robert. *When Capitalists Collide: Business Conflict and the End of Empire in Egypt.* Berkeley: University of California Press, 1995.

Waisman, Carlos. "Capitalism, the Market, and Democracy." *American Behavioral Scientist* 35:4–5 (March–June 1992): 500–516.

Waldner, David. *State Building and Late Development.* Ithaca, N.Y.: Cornell University Press, 1999.

Waterbury, John. *The Egypt of Nasser and Sadat: The Political Economy of Two Regimes.* Princeton, N.J.: Princeton University Press, 1983.

———. "The Political Management of Adjustment and Reform." In *Fragile Coalitions: The Politics of Economic Adjustment,* edited by Joan Nelson, 39–56. New Brunswick, N.J.: Overseas Development Council, 1989.

———. "The Heart of the Matter? Public Enterprise and the Adjustment Process." In *The Politics of Economic Adjustment,* edited by Stephan Haggard and Robert Kaufman, 182–217. Princeton, N.J.: Princeton University Press, 1992.

———."Democracy Without Democrats: The Potential for Political Liberalization in the Middle East." In *Democracy without Democrats: The Renewal of Politics in the Muslim World,* edited by Ghassan Salame, 23–47. London: I.B. Taurius, 1994.

———, and Alan Richards. *A Political Economy of the Middle East.* Boulder, Colo.: Westview, 1996.

Wedeen, Lisa. "Conceptualizing Culture: Possibilities for Political Science." *American Political Science Review* 96:4 (December 2002): 713–738.

"Who's Who in Syria's Leadership." *BBC News,* March 3, 2005. http://news.bbc.co .uk/2/hi/middle_east/4314787.stm.

Wickham, Carrie Rosefsky. "The Path to Moderation: Strategy and Learning in the Formation of Egypt's Wasat Party." *Comparative Politics* 36:2 (January 2004): 205–228.

Williamson, John. "What Washington Means by Policy Reform." In *Latin American Adjustment,* edited by John Williamson, 7–20. Washington, D.C.: Institute for International Economics, 1990.

———, ed. *The Political Economy of Policy Reform.* Washington, D.C.: IIE, 1994.

"Workers Strike against Algerian Government." United Press International, March 12, 1991.

"Workers Vow to Protest in September." *Info-Prod Research,* August 26, 1998.

World Bank. External Data/Statistics 2006.

Yamine, Jeannie. "Egypt's Social Fund for Development." Press Release no. 96/25/ MENA, Washington, D.C.: World Bank, 1996.

Yousef, Tarik. *Employment, Development, and the Social Contract in the Middle East and North Africa*. Washington, D.C.: World Bank, 2004.

Zaki, Moheb. *Civil Society and Democratization in Egypt, 1981–1994*. Cairo: Ibn Khaldun Center, 1994.

Zartman, I. William. "Opposition as Support of the State." In *Beyond Coercion: The Durability of the Arab State*, edited by Adeed Dawisha and I. William Zartman, 61–87. London: Croom Helm, 1988.

———. "Algeria at Forty: A Midlife Crisis." *Journal of North African Studies* 9:2 (Summer 2004): 216–222.

"Zilzāl al-arbiʻāʻ 21 May 2003: Hazzat arÃiyya jadīda wa-akthar min 4000 qatīl fī l-zilzāl al-awwal" *Algeria Voice,* http://www.algeria-voice.org/Eco-So/Eco-So10/hauptteil_eco-so10.html (site now discontinued).

Zolberg, Aristide R. *Creating Political Order: The Party States of West Africa*. Chicago: McNally, 1966.

Zussman, Mira. *Development and Disenchantment in Rural Tunisia: The Bourguiba Years*. Boulder, Colo.: Westview Press, 1992.

INDEX

Initial articles in titles (The, L') in all language and initial Arabic name particles (e.g., al-) are ignored in alphabetization. Page numbers in italics refer to tables.

Abbas, Ferhat, 45, 68
'Abboud, Ahmad, 55
Abd al Qadir, 218n51
'Abd al-Rahman, Umar, 101, 102, 104
'Abdou, Muhammad, 44–45
Abdullah, Crown Prince of Saudi
  Arabia, 109
Abou-Al-Enein, Mohammed, 116
Aboud, Hichem, 164, 166, 236n325
Abu-Dan, Mohammad Safi, 143
Achour, Habib, 172, 173
ACPC (Anti-Trust and Competition
  Protection Commission), Egypt,
  203–204
actors. *See* political actors
'Aflaq, Michel, 39, 41, 59, 60, 65,
  218n33
agrarian oligarchy, 36
Agrarian Reform Law (1952), Egypt,
  53, 118
Agrarian Reform Law, Syria, 62
Agrarian Relations Law (1958), UAR, 62
Agricultural Credit and Development
  Bank, Egypt, 99
Al-'Ahd Party, Algeria, 163
Ahmed, Hocine A't, 149
Al Alfi, Ibrahim, 116
Algeria
    army's political power in,
      146–147
    autogestion self-management
      movement, 71, 167
    Black October (1988), 146
    as bunker state, 185, 186
    civil war between regime and
      Islamists, 145
    competition legislation in, 204

constitution of 1989, 151
Council of the Nation, 148
as dominant-party regime, 206,
  243n26
earthquake of 2003, 165
European population and land
  ownership, 42–43, *43*, 218n47
French colonialism in, 42–43
government in exile, 67–68
identity politics in, 147
influence of, 16
Islamic reform movement, 44–45
military coup of 1992, 151
multiparty politics and elections.
  See under multiparty politics
  and elections
nationalist movements, 42–45,
  218n51
new authoritarianism, 145–169;
  corporatist controls under,
  150; corruption in government, 164–166; deindustrialization and, 187; economic
  reforms, 161–163; increased
  presidentialism under
  Bouteflika, 155; landlord
  and crony capitalism in, 145;
  legitimacy of regime, 168–
  169; multiple trade unions
  permitted, 151, 162; political institutions, 146–157;
  privileged groups in, 166;
  protests against Benjedid's
  economic policies, 150–151;
  reemergence of military
  influence, 155, 235n298; as
  regime in transition, 184; rent

STEPHEN J. KING is Associate Professor of Government at Georgetown University. He is the author of *Liberalization against Democracy: The Local Politics of Economic Reform in Tunisia* (Indiana University Press, 2003).